Gendered Configurations of Humans and Machines

L'AGENda

Vol. 8

edited by Landesarbeitsgemeinschaft der Einrichtungen für Frauen- und Geschlechterforschung in Niedersachsen (LAGEN)

Series edited by the speakers of LAGEN
Prof. Dr. Corinna Onnen (University of Vechta, Germany) and
Prof. Dr. Susanne Rode-Breymann (Hanover University of Music, Drama and Media, Germany).

Organisation and programme content by the members of the Editorial Board:

Prof. Dr. Melanie Kubandt (University of Vechta, Germany)
Dr. Tanja Kubes (TU Munich, Germany)
Dr. Anna Orlikowski (University of Vechta, Germany)
Joana Rieck, M.A. (Leibniz University Hannover, Germany)
PD Dr. Rita Stein-Redent (University of Vechta)
Prof. Dr. Bettina Wahrig (TU Braunschweig)

The Editorial Board und the series editors are supported by
Jördis Grabow, M.A. (Coordination of LAGEN).

All articles in this volume have been subjected to a Peer Review for quality control, in the manner of scientific journals. We owe many thanks to all reviewers, whose comments have contributed greatly to this book.

Jan Büssers
Anja Faulhaber
Myriam Raboldt
Rebecca Wiesner (eds.)

Gendered Configurations of Humans and Machines

Interdisciplinary Contributions

With the cooperation of
Prof. Dr.-Ing. Corinna Bath, Technische Universität Braunschweig,
Germany
Prof. Dr. Bettina Wahrig, Technische Universität Braunschweig,
Germany

Verlag Barbara Budrich
Opladen • Berlin • Toronto 2021

A CIP catalogue record for this book is available from
Die Deutsche Bibliothek (The German Library)

© 2021 by Verlag Barbara Budrich GmbH, Opladen, Berlin & Toronto
www.budrich.eu

    ISBN   978-3-8474-2494-9
    eISBN 978-3-8474-1646-3
    DOI   10.3224/84742494

Die Deutsche Bibliothek – CIP-Einheitsaufnahme
Ein Titeldatensatz für die Publikation ist bei der Deutschen Bibliothek erhältlich.

Verlag Barbara Budrich GmbH
Stauffenbergstr. 7. D-51379 Leverkusen Opladen, Germany

86 Delma Drive. Toronto, ON M8W 4P6 Canada
www.barbara-budrich.net

Jacket illustration by Bettina Lehfeldt, Kleinmachnow, Germany –
www.lehfeldtgraphic.de

Content

Greeting

Juliette Wedl

A lot of time has passed since the hours I spent with Bettina Wahrig in 2011 working on the application for the Maria-Goeppert-Mayer Professorship[1] "Gender, Technology and Mobility" ("Gender, Technik und Mobilität"). It has been more than nine years since this spontaneous idea, which has matured more and more into an ambitious concept, culminating in a professorship held by Prof. Dr.-Ing. Corinna Bath at the Faculties of Mechanical Engineering of the Technische Universität Braunschweig and the Ostfalia University of Applied Sciences since the end of 2012. In that period, the activities of the working group "Gender, Technology and Mobility" (GTM) have created a number of innovative impulses for both universities: The outcomes of gender studies have found their way into teaching and research at both institutions. To name just two initiatives, the booklet "Gender, Technology and Mobility" (Bath 2015) outlined the general ideas and context of the new research field; and, most recently, the working group's post-doctoral researcher, Dr Sandra Buchmüller, was granted the Junior Research Project "Human Demands of Sustainable Aviation"[2] in the Cluster of Excellence "Sustainable and Energy Efficient Aviation" (SE²A) funded by the German Research Foundation (DFG). This project aims at using participatory methods to research the interests and needs of different stakeholders and their diverse life situations regarding the future of aviation. The results will be integrated into technology development processes. The other initiative mentioned, the booklet, set out to explain the importance of the perspective of gender for engineering sciences, a perspective that is now an integral part of the Cluster of Excellence.

In addition to the doctoral program, which I will go into in a moment, the project "GenderING. Gender Studies in the Engineering Sciences" (Draude

---

[1] The Maria Goeppert Mayer Program for International Gender Studies was launched in Lower Saxony in 2001. With this program, the Ministry of Science and Culture (MWK) aims to promote, strengthen and internationalize women's and gender studies in the state of Lower Saxony. Through this program, the creation of centers for gender studies was supported, many guest professorships were made possible, and with the last two calls for proposals in 2011 and 2017, regular professorships focussing on or including gender research were established at universities in Lower Saxony. The TU Braunschweig and Ostfalia HaW successfully applied for funding within this framework.

[2] Project page: https://www.tu-braunschweig.de/gtm/human-demands-of-sustainable-aviation.

n.y.) exemplifies the participatory and egalitarian approach of the GTM research team. The project supported interdisciplinary cooperation between engineering sciences and gender studies by enabling actors to meet as equals in research and teaching. The aim of the project was to take into account the analytical findings of gender-technoscience research on the one hand and the methods of research and development and the professional cultures of engineering sciences on the other. Accordingly, in the project GenderING,[3] a tandem team from both subjects exemplarily reconceptualized the course "Introduction to Car Body Development" ("Einführung in die Karosserie-entwicklung") at the Institute for Engineering Design at TU Braunschweig, combining findings from gender studies with engineering science and integrating them into teaching. This concept of translation between disciplinary cultures was also applied to the course "Automated Driving"[4] ("Automatisiertes Fahren"), and teaching experiences from that course led to a scientific collaboration (see Buchmüller et al. 2018).

The GenderING projects show that interdisciplinarity contributes to the development of "socio-political competencies as important key competences"[5] (Leicht-Scholten 2018) in the engineering sciences. Entangling different disciplinary perspectives with the teaching and practice of engineering helps to open these disciplines towards questions of gender and diversity in terms of didactics, content, and personnel, attracting new groups of students to the engineering sciences. Through the influence of gender studies, taking the forms of research on inequality and reflection on science and technology, on engineering classes and the practice of engineering that focuses on development tasks, technical developments can be geared more closely towards the real needs of users, instead of being based on stereotypical assumptions. Moreover, an orientation towards research-based and problem-based learning appeals to other types of learners, and the consideration of the social aspects of technology appeals to new groups of students, making engineering sciences more attractive to diverse target groups. This is a forward-looking answer to the problems of today, which engineering sciences also must face.

The doctoral program "Gendered Configurations of Humans and Machines. Interdisciplinary Analyses of Technology (KoMMa.G)," established in 2017 and funded by the Ministry of Science and Culture of Lower Saxony, is an outstanding enterprise when it comes to interlinking gender and engineering perspectives. By focusing on the category of gender from a

---

3   The year-long GenderING project was funded within the innovation program Good Teaching; the follow-up project within the transfer program. Both funding instruments are part of the BMBF project teach4TU at the TU Braunschweig and part of the federal and state program for better study conditions and more quality in teaching. More information: www.tu-braunschweig.de/teach4tu.

4   For more information, visit https://www.tu-braunschweig.de/gendering-automatisiertes-fahren.

5   Translated from the German publication.

transdisciplinary perspective, it investigates how human-machine configurations that support inequality and injustice emerge and aims to propose changes to address that inequality. The challenges of transdiciplinary cooperation and communication between doctoral students and their supervisors across the traditional boundaries – the program included disciplines from humanities, social sciences, and media studies, on the one hand, and natural sciences, technology, and engineering on the other – became clear in the four years of the program, demonstrating the enormous innovative potential of concrete research and learning exchange. In the course of KoMMa.G, the hurdles of the so-called *great interdisciplinarity* became just as apparent as the promotion of mutual understanding – although much remains to be done before such transdisciplinary research collaborations matter in Germany. In view of this, the professorship "Gender, Technology and Mobility," though installed only recently, has already had a lasting impact on gender and technoscience research. The present volume, the result of the final conference of the doctoral program, and the work of the doctoral students will contribute to attracting international attention to these achievements in Braunschweig. I wish all those involved every success and all readers an informative read!

References

Bath, Corinna (2015): Gender, Technik und Mobilität: Innovative, soziotechnische Lösungen für gesellschaftliche, wissenschaftliche und wirtschaftliche Herausforderungen. Braunschweig: Technische Universität Braunschweig. Available at https://www.tu-braunschweig.de/index.php?eID=dumpFile&t=f&f=84793&token=473da4057d98ba748f78335053 1a84c42bba3279, last accessed October 13, 2020.

Buchmüller, Sandra et al. (2018): To Whom Does the Driver's Seat Belong in the Future? A Case of Negotiation Between Gender Studies and Automotive Engineering. In: GenderIT '18: Proceedings of the 4th Conference on Gender & IT, pp. 165–174.

Draude, Claude (n.y.): Handreichung zur Integration von Gender- und Diversity-Aspekten in die ingenieurwissenschaftliche Lehre. [Developed in the project "GenderING. Gender Studies in the Engineering Sciences" ("GenderING. Gender Studies in die Ingenieurwissenschaften") by Prof. Dr.-Ing. Corinna Bath, Dr. Claude Draude, Prof. Dr.-Ing. Thomas Vietor and Dipl.-Ing. Nico Selle] Braunschweig: TU Braunschweig. Available at https://www.tu-braunschweig. de/index.php?eID=dumpFile&t=f&f=35467&token=81aaabe567974a092e530d8 0240e315f469e7467, last accessed October 13, 2020.

Leicht-Scholten, Carmen (2018): Sozial verantwortliche Technikwissenschaften: Der Beitrag der Geschlechterforschung für Forschung, Entwicklung und Ausbildung. In: Kortendiek, Beate et al. (eds.): Handbuch Interdisziplinäre Geschlechterforschung. Wiesbaden: Springer VS, pp. 699–707.

Editors' Note

Jan Büssers, Anja Faulhaber, Myriam Raboldt and Rebecca Wiesner

This volume is a collection of contributions deriving from the "Interdisciplinary Conference on the Relations of Humans, Machines and Gender" which took place in Braunschweig (October 16–19, 2019). It aims to give insights into the configurations of humans and machines, taking the perspective of gender studies from various disciplinary viewpoints – including contributions from the humanities and STEM (short for natural sciences, technology, engineering, and mathematics). In its range, the volume mirrors the diversity of disciplines involved in our doctoral program, "Gendered Configurations of Humans and Machines" (abbreviation: KoMMa.G), a joint endeavor of Technische Universität Braunschweig, Ostfalia University of Applied Sciences and Braunschweig University of Art (2017–2020).[1]

Finding companions in pursuing such an interdisciplinary approach to reflect on science, technology, and gender from various disciplinary angles was (and is) an aim of the conference and this volume. Interdisciplinary approaches are necessary if we are to address contemporary challenges successfully. But the fruitfulness of this work must not overshadow the obstacles that such projects have to overcome. Having learned how demanding and time-consuming working in interdisciplinary contexts can be ourselves, this volume is a plea for staying with the trouble and making kin along this winding road.

We thank the Niedersächsischen Ministerium für Wissenschaft und Kultur for supporting our research with scholarships and grants with which we were able to finance the conference and this volume. Furthermore, our special thanks go to Corinna Bath and Bettina Wahrig for their ambitious work as speakers of the doctoral program and their support in the making of this volume. The same goes for our coordinators, Corinna Melcher and Annette Bartsch, whose work not only guided us through all stages of the doctoral program but who were also incredibly helpful in making the conference happen. Our gratitude for doing such a great job in finalizing the texts for this volume and staying with the trouble of bringing together all the different styles of our texts goes out to Thomas Nyckel, the internal copy-editor of this volume. In this manner, we are also very grateful for the wonderful

---

1   More details on the development of the KoMMa.G-program can be found in Corinna Bath's and Bettina Wahrig's "Introduction" to this volume.

work of Anna Panagiotou and all her helpful advice for improving these texts as the proof-reader of this volume. We thank all of the authors for their contributions to the conference as well as this volume. None of this could have been achieved without the care, time and attention of everyone participating. Last but not least, we would like to thank our publisher, Barbara Budrich, and the series L'AGENda for publishing our book. A special thanks to Vivian Sper for her supportiveness in answering all of our questions in the publishing process.

So, by turning the page, we invite you as the reader to join our endeavor: meeting us halfway in our texts, entangling with our thoughts and maybe, through enjoying and struggling with these texts, becoming a companion in our pursuit of reconfiguring human-machine relations and doing interdisciplinary work by overcoming the seemingly distinct boundaries of humanities and STEM.

Looking Through the Mirror: The PhD Program KoMMa.G[1]

Bettina Wahrig and Corinna Bath

1. Introduction

Can you look through a mirror? Of course not. But yet… Plain mirrors usually have a reflective *and* a transparent component. A transparent surface, like water or glass, will reflect some of the light rays falling on it, depending on the angle of incidence and the perspective of the onlooker. By using the reflecting surface of this volume, which was the last joint project of the members of the PhD program "Gendered Configurations of Humans and Machines" ("Konfigurationen von Mensch, Maschine und Geschlecht, KoMMa.G," 2017–2020) we are looking back at three years of intensive and often joyful collaboration and striving to catch a glimpse of the future. Hence our paradoxical title "Looking through the mirror," i.e., casting a glance both backwards and ahead, taking account of the recent past and guessing what may become of that endeavor in the future. The conference itself was organized by the PhD researchers in KoMMa.G, and this volume is also a fruit of their initiative.

Over the past three years of working in the PhD program KoMMa.G, funded by the Ministry of Science and Culture in Lower Saxony, our PhD researchers and the Principal Investigators (PI) have held conversations at the intersections of a broad range of disciplines. The initial fifteen principal investigators and PhD projects represented disciplines cutting across the fields of technology and engineering, natural sciences, social sciences, science and technology studies (STS), film and media studies, and history of science. We also garnered associated investigators from literary studies, history, and informatics, to name just the most important ones. The overall aim of this project was to understand gender relations and implicit gendering within the disciplinary fields of science and engineering. In this context, our questions

---

[1]   This short preface is the written and overhauled version of our welcome address to the final conference of the Doctoral Program "Gendered Configurations of Humans and Machines" ("Konfigurationen von Mensch, Maschine und Geschlecht, KoMMa.G," 2017–2020) held in October 2019 in Braunschweig.

were: How do different forms of gender knowledge arise within these fields? In what way do they play out at the sites where knowledge and technologies are produced? How do technologies configure gender as a structural-symbolic category of inequality and, vice versa, how does gender configure knowledge and technologies? Our PhD researchers, previously educated in science, engineering, or the social sciences and humanities, acquired knowledge about other disciplines and about the way Gender and Queer Studies provide frames of understanding and analyzing them. They did so by actively participating in workshops, seminars and discussions, and through invited guest lectures, many of which they organized themselves. They also developed and organized the conference documented in this volume. Consequently, PhD researchers from our program are its principal editors.

Within the limited time of three years' funding, and in addition to working on their own projects, the PhD researchers and the Principal Investigators have taught each other what their disciplines of origin are about. The PhD researchers have nudged their mentors and inspired one another to cast a fresh look at their fields of research. They reframed their habitual disciplinary perspectives by gazing through the looking glass of unfamiliar research methods and approaches that they had not yet considered.

The PhD researchers' short accounts of their completed and ongoing work included in this volume testify to the difficulties of developing an inter- and transdisciplinary perspective, inspired by questions arising from different strands of Gender Studies, but centered on a given research topic in their disciplines of origin. The task of combining innovative research & development (R&D) with current approaches in gender studies, or, vice versa, of undertaking a journey into the world of R&D, equipped with a gender toolbox taken from the arts and media or social studies, has been challenging. It is an endeavor, an issue of daily struggles, of getting lost, of misunderstanding each other, and of eventually making sense of that incomprehension. This might even lead us to a short, and paradoxical, definition of *interdisciplinarity* and *transdisciplinarity*: Interdisciplinary and transdisciplinary work are the process of NOT understanding each other, which then makes us start to spell out WHY these moments of misunderstanding continue to happen, with the effect of either transforming well-trodden paths or clinging to the traditional epistemologies we have been taught. With this definition – or, to phrase it more modestly – with this formula for what happens at the intersections between disciplines, we have already taken the step from *reflecting on* science, technology, and gender to *reflecting on the way we perform this reflection*. But on what does this reflection on reflection depend? We intended – and still intend – to tap into inter- and transdisciplinary reflection as a resource to understand better how we, as researchers and as humans, change and are changed in a series of co-configurations in technology-driven processes (see among others Barad 2007; Barla 2019; Suchman 2007; 2012).

The necessity of such a transdisciplinary reflection process in a globalized, technology-driven world, which is thoroughly structured by inequality and by dangerously anti- or a-social power relationships, is highlighted by the central research object of our PhD program, namely the growingly complex human-machine configurations, as we formulated in our project outline: "Machines, which can be understood as object-centered technologies, open up new possibilities for mobility and communication, they relieve us of tedious tasks, and allow us to share information or overcome physical limitations and geographical borders. At the same time, technical products influence the way we think, act, and feel, i.e., our forms of subjectification. Machines are thus not only configured by humans, but they represent an essential part of the (re)configuration of the human [...]. The same applies more generally to technical artifacts in research and development."[2]

Gender Studies in STS, Queer Studies and approaches to intersectionality have helped us to contextualize scientific and technological developments within the larger picture of social interaction, to understand research practices and disciplinary cultures, to conceptualize their economical, juridical, and political frameworks (Cipolla et al. 2017; Escobar 2018; Harding 2015; Suchman 2008; Thakor/Molldrem 2017; Verran 2002; Wajcman 2010). Science and technology are social enterprises; they constitute webs of signification and power relationships, to which we all belong. Like the challenges of the climate crisis, the ongoing pandemic is a striking example of how urgently we need approaches encompassing and entangling cultural, historical, and techno-scientific insights, in addition to a new understanding of what it means to be human, in order to solve the current existential global problems (see among other Bath et al. 2017; Haraway 2016; Puig de la Bellacasa 2017; Stengers 2015; Tsing 2017).

2. How to Conceptualize an Interdisciplinary PhD Program

When, together with the other PIs, we started to write up the proposal for the doctoral program back in 2015, we were confronted with the challenge of how to organize a joint exploration of research fields and methods. At first, each of us developed outlines of case studies for possible PhD projects. For example, we sketched out projects touching on gender aspects in the ergonomics of human-computer interaction, gender in the planning processes of steel construction or, the task of developing a revision of actor-network theories with the aid of the critical tools developed by gender studies.

---

2   See: https://www.tu-braunschweig.de/kommag, last accessed August 11, 2020.

Thus, in order to create a living and productive atmosphere of interdisciplinarity, we needed a space for mutual translations and collaborations. KoMMa.G turned out to be such a space. How did we conceptualize this space? We initially aimed at a tandem or double supervision for PhD projects, so that each project would have one supervisor with a science or engineering background and one with a gender studies background. These tandems, we thought, would be able to inform each other both on the thematic side and the methodological side. For example, how are gender relations and lab automation entangled? The tandem project for this research in pharmacy was to be located in the history of science: Can prosthetics re-constitute the cis-male body? In both projects in this tandem, artifacts and humans were intermixed and entangled. But how do lab automation and the development of prosthetics in the wider sense resonate? How do human-artifact relations change human-human relations and vice versa? In the course of the program, the first project (on lab automation) has been realized, the second one (on prosthetics) thoroughly modified.

In hindsight, we can name some more pairs of projects that mirror each other somehow. Still, in the period of refining the program, we soon realized that this approach was too schematic because we were encompassing such a large number of different disciplines. We were still confident that resonances between the PhD projects would arise over time, and we had already detected quite a number of them. But on further elaboration, they turned out to be elusive, and, more importantly, the thematic interactions were not simple resonances, but rather patterns of resonances and interferences, like the patterns one may see on a liquid surface observed from different angles and over an extended period. Moreover, we had to adapt the formal requirements of the curriculum and the supervision of doctoral students to the regulations of three different universities. A schematic dual mentoring would have brought too many structural inequalities into the group.

Therefore, we decided to propose another model of mutual interdisciplinary instruction: We defined four research areas and allocated between three and five PhD projects to each, making sure that experts both for gender studies and for science and engineering were present in every group of potential supervisors. The four research areas were *Abstractions and Modeling*; *Creativity and Design*; *Materialization, Virtualization, Representation*; and *Networks and Emotions*. This concept of structuring the program and facilitating interdisciplinarity convinced the reviewers of our proposal. Thus, in 2016, we received the funding for the PhD program by the Ministry of Science and Education in Lower Saxony.

3. Working with PhD Researchers and Their Supervisors Across Disciplines

We started our program in January 2017 with eighteen PhD researchers. Fifteen of them received a three-year grant, and three were associated with the PhD program. They were, and continue to be, supervised by fourteen professors at eleven institutes or departments from three universities in and around Braunschweig: The TU Braunschweig, the Ostfalia University for Applied Sciences and the Braunschweig University of Arts.

As expected, the doctoral students brought a large number of new perspectives into the program. Many of them joined the research areas with projects of their own.[3] As a consequence, the dynamics emanating from the interdisciplinarity within the four groups differed enormously from what we had expected and among these research areas. Although the backbone of the accompanying curriculum was stable, these differences necessitated repeated adjustments of the program's details.

Looking back, we might say that the fruitful process of *not understanding* each other went on throughout the program, and we continuously got better at it. Understanding and being engaged in interdisciplinary processes is a complex skill that involves capacities of interpersonal and trans-methodological communication, but also of finding one's place in an array of existing disciplinary fields. From the beginning, we encouraged the PhD researchers and the Principal Investigators to look for individual paths of qualification in a well-defined discipline, while also gathering experience in interdisciplinary work. We placed a relatively strong emphasis on disciplinary frameworks in view of the fact that, after receiving their doctoral degree, PhD researchers will have to gain access to established professional and disciplinary fields, even though, in the third millennium, professional work is undergoing enormous changes. This also applies to research and development. The balance between intradisciplinary and inter-/transdisciplinary work remained difficult for almost every one of us. In nearly all the projects, research tandems, and clusters, it was continuously negotiated and re-negotiated.

In spite of all of us having to handle this demanding task, we look back on one element of our curriculum as particularly successful, namely the workshops. These were our discursive and experimental spaces for the reflection of and training in inter- and transdisciplinary research. These workshops

---

3   One of the first experiences of interdisciplinarity we had when discussing in the group of PIs were differences in the recruiting processes of the PhD researchers: Graduate programs in the social sciences and the humanities usually recruit PhD researchers by asking them to come up with their own project proposal and announce decisive criteria for being selected for the program. In contrast, supervisors in sciences and engineering offer pre-defined PhD projects within the framework of their own working programs.

were conceptualized and organized by the PhD researchers themselves, who introduced other members of their respective groups to the most important theoretical concepts, methods, and practices of their own (disciplinary) field. On the request of the PhD researchers, the Principal Investigators also gave broader, additional information about their fields and specific methods of research during the workshops. Our PhD program was a program *on the move*, with workshop meetings at different locations within the participating universities. We rarely used one meeting room twice, since we wanted to see the PIs and PhD researchers *at work* in their academic homes: in seminar rooms, libraries, steel construction halls, simulator labs near the airfield, etc. We climbed simulators, watched and analyzed films, worked hard to understand texts, while saying hello to the robot Pepper, filling heaps of flipcharts, talking/walking, and playing the "lotto of identities."[4]

The concept of the workshops and their realization gave rise to new questions linking science and technology with gender studies. To name just a few examples: What are the concepts and practices behind feedback control systems, programming, robotics, simulators, test and interview techniques, ethnographic research, or life science research? What are Gender and Queer Studies, and how do they relate to postcolonial studies? Is research always *politics by other means* (Haraway 1986) and if so, how do we as researchers position ourselves explicitly? How can we combine cultures of innovation with concepts of care and responsibility?

4. Looking Through the Mirror: Impacting Future Research and Technologies

Given the broad range of disciplines and research questions, the projects of the program could only include a small number of case studies on the gendered relations and entanglements of humans and machines, both in science and engineering, and in their representations in media and film. Theoretical-methodological projects complemented these case studies. Now, at the end of the funding period, we understand some of those entanglements better. However, since research, which aims at providing us with answers to questions, necessarily ends up with yet more questions, we have also identified new research lacunae. Some of these are specific to individual projects. Others concern the central question of the program, namely, how to integrate reflex-

---

4   The "Identitätenlotto" is a game to explore diverse identities. It aims at playfully introducing intersectional gender studies to educational settings and was developed by Juliette Wedl (Braunschweig Competence Centre for Gender & Diversity Studies) and her team: https://identitaetenlotto.de/, last accessed October 25, 2020.

ive (or diffractive) capacities, inspired by Gender Studies, into engineering processes.

Moreover, it turned out that the character of Gender Studies itself was a matter of dispute, both among the Principal Investigators and among the PhD researchers. Most of us agreed that Gender Studies are more than taking account of gender differences in the development of, access to, and use of technologies, although these are still important questions to ask. Gender and Queer Studies open up ways of asking how other categories of inequality come into the world, how the binary gender system can be diversified, how gendered power relations materialize in machines, technologies, and knowledge apparatuses, how gendered social structures stubbornly persist . Some of the differences among us – both senior and PhD researchers – boiled down to contrasting epistemologies, some to different cultures of living and researching. Depending on how questions of identity, hierarchies, and materiality are answered, the category of gender may be framed in many different and, sometimes, conflicting ways. How relevant, however, were those ontological and epistemological questions? Would the differences arising from them impede the common struggle for a more sustainable and just environment? Do we need new terminologies and methodologies for describing how we want to produce knowledge and technologies, such as the framework of agential realism (Barad 2007) or the concept of the Chthulucene (Haraway 2016)?

The problematic status of disciplines in general is just another essential facet of understanding the role of Gender and Queer Studies as catalysts for innovation and interdisciplinary work. In the academic world, disciplines are considered necessary in order to create consensus about methods and develop them further. But disciplines and their innate hierarchical order can also impede innovation, both at an institutional level and in the professional fields for which our graduates are training. The PhD researchers in KoMMa.G have to get their degree within *one* particular discipline. This was and still is creating frictions, since we have been asking the PhD researchers to engage in a self-contradictory process. In (post-)industrial academia, disciplines do not have fixed boundaries. Shifts and reconfigurations are happening on a daily basis, yet the etymological kinship between *disciplining* and *discipline* is still significant. *Discipline* is one of the many academic names for *power*. This is one of the reasons why we will have to continue fighting against them, with them, and over them. But as long as we (can) keep arguing, there is still hope.

Disciplining and overcoming disciplinary boundaries is not only an issue of content and methods but also a matter of time and resources. It has often been stated that PhD projects, in general, can hardly ever be completed within three years. This is even more true of transdisciplinary projects. Thus, we are happy to see that a considerable number of the KoMMa.G projects are in, or near, completion. Moreover, some of the graduates have found new work opportunities that enable them to continue their research. But these individual solutions are not satisfying. Gender studies and the institutionalizing of inter- and transdisciplinary research at the intersection of engineering/science and social sciences/humanities need more support from politics, research, and funding institutions.

Thinking out of the box takes time, and it is urgently needed to meet current problems all around the world. We are convinced that Gender and Queer Studies contribute to thinking and acting beyond established models and concepts, both within given disciplines and for establishing research across disciplinary boundaries. Future projects can rely on these strengths. Reflections on science from a perspective of responsibility, care, and democracy, which are at the core of Gender and Queer Studies, are currently needed to address the issues at the top of the world's agenda: Global justice, the fight against racism and antisemitism, the struggle for a sustainable future, and, lately, a globally just and effective response to the current pandemic, which highlights the shortcomings of societies that have neglected concepts of mutualism, relating, equality, and care.

The PIs of this PhD program and some new allies have already started further initiatives, and we hope to continue our collaboration in the future. We, furthermore, welcome and invite all engaged researchers that participated in KoMMa.G, its final conference, this publication, and beyond – to elaborate Gender and Queer Studies as well as science and technology studies in order to join in this vast enterprise of entangling Gender Studies with science and engineering.

5. Gendered Configurations of Humans and Machines: About This Volume

Before we come to the single contributions, we would like to mention some of the most salient points of reference both for the past work of the doctoral program and for the contributions collected in this volume. As mentioned above, the joint venture of transdisciplinary experience and theoretical reflection was one of the pillars of the program, both in research and postgraduate teaching. The introduction of the concept of experience was one of the early interventions by feminist theory (Alcoff/Potter 1993). This move had an impact on more traditional accounts in STS, centering on experiments and observations (e.g. Latour 1987). Experience matters. It mediates between past and present, and it is permeated by power relationships. In different ways, and amongst many others, Donna Haraway and Michel Foucault (Foucault 1971: 10 and passim; Foucault 1996: 85) have insisted on this. Donna Haraway, with a sharp eye on gender woven into power relationships within knowledge production (Haraway 1997), has not only elaborated on this, but she is also suggesting communication practices among humans, and between humans and non-humans, avoiding mutual othering in order to invent livable futures (Haraway 2016). Apparatuses of knowledge production are situated in experiences and power relations.

Questioning the sovereign subject of knowledge has been a recurrent topic in feminist philosophy. With Judith Butler's interventions (1990; 1993), this type of criticism has been firmly established in Gender Studies since the 1990s. These critical accounts of knowledge production make us question traditional basic assumptions like mind-matter hierarchies and rigid categorization systems. Networks of subject-object hybrids are the sites of new insights, and this is the ground for deranging implicit assumptions in science and engineering such as the I-methodology (Akrich 1995; Rommes 2002) or methodological dogmatism (Wajcman 2004: 38). By dismantling the distinction between being and knowing, Karen Barad (2007) has developed one more important account in this respect. She moves away from the differentiation of ontology and epistemology inherent in those assumptions and suggests a relational attitude towards practices producing scientific and technological knowledge. Her contributions most explicitly linked feminist theory to *response-able* knowledge and technology production (Barad 2018) and have inspired many of the PhD projects in this volume.

We would now like to make a few remarks on the contributions assembled in this volume, which documented the concluding conference of the "KoMMa.G" program, held between the 16th and the 19th of October 2020 in Braunschweig. This volume collects the elaborated versions of contributions from our PhD researchers, of papers presented on the basis of submitted abstracts, and invited keynotes of the conference. There are many thematic overlaps between the sections, and we also see some common threads running through most of the papers. One of those threads is the challenge of a rapidly changing, already technology-imbibed/infused world, a process that is often dubbed *digitalization* in public discourse, but also *rationalization* and *automation*. Artificial intelligence, robots and big data are on top of the agenda of science policy makers, and hence also of those scientists who are trying to keep pace with an ever-accelerating process of *technological innovation*. With this volume, we aim at describing and questioning this narrow understanding of innovation as an ever-growing avalanche of *technological fixes* to problems we no longer have the time to understand. Many of the papers collected here aim at understanding these problems. They will lay the power relationships in these processes bare and they will present ways of *bringing the human factor back in*. Feminist science and technology studies have for several decades contributed to analyzing science and technology concerning the power relationships interwoven in the configurations of humans and machines, mediated by artifacts and dispositives. How do these relationships play out in fields like communications, arts, body policy and body politics, design, and everyday life? Do the general terms *humans* and *machines* sufficiently address the challenges that we so urgently need to confront, such as climate change, ongoing colonial and postcolonial violence, gender discrimination, etc.? In short, do we need new terminologies, concepts, and agencies against the current tendency of proposing old, violent, dysfunctional solutions to the problems these concepts of the modern or postmodern human and machine have caused? How can we conceive of a new relatedness and togetherness, beyond myths and dominance, but also imaginative enough to help technological change onto the path of "response-ability" (Barad 2018; Haraway 2008), of understanding ourselves as being able to respond to the current problems in the world, including a de-centering of the human, for instance in the sense of "critters" (Haraway 2016)?

6. Structure of the Volume and Contributions: A Short Overview

The contributions in this edited collection are organized into four sections that reflect the structure of the conference program. Between the conference and the writing of this volume, some contributions have been allocated to a different section. This illustrates that clear-cut boundaries between the thematic blocks are hard to find. We hope that the resonances between contributions are noticeable to the readers of this volume, beyond ourselves and the editors.

The first section "Interdisciplinarity: Boundaries, Transgressions and Politics" engages with tensions between disciplinary approaches on the level of collaboration and addresses methodological questions immanent in research projects. Diffractions are detected in a guided tour through Braunschweig (Büssers), in the technical problem of tread profiles (Metzger), and also in cross-cultural aspects of fiction and non-fiction reflecting the phenomenon of so-called *guest workers* of the 1960s (Dayıoğlu-Yücel). Like Barad's diffractive approach, Actor Network Theories are instrumental for methodological reflection in Gender Studies (Bednarek), and we also find an account of how the discipline-transgressing work of interdisciplinarity, in turn, disciplined our PhD researchers (Heuer/Sonneck).

"Artificial Intelligence * Bodies as Artefacts" is the title of the second section, which provides a tour-de-force through gender-biased algorithms (Wellner), problems of CATPCHAs (Nyckel) and metaphysical machines (Zakablukovskij), while in the wake of a waning cisgender identity, the individual body, situated between self-fashioning and naturalization, is becoming fragile (Raboldt). Fragile natural bodies may, in some cases, be reinforced with "bullet-proof coffee" and other nutrition-based biohacking techniques (Trittelvitz).

The third section, "Humans and Machines in Everyday Life," juxtaposes different technologies of human-machine interaction with the question of how *Verlässlichkeit* – the double capacity of being relied on and of being left (Crutzen) – could help us conceive technologies of the future. Emotions can lure us forward into innovations, while simultaneously propelling our roots of traditional personal identities yet further into the ground. Renewable energies, calculating their own in- and output can provide owners with "solar delight" (Lorenz-Meyer). Can Crutzen's vision of *Verlässlichkeit* be transferred to the reliability of flight assistant systems (Faulhaber)? Mhealth applications are another instance of the precarious reliability and the open question of respons-ability within apps and the Internet of Things (Gabel). Laboratory robots can only succeed with labor that is strictly regulated, hence, in a sense, automated – and they apparently have to be humanized and gendered in turn (Wiesner). Can these technical dispositives safely and respons-ably be *left alone*?

The fourth section, "Digitalization und Cultures of Translation" opens up yet another variety of perspectives on the relationships between humans and human-made artifacts. Digital technologies have the potential of communicating and mediating between different cultures of knowledge, of building bridges between the digital age and other local/regional cultural techniques. In those connections, identities both change and get stabilized (Verran). New transcultural concepts are also needed for intersectional approaches to the tech professions. Following the trajectories of female doctoral researchers from India and China to Germany puts male connotations of computer science into question, particularly the assumption that informatics and computer science are a domain of white males everywhere in the world (Losch). Digitalization enables new bridges between performance and teaching (Leuschner/Petersen) and has inspired teaching experiments that successfully bridge the apparent gap between the arts and academic teaching (Britton). Yet, the making of new, un-gendered identities is no safe harbor regarding global surveillance. What are we afraid of? A new breed of digital monsters, the(ir) kingdom of bullshit, or rather the unruly versions of feminist media studies that bring them to our attention (Dannenberg)?

Not as a consequence and not as a final fiction, but as a reading that can make us start everything all over again, "Zero" (Pumará) is both a fictional and a non-fictional text that helps us fall into the abyss of not knowing how to think and write.

Acknowledgements

Our special thanks first go to the Ministry of Research and Education in the state of Lower Saxony for the funding of the grants and the program, including this conference. Moreover, we thank the three universities, Technische Universität Braunschweig, Ostfalia University of Applied Sciences and the University of the Arts, Braunschweig for their support and the funding of the coordination position. We thank the professors involved in the program as supervisors and all the PhD researchers.

For their commitment while preparing this event, we would like to thank the conference organization team: Myriam Raboldt, Anja Faulhaber, Jan Büssers, Rebecca Wiesner, and Katharina Losch. Thanks to all the doctoral researchers for their hard work and efforts throughout the program, for the joy they have provided us with by making progress, and for persevering whenever they met institutional but also methodological and conceptual obstacles.

Moreover, we thank the two coordinators, Corinna Melcher und Annette Bartsch, for their continuing support of the project, and also for their unrelenting and most reliable support throughout the working time of KoMMa.G.

As usual, Anna Panagiotou's work as an English-language copy-editor with her impeccable attention to detail, not only for this volume, has been invaluable.

Last, but not least, we thank Thomas Nyckel for his engaged copy-editing and communication work. Without his efforts, we would not have been able to send this book to the publisher.

References

Akrich, Madeleine (1995): User Representations: Practices, Methods and Sociology. In: Rip, Arie et al. (eds.): Managing Technology in Society. London/New York: Pinter, pp. 167–184.

Alcoff, Linda/Potter, Elizabeth (eds.) (1993): Feminist Epistemologies. New York: Routledge.

Barad, Karen (2007): Meeting the Universe Halfway: Quantum Physics and the Entanglement of Matter and Meaning. Durham/London: Duke University Press.

Barad, Karen (2018): On Touching – The Inhuman That Therefore I Am (v1.1). In: Witzgall, Susanne/Stakemeier, Kerstin (eds.): Power of Material – Politics of Materiality. Zürich/Berlin: Diaphanes, pp. 153–164.

Barla, Josef (2019): The Techno-Apparatus of Bodily Production: A New Materialist Theory of Technology and the Body. Bielefeld: Transcript.

Bath, Corinna et al. (eds.) (2017): Verantwortung und Un/Verfügbarkeit: Impulse und Zugänge eines (neo)materialistischen Feminismus. Münster: Westfälisches Dampfboot.

Butler, Judith (1990): Gender Trouble: Feminism and the Subversion of Identity. New York: Routledge.

Butler, Judith (1993): Bodies That Matter. New York: Routledge.

Cipolla, Cyd et al. (eds.) (2017): Queer Feminist Science Studies: A Reader. Seattle, WA: University of Washington Press.

Escobar, Arturo (2018): Designs for the Pluriverse: Radical Interdependence, Autonomy, and the Making of Worlds. Durham, N.C.: Duke University Press.

Foucault, Michel (1971): L'Ordre du Discours. Paris: Gallimard.

Foucault, Michel (1996): Der Mensch ist ein Erfahrungstier: Gespräch mit Ducio Trombadori. Frankfurt am Main: Suhrkamp.

Haraway, Donna (1986): Primatology is Politics by Other Means. In: Bleier, Ruth (ed.): Feminist Approaches to Science. New York: Pergamon, pp. 77–118.

Haraway, Donna (1997): Modest_Witness@Second_Millennium. FemaleMan©_ Meets_OncoMouseTM. New York: Routledge.

Haraway, Donna (2008): *When Species Meet.* Minnesota: University of Minnesota Press.

Haraway, Donna (2016): Staying with the Trouble: Making Kin in the Chthulucene. Durham, N.C.: Duke University Press.

Harding, Sandra (2015): Objectivity and Diversity: Another Logic of Scientific Research. Chicago: University of Chicago Press.

Latour, Bruno (1987): Science in Action: How to Follow Scientist and Engineers through Society. Cambridge, MA: Harvard University Press.

Puig de la Bellacasa, Maria (2017): Matters of Care: Speculative Ethics in More Than Human Worlds. Minnesota: University of Minnesota Press.

Rommes, Els (2002): Gender Scripts and the Internet: The Design and Use of Amsterdam's Digital City. Enschede: Twente University Press.

Stengers, Isabelle (2015): In Catastrophic Times: Resisting the Coming Barbarism. Milton Keynes, UK: Open Humanities Press.

Suchman, Lucy (2007): Human-Machine Reconfigurations: Plans and Situated Action. 2nd ed. Cambridge: Cambridge University Press.

Suchman, Lucy (2008): Feminist STS and the Sciences of the Artificial. In: Hackett, Edward J. (ed.): New Handbook of Science and Technology Studies. 3rd ed. Cambridge, MA: MIT Press, pp. 139–163.

Suchman, Lucy (2012): Configuration. In: Lury, Celia/Wakeford, Nina (eds.): Inventive Methods: The Happening of the Social. New York: Routledge, pp. 48–60.

Thakor, Mitali/Molldrem, Stephen (2017): Genealogies and Futures of Queer Science and Technology Studies. In: *Catalyst: Feminism, Theory, Technoscience* 3, 1, pp. 1–15.

Tsing, Anna Lowenhaupt (2017): The Mushroom at the End of the World: On the Possibility of Life in Capitalist Ruins. Princeton: Princeton University Press.

Verran, Helen (2002): A Postcolonial Moment in Science Studies: Alternative Firing Regimes of Environmental Scientists and Aboriginal Landowners. In: Social Studies of Science 32, pp. 729–762.

Wajcman, Judy (2004): TechnoFeminism. Cambridge, UK: Polity Press.

Wajcman, Judy (2010): Feminist Theories of Technology. Cambridge Journal of Economics 34, 1, pp. 143–152.

Interdisciplinarity: Boundaries, Transgression and Politics

InSights – A Critical Review of an Interdisciplinary Doctoral Program

Tanja Heuer and Jennifer Sonneck

1. Introduction

In general, being able to work in an interdisciplinary team is becoming increasingly important. When it comes to working and researching innovatively and successfully, interdisciplinarity is the buzzword, particularly regarding how crossing disciplinary boundaries can enrich research and learning across fields. However, while, on the one hand, interdisciplinary courses seem promising, on the other hand, many scientists believe that in order to work in an interdisciplinary way, you have to be firmly rooted within one discipline first (Weber 2011: 105–107). Additionally, interdisciplinary work is very challenging and involves new stumbling blocks, like language barriers, group dynamic problems, or discipline-specific subcultures (Brewer 1999; Lerch 2017). Certain topics and problems are so complex that they have to be dealt with by several disciplines in order to make the overall picture clearer, so they can be solved. KoMMa.G (Gendered Configurations of Humans and Machines – Interdisciplinary Analyses of Technology)[1] was designed with this kind of complex problem in mind: the interdisciplinary doctoral program should give an idea of how interdisciplinarity works (or can work) in general.

The doctoral program "Gendered Configurations of Humans and Machines – Interdisciplinary Analyses of Technology" was focused on inter- and transdisciplinary questions. It was an ongoing cooperation between three universities: Technical University of Braunschweig, Ostfalia University of Applied Sciences and the Braunschweig University of Art. The program has awarded fifteen scholarships within different disciplines. The idea was to work across the boundaries of the social sciences, media studies, humanities, as well as the natural and engineering sciences, for three years. For the reader to understand the perspective of the authors, we present here our research interests:

Tanja Heuer: Social robotics is a growing field, especially in the assistance and health care sector. Social means providing communication in some

---

1   https://www.tu-braunschweig.de/kommag.

way, providing companionship. In order to reach the full potential of functionalities and communication skills, the collection of personal information is required. To foster acceptance and trust, privacy and the accompanying legal issues need to be a part of the design process and users need to be sensitized to them. Relevant research areas are computer science, mechanical engineering, participatory design, and privacy.

Jennifer Sonneck: The subject of the author's research is the planning process of projects in construction engineering, especially in steel construction. The main research question is: How do existing planning strategies represent the issues particular to steel construction (prefabricated elements, pre-planning, the central role of scheduling) and what are the challenges? The work belongs both to the field of Design and Communication Strategy and to that of construction engineering. To answer the research questions, the research draws upon design studies, gender studies, science and technology studies, as well as the philosophy of science.

The PhD program has organized workshops and talks in which various speakers reported on their experiences and their personal definitions of interdisciplinarity. We learned about different approaches to interdisciplinary work, what the assumed requirements are, and how to design interdisciplinary cooperation. In the next step, it was up to the program fellows to sharpen their personal views and to exchange ideas. Workshops were designed in various formats, and with the help of laboratory visits the program ensured the transfer of theory to practice. There was plenty of space for interdisciplinary exchange, including summer schools and conferences. The ability to see beyond the end of one's nose and the constant encouragement of exchange resulted in fruitful discussions and lively cross talks. The following two sections describe our personal perspectives on the opportunities and challenges we experienced within the three years of the doctoral program. All conclusions are outcomes of our personal *engineering perspective* and do not represent all of us at the program. By describing our experiences, we want to point out that true interdisciplinarity is not that easy to achieve and means a lot of work and openness, even though there is a lot of literature about this topic, and that theoretical and practical approaches still differ (Borrego et al. 2010).

2. Opportunities

Such an interdisciplinary program should emphasize its positive effects, especially those that emerge from the different workshops. Some of the positive features that we experienced for ourselves during the last three years are reflected in this section.

The overcoming of interdisciplinary boundaries needs to be primary and considered as an overall goal. With the help of different kinds of workshops and meetings, we could exchange information and opinions in a multidisciplinary way. The workshops organized by the fellows themselves were especially significant in providing input. In particular, they had two main positive outcomes, which might also help beyond the academic life. The workshops improved mediation skills by requiring participants to describe their own research discipline to non-experts. Very specific information needed to be *translated* in an understandable way for non-experts in this field of research, where not only language, but also practical and creative methods, helped each person communicate their message. We had to learn that certain terms and expressions need to be explained to other discipline cultures and might have different meanings. Thereby, the participants' own scientific position was strengthened as they were forced to think about conveying their research topic and specific goals.

Besides the presentation of individual work, there was the ability to cross-link exchanges and the discovery of new methodologies and information within different disciplines. We got input from other perspectives and were forced to think outside the box, which can lead to a more open-minded attitude regarding other opinions and views. Additionally, it allowed us to integrate new methodologies and views into our own projects, connect the new information to familiar theories, and broaden our horizons.

3. Challenges

The elements that were highlighted as opportunities were also quite challenging, something we would like to reflect on in this section. Preparing for and following up on such workshops is very time- and energy-consuming, despite the opportunity for interesting input from other disciplines. The absence of a common language, which was time-consuming as well, raised additional issues. According to Bracken et al. (2006), shared vocabulary among disciplines is an important basis on which to build trust and discuss. We could perhaps have learned such a common language within these meetings – however, this only happened partially. A common language could have helped and simplified discussions, making them more in-depth, but, in our opinion, it is way more important to accept other disciplines and their views and be aware of different languages (Bösl/Schatz 2019: 117).

Furthermore, there was only limited benefit from these workshops because of the variety of research topics and everyone writing their thesis from within their own discipline. The absence of a common goal makes being open-minded to other researchers' input and the diversity of perspectives even more difficult. The subjects were so variable that we were not able to find overall topics or methods that were interesting for everyone, which was confirmed to be very difficult and challenging by Pohl et al. (2008). Another problem was that, except for these meetings, everyone was working on their own without any connection to any other project. The gaps between so many different research areas were bigger than ever expected and bridging these gaps was way too time-, work-, and energy-consuming. To reduce the stress and energy spent on finding a common language, it got way easier to stay together with people within each one's own or similar disciplines, who also know the relevant theories and methods.

4. Discussion and Conclusion

The benefits of interdisciplinary cooperation are not without disadvantages. There are positive aspects, but there are also challenges to be faced.

We had a similar experience in our graduate program – practicing inter-disciplinarity is more complicated than expected. We could not simply start discussing and exchanging right away. First of all, we had to clarify questions, such as what is interdisciplinary research and how is it defined by everyone? One of the first results was the realization that there is no widely accepted definition of interdisciplinarity, which makes finding a basis for discussion even harder. Furthermore, we realized that we have to discuss and to learn different definitions and views. STEM (science, technology, engineering, and mathematics) is a large area and can be seen as an interdisciplinary program in itself (Lavadia et al. 2018). The goal was the exchange of professional and technical skills among engineers and scientists, which worked better because of common projects to work on. The overall outcome was presented as positive and most of the skills could be adapted. If similar subjects need time and a basis to work on, a group of completely different disciplines needs even longer. A suitable statement regarding bringing different views together is given by Borrego et al. (2010) who *"argue that humanists operationalize integration as critical awareness, while engineers and scientists operationalize it as teamwork,"* which explains the difficulties of establishing a common language very accurately.

The multiplicity of views and attitudes concerning different topics means being tolerant and respectful towards other disciplines is very important. We have learned that there is often a negative attitude towards new and unknown disciplines, research methods, and collaborations. This attitude often makes constructive exchange impossible. Foreign disciplines are often underestimated and their internal research potential is not recognized. Disciplines should all be treated equally, without judgment on the relevance of their topics, which might be difficult to make when you do not completely understand the focus of certain subjects. The broadening of your horizons and intrinsic motivation are the basis for participating in an interdisciplinary program. It should not only be seen as a painstaking process, but as learning for life. We have discovered that exchanging ideas about different research methods might be the most important part. This is where you get to know the different interfaces of the individual disciplines. Another important factor is a responsible moderator, who knows how to sometimes end an inexpedient discussion.

Regardless of the composition of interdisciplinary teams, interdisciplinary work is always time-consuming, sometimes energy-consuming, and takes collaborative teamwork. If you accept these facts and bite the bullet, you will advance in your own research, especially with regards to critical thinking, communication, and creativity. In our opinion, complex problems can only be solved with the help of interdisciplinary approaches. Transparency and participation in a doctoral program must be guaranteed by all researchers. We anticipate that our insights will have applications beyond our context, in other interdisciplinary programs. Interdisciplinary techniques and co-operations are not only important in order to learn about other disciplines, but rather to best carry out your own research and enrich your own discipline. Nevertheless, the basic conditions need to fit the entire stakeholder group and it is a give-and-take that might be difficult if expectations are not clear from the beginning. Be open-minded and do not judge.

References

Borrego, Maura/Newswander, Lynita K. (2010): Definitions of Interdisciplinary Research: Toward Graduate-Level Interdisciplinary Learning Outcomes. In: The Review of Higher Education 34, 1, pp. 61–84.

Bracken, Louise J./Oughton, Elizabeth A. (2006): 'What Do You Mean?' The Importance of Language in Developing Interdisciplinary Research. In: Transactions of the Institute of British Geographers 31, 3, pp. 371–382.

Brewer, Garry D. (1999): The Challenges of Interdisciplinarity. In: Policy Sciences 32, 4, pp. 327–337.

Bösl, Elsbeth/Schatz, Desiree (2019): Wissenschafts- und Technikgeschichte in „Interdisziplinären" Master-Studiengängen: Ein Erfahrungsbericht aus München. In: Popplow, Marcus (ed.): Technik- und Wissenschaftsgeschichte in der universitären Lehre: Formate, Adressaten, Konzepte. Karlsruhe: KIT, pp. 109–127.

Lavadia, Courtney et al. (2018): Student and Faculty Perspectives on Effectiveness of an Interdisciplinary Graduate Engineering Program. In: 2018 IEEE Frontiers in Education Conference (FIE), pp. 1–7.

Lerch, Sebastian (2017): Interdisziplinäre Kompetenzen. Stuttgart: UTB, pp. 15–21.

Pohl, Christian/Hirsch Hadorn, Gertrude (2008): Methodological Challenges of Transdisciplinary Research. In: Natures Sciences Sociétés 16, pp. 111–121. Available at https://www.nss-journal.org/articles/nss/abs/2008/02/nss8204/nss82 04.html, last accessed September 25, 2020.

Weber, Jutta (ed.) (2011): Interdisziplinierung? Zur Übersetzungspolitik einer neuen Technowissenschaftskultur. In: Interdisziplinierung? Zum Wissenstransfer zwischen den Geistes-, Sozial- und Technowissenschaften. Bielefeld: Transcript, pp. 83–112.

Diffracting Braunschweig: Outlines of a (Neo)Materialist Concept of Meeting and Spatiotemporality

Jan Büssers

1. Introduction

This contribution is a homage to Braunschweig – the city that provided the geographical space for the PhD program "Gendered Configurations of Humans and Machines" (KoMMa.G). Furthermore, it is an entanglement of a guided city tour that took place during the "Interdisciplinary Conference on the Relations of Humans, Machines and Gender" (Braunschweig, October 16–19, 2019) and my current work on a PhD thesis on the differences of the (neo)materialist approaches of Ernst Bloch and Karen Barad. This entanglement aims at showing that a city is a material place in time, where human and nonhuman agents meet, live, and die alongside one another. This text tries, therefore, to explore an application of the neomaterialist readings of modalities, relationality, and situatedness in space and time, i.e. exploring spatiotemporality. It takes the event of a guided city tour and Braunschweig as real, i.e. actual, examples and aims at (1) insights into what approaching a city with a focus on spatiotemporality in a (neo)materialist manner might mean, (2) applying this approach to Braunschweig and meetings that take place in a city more generally, and (3) concluding with remarks on leaving the city, i.e. looking backwards and forwards.

2. Approaching Braunschweig – Groundwork

Real, i.e. actual, places in time/s have been the subjects of philosophers throughout the ages. For example, the materialist philosopher Ernst Bloch takes an interest in geographical places and experiences, dedicating the second volume of "Verfremdungen" to "Geographica" (Bloch 1964). There, he reflects on places where he had lived, or places and sights that he had visited. It is a volume written over many years and, accordingly, in many places. A striking text is "Ludwigshafen-Mannheim"[1], written in 1928, in which Bloch writes about his hometown Ludwigshafen (probably in his childhood memories) and Mannheim, the city nearby. The text reflects the different material conditions, the societal as well as the economic and cultural ones, that shaped the face of these neighboring cities, which are separated by more than the river Rhine (Bloch 1964: 13–17). In a similar vein, Walter Benjamin's "Arcades Project"[2] is an unfinished masterpiece about Paris in the 19th century. In this fragmentary work, the materialist basis of history reveals itself in the many-splendored face(t)s of a city built, re-built, and re-shaped numerous times in history. It is the tale of a city that has become, in Benjamin's reading, the capital of the 19th century. In contrast to Bloch's memories of Ludwigshafen and Mannheim, Benjamin describes a place at a time when he had not yet been born[3], in order to bear witness to the things he described.

The neomaterialist thinker Karen Barad has used Walter Benjamin's work (including the Arcades Project, among others) to reflect on temporalities flashing up – traversing one another. Approaching a city, therefore, might mean "diffract[ing] the past through the present moment, like the play of light inside a crystal." (Barad 2017: 22) Thereby, the past becomes present in the state of its having become this very city, as it can be seen right now – and already being on the brink of becoming something else, harboring a tendency towards a future transformation. "»Thick-now« is an identifying phrase that I use to invoke the thick sense of multiple historicities and temporalities that exist in any given moment." (Barad 2017: 76) This "thick-now" is a spatio-temporal phrase that flashes up in the very givenness of a moment and in-cludes all the traces of the past and the potentiality of any given moment in it.

---

1 This text can also be also be found in "Erbschaft dieser Zeit" (Bloch 1985: 218–211), which would also provide fruitful insights to spatiotemporality from a Blochian point of view, reflecting on Nazism in Germany and his concept of (un)simultaneity.

2 The German edition was published as the fifth volume of his selected works (Benjamin 1991).

3 Similar to Ernst Bloch, Walter Benjamin wrote about his own childhood in "Berliner Kindheit um 1900" (1987). As the title suggests, it is also a work on growing up at a certain place in time. Instead of Ludwigshafen, it is about Berlin at the very beginning of the 20th century. It is a recollection of places, things, and, in a Baradian sense, critters in a city that matter to a child, written down in the 1930s when the author himself became witness to the rise of Nazism. Berlin and Nazi Germany became places that were hostile to Jewish think-ers, such as Benjamin, but that remained vivid in his memories and materialized again in his writings. Berlin was a place that he was not able to see again. He committed suicide during his flight in 1940, when all hope for a safe haven was gone, denied permission to cross the border from France to Spain in the Pyrenees (from where he wanted to head for the USA) and fearing extradition to the Gestapo (for a detailed witness report, see Scholem 2016: 279–282).

Thus, it also entails the potential otherness of the past that has not come to pass, but that could have been possible.

So, what is to be seen on a guided city tour? The perspective of participants will be what new materialists, especially Karen Barad, might call a superposition: "*Jetztzeit* [J.B.: now-time] is a crystallization of times, of multiple temporalities, blasted out of the continuum of history: a superposition of times – moments from the past – existing in the thick-now of the present moment." (Barad 2017: 33) A city grown at a certain point in and over time is always a simultaneity of artifacts and buildings of various times, and only upon meeting them in the very now of a moment in time, do moments of the past shoot through time into presence.

Barad's approach is thereby also radically queer[4], since it questions fixed identities and pleads for an agentive approach to reality – one in which "[a]ll real living is meeting. And each meeting matters." (Barad 2007: 353) These meetings happen with critters of all kinds – as she jokingly sums up in one of her works: "queer critters that will be introduced in this section include lightning, neuronal receptor cells in stingrays, a phantom species of dinoflagellates, academics (a strange species), and atoms." (Barad 2012b: 33) So, it might also be appropriate to call Braunschweig itself a critter to be met – thus, approaching the thick-now of a city is like being confronted with a lively, mutating, and always changing critter. For certain, a critter that one cannot expect to be the same when encountered once again – *tempora mutantur, nos et mutamur in illis.*[5]

3. Approaching Braunschweig – On Foot and through Time

A group of international scholars set foot to explore Braunschweig on a guided city tour on the third evening of the "Interdisciplinary Conference on the Relations of Humans, Machines and Gender" (October 18, 2019). Starting at the University of Arts (Braunschweig), their track led them by old cemeteries, over a bridge crossing the river Oker, through a no-more-existing, i.e. virtual, gate to the old part of the town, then, via several squares, all the way to the Cathedral and the iconic lion statue in front of the Dankwarderode

---

4   As Karen Barad explains in an interview: "Indeed, given that »queer« is a radical questioning of identity and binaries, including the nature/culture binary, I explain, based on a detailed consideration of recent experimental findings, that all sorts of seeming impossibilities are indeed possible, including the queerness of causality, matter, space, and time. [...] »Queer« is itself a lively, mutating organism, a desiring radical openness, an edgy protean differentiating multiplicity, an agential dis/continuity, an enfolded reiteratively materializing promiscuously inventive spatiotemporality." (Barad 2012a: 81)

5   Loosely translated: "Times change, and we change with them."

Castle, which had already been illuminated by the evening lightings. Having been given hints at the historic background and the geographical situatedness of Braunschweig, words shed a light at what was materially there and on things that would have been there at this very place in a different time – times when Braunschweig was a duchy, or when its most iconic figure, Henry the Lion, walked the streets of medieval Braunschweig. Those words also shined a light on the dark spots of history, e.g. the precariousness of Jewish life through the ages, or Nazism and the destruction of vast parts of Braunschweig during World War II. Rebuilding Braunschweig in the decades after its destruction must have been the most severe imprint of time on its current look – building a city for the people and their needs at a certain time is confronted with the partial rebuilding of historic places.

Braunschweig is an assemblage of built and restored historic buildings and monuments alongside a travesty of seemingly old parts that actually are just restored or re-built facades of what once was there. Braunschweig is a lively mutating organism made of stone, wood, glass, steel, and the people and all the other critters living and dying in it. It is shaped by a play of materials in and at humans' hands, bearing witness to what was feasible for construction at a certain place in time. But a city is always more than humans inhabiting their buildings: it is also co-created by all the nonhuman animals that find their niches and ways of living in the city; it is moreover shaped by geographical conditions, climate, and vegetation. Today's visible Braunschweig is the result of constant building and rebuilding, constructing and de(con)structing, weathering and renovating.

Contextualizing spatiotemporality, Braunschweig also literally houses time itself. The Physikalisch-Technische Bundesanstalt is home to atomic clocks defining exact time. In her work, Karen Barad names three clocks that matter to her "telling time/s": (1) the "Doomsday Clock" as it "represents scientists' estimation of our proximity to global catastrophe" (Barad 2018: 207), (2) the clocks in Hiroshima that stopped on August 6, 1945 at 8:15 a.m., the very moment when the nuclear bomb had just exploded, and (3) the atomic clocks, just like the ones in Braunschweig, that synchronize "[g]lobal time, universal time, cosmic time – all keeping rhythm with the smallest bits of matter" (Barad 2018: 209). Braunschweig is such a place, where time materializes in apparatuses. But as Barad continues, quoting Benjamin: "Clock time is what Walter Benjamin poignantly calls »homogenous empty time«." (Barad 2018: 210) Only in relating a lived life and the actual meetings of entities in the world does the regime of empty clock time help situate happenings in their spatiotemporality – just like the walk through Braunschweig on October 18, 2019 that started by meeting at 5:30 p.m. outside the University of Arts – because every meeting matters.

4. Conclusions – Leaving Braunschweig

Looking back towards a city, leaving it, means literally also taking along memories – taking it to other places at other times, being able to compare, and, most importantly, being able to report and make stories of a place in time just like Ernst Bloch and Walter Benjamin did in their own manners.

Cities like Braunschweig are unfinished in the best sense of Blochian[6] thinking. They are open to lives lived within them – lives lived by all critters: human alongside non-human agents. Upon returning, this unfinished quality might be seen in what has changed since the last visit, but, more importantly, it would have to be seen in the potentiality of a city at a certain time, in its not-yet, another Blochian term for what seems realistically possible at a certain time and might become reality – a utopian negativity inside the thick-now of the present city. Braunschweig is not a utopia, it is a fixed place, a topos, that will change and can be intentionally changed (in time).

So, leaving Braunschweig and one distant day thinking back to what might have been seen at the city tour could mean trying to find the identifying, most iconic element of this very city – in this case probably the lion(s). There are lions made of metal, stone, paint, carved in wood, and so on, but there are no lions of flesh and bone[7] to be found in the current city of Braunschweig. Not even the zoo has lions, although it is currently home to tigers and a cheetah. As Hans Blumenberg writes "a world without lions would be dreary" (Blumenberg 2013: 77), and even though it lacks a living lion right now, *Braunschweig without its lion(s) would be dreary as well*.

---

6   Ernst Bloch sees the world as unfinished – placed into human hands to be fulfilled. This is a recurring topic in Bloch's work, which can already be found in "Geist der Utopie" (1918/1923).

7   Except for Henry's bones resting in the crypt underneath the cathedral.

References

Barad, Karen (2007): Meeting the Universe Halfway. Quantum Physics and the Entanglement of Matter and Meaning. Durham/London: Duke University Press.

Barad, Karen (2012a): Intra-actions. Interview of Karen Barad by Adam Kleinman. In: Mousse 34, pp. 76–81.

Barad, Karen (2012b): Nature's Queer Performativity. In: Kvinder, Køn og forskning. Feminist Materialism 1–2, pp. 25–53.

Barad, Karen (2017): What Flashes Up: Theological-Political-Scientific Fragments. In: Keller, Catherine/Rubenstein, Mary-Jane (eds.): Entangled Worlds. Religion, Science, and New Materialism. New York (NY): Fordham University Press, pp. 21–88.

Barad, Karen (2018): Troubling Time/s and Ecologies of Nothingness: Re-turning, Re-membering, and Facing the Incalculable. In: Fritsch, Matthias et al. (eds.): Eco-Deconstruction. Derrida and Environmental Philosophy. New York (NY): Fordham University Press, pp. 206–248.

Benjamin, Walter (1987): Berliner Kindheit um 1900. Mit einem Nachwort von Theodor W. Adorno. Frankfurt am Main: Suhrkamp.

Benjamin, Walter (1991): Das Passagen-Werk. Gesammelte Schriften Band V. Frankfurt am Main: Suhrkamp.

Bloch, Ernst (1964): Verfremdungen II. Geographica. Frankfurt am Main: Suhrkamp.

Bloch, Ernst (1985): Erbschaft dieser Zeit. Frankfurt am Main: Suhrkamp.

Blumenberg, Hans (2013): Löwen. Berlin: Suhrkamp.

Scholem, Gershom (2016): Walter Benjamin – die Geschichte einer Freundschaft. Berlin: Suhrkamp.

Of Egg Machines and Tread Profiles: On the Shaping of Materiality and Knowledge by Apparatuses

Max Metzger

1. Where to Start

At the international Rad-Schiene-Tagung in 2015, Thomas Kolbe (2015) presented his finding that the German tread profile[1] S1002 is no longer a wear profile[2] and is shaping itself differently than originally intended. The wheel is losing material in a different manner than expected and the tread profile is changing form. As a result, this type of tread profile requires optimization. But optimizing solely as a railway engineer does not seem to me to be a promising approach. I doubt that there is such a thing as THE right tread profile to find. Instead, it is always influenced by maxims given by people, politics, standards, developers, optimizers... Hence, I wanted to combine my task of optimizing the tread profile with feminist science and technology studies. I especially draw on Karen Barad's *agential realism* (Barad 2007: 132–185 [Chapter 4]), entangling her theory with my optimization project. *Agential realism* has been applied to many fields, such as engineering, e.g. by Waltraud Ernst (2017) and informatics, e.g. by Corinna Bath (2014).

In the following, I will describe two *apparatuses* (Barad 2007: 169–170) and the line of thought that led to one of the core research questions of my doctoral thesis.

---

[1] The wheel of a train has a specific tread profile, as shown in Figure 3. The geometrical form of the tread profile influences the running behaviour of the train. Furthermore, the wheel's surface needs to be smooth and clean.

[2] A wear profile is a tread profile derived from the form of the profile after long-time usage. The S1002 was developed in the 1960ies.

2. A Thought Experiment – The Egg Machine

The Egg Machine can prepare marvelous fried eggs. It is the only known method for preparing eggs. If there had been more methods, the Egg Machine would have been able to prepare eggs accordingly.

Figure 1: The Egg Machine

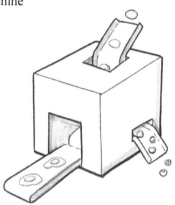

Source: Facundo Guitterez and Max Metzger

What has happened in the world where the Egg Machine exists? As you probably know, there are more ways to prepare an egg than frying it. You can poach, boil, or scramble it. You can use eggs with loads of other ingredients to make several different dishes. Now, imagine the invention of the Egg Machine, which can prepare marvelous fried eggs. In consequence, everybody is starting to use the Egg Machine for preparing eggs. If we jump 400 years ahead in time and we ask someone how they prepare their eggs, their answer would probably be "I use the Egg Machine." To the question "Can an egg be prepared with another method?", they would answer "No, they can only be fried, otherwise the Egg Machine would have been able to prepare them in more ways." And whoosh, we are in the story as told above. The most amazing thing has happened: The Egg Machine has shaped what is possible to do with eggs.

That thought experiment might seem totally absurd and counterintuitive. Why should something like this happen? And I agree, the thought experiment is absurd. But if instead of the Egg Machine we have an *apparatus* where the underlying process is not understood by the users, but only by the people who constructed and introduced this *apparatus*, then the story might change. It would probably take a lot less than 400 years until this *apparatus* shapes the only possible method of doing something. (Götschel/Metzger 2017)

3. A Regularly-Used Tool

Figure 2: Track Gauge Measuring Device

Source: Heribert Lehna

Going back to railway engineering, there are a lot of fixed values, e.g. the gauge between the tracks for ensuring the safe running behavior of trains. If the track gauge is too wide, the train becomes unstable at high velocities and safety against derailment is no longer ensured. If the track gauge is too narrow, the wheel of the train can be restrained in curves and the added force can lead to derailment. Hence, a track gauge should stay inside the obligatory range to create a safe running environment for trains. In Germany, the track gauge is typically 1435 mm (+20 mm, −5 mm)[3]. There is a specific tool called Track Gauge Measuring Device[4] (TGMD) for measuring the gauge, as shown in Figure 2. The device is placed on top of the tracks, making it possible to measure the distance between the rails. Moreover, the distance has to be measured 10 mm underneath the top of the rail, a parameter that is built into the TGMD.

According to *agential realism*, we have a *phenomenon* (Barad 2007: 139–140) consisting of rails, the gauge, the TGMD, the person measuring, the weather, etc. This *phenomenon* can be *cut* (Barad 2007: 148) in several

---

3   For the national railway network. For light railway networks, the track gauge can vary from 1000 mm up to 1500 mm. There are also some local railway networks with different track gauges.
4   In German this is called *Spurweitenmessgerät*.

ways[5]: One is the *cutting* between (1) the rails, with a specific gauge, and (2) the TGMD positioned by the measurer. The weather influences the friction between the surface of the rails and the TGMD, and also the situational attitude of the person measuring. The construction of the TGMD ensures more or less that the TGMD is positioned in the *right*[6] manner so that the track gauge can be measured accordingly. Another *cutting* is between (1) the positioned TGMD, whose *correct* position on the rails depends on friction, dirt, etc., and (2) the measurer. There are several ways for the person measuring to get the desired data from the TGMD: Either by reading the value shown on a digital display integrated into the TGMD or by using the analog scale, which is also part of the TGMD. This *cut* enables the measuring person to take measures depending on weather conditions, situational attitude, eyesight, and further "interfering" circumstances[7] (Metzger 2018).

The implications of the first described *cut* are particularly interesting in this example. The *right* fit in accordance to the agreed-upon standards is inscribed in the *apparatus* used for the measurement, the TGMD. The result of the measurement lies beneath the construction of the *apparatus*: by using it, the result is pre-shaped. Although this might seem trivial – because a lot of tools are produced for a specific purpose and are refined to meet the *right* prerequisites, so that the measured value is in accordance to the needs of the analysis – it becomes tricky when a tool is far more complex and covers more functions or when a tool, like the Egg Machine in the thought experiment, gains the power to shape what is known. With the TGMD, we have an example that, firstly, shows how Barad's *agential realism,* especially the *agential cut,* can be applied to something like engineering and, secondly, helps us to understand that with the change of perspective via different *cuts*, we are getting a different understanding of the *phenomenon* at hand. These results already start pointing in a direction where the *apparatus* and the *phenomenon* become far more complex and an interesting site for a deeper dive.

5   A dimension which is not part of the example is time. The question arises of whether the two cuts are taken at the same time or whether one is following the other. Time can be understood in a non-classical way as pointed out by Barad (2007: 179–182).

6   I also work in railway engineering, where words like *right, correct,* and *well done* are used by me and others on a regular basis. I highlighted these words to show the inscribed and intended expectations for the topic at hand. In using these phrases to evaluate whether something meets specific expectations or not normatively, these expectations are (re)produced, including by me in this text. I think using these words is problematic and needs to be highlighted.

7   To reduce the impact of these circumstances the engineers tend to take multiple measures. This enables the engineer to calculate error margins that describe the uncertainty of the measurement.

4. A Tool for Tread Profile Optimization

Figure 3: Tread Profile

Source: Max Metzger

Nowadays, tread profile optimization is not done by running tests with trains. This has not always been the case: in the past, optimization tests were carried out on trains and wagons and the researchers identified a threshold value that needed to be met. This threshold value ensured that most trains and wagons wouldn't derail. This kind of method cannot be applied any more. The amounts of money and time spent need to be reduced[8] and, furthermore, it is too risky to let trains and wagons derail for the purpose of optimization. Additionally, current theories are more complex, and a lot of variables need to be taken into account. There are 23 parameters (Metzger 2015) that can vary in derailment alone. Further parameters originating from other criteria, like running stability, the comfort of the passengers, or noise emission, also influence the optimal tread profile and need to be taken into account. This huge number of parameters is not analytically solvable, so we need to model and simulate the behavior of the train with different tread profiles. Current simulation programs on the market are highly complex and the implementation of the underlying theory of aspects such as movement equations or contact mechanics is not easily understandable. Users of the programs for simulating wheel-rail contact have to trust that the implementation of the theories[9] was

---

8   The need for spending less money and time is at least a given for the current primacy of our society: the economy.

9   Interestingly, the contact behavior theories by Joost Jacques Kalker (1973) and it's realization by Kalker (1982) or Oldrich Polach (1990) between the wheel and the rail are just an

done well. In consequence, the programs are calculating something that might be what the user is hoping for (or might not). The understanding of the programs, the inscribed restrictions, and the understanding of the results of the simulations are becoming really difficult, if not impossible. Furthermore, it is not evident which results were pre-shaped by the structure of the programs, as shown in the example of the TGMD.

5. Where to Go from Here

The absurdity of the Egg Machine and the triviality of the TGMD vanish when looking at such complex *apparatuses* as simulation programs. Those programs shape, inside the *phenomena* they are part of, a lot of what is gained by the *agential cut*, without the user even noticing what has already been created through the use of such complex *apparatuses*.

In my PhD project, I aim to get a better understanding of the power of programs in the knowledge production process, explicitly applied to tread profile optimization.

approximation for describing what is happening a bit better then Heinrich Hertz's classical contact theory (1881). But it still is a rough approximation, since what exactly is happening in the wheel-rail contact is not yet understood.

References

Barad, Karen (2007): Meeting the Universe Halfway: Quantum Physics and the Entanglement of Matter and Meaning. Durham/London: Duke University Press.

Bath, Corinna (2014): Diffractive Design. In: Marsden, Nicola/Kempf, Ute (eds.): GENDER-UseIT: HCI, Usability und UX unter Gendergesichtspunkten. Oldenbourg: De Gruyter. pp. 27–36.

Ernst, Waltraud (2017): Emancipatory Interferences with Machines? In: International Journal of Gender, Science and Technology 9, 2, pp. 178–196.

Götschel, Helene/Metzger, Max (2017): Die Verschränkung von Technik und Kultur. In: Die Ingenieurin 124, pp. 20–22.

Hertz, Heinrich (1881): Über die Berührung fester elastischer Körper. In: Journal für die reine und angewandte Mathematik 92, pp. 156–171.

Kalker, Joost Jacques (1973): On the Rolling Contact of Two Elastic Bodies in the Presence of Dry Friction. Diss. Delft: Delft University of Technology. Laboratory of Engineering Mechanics.

Kalker, Joost Jacques (1982). A Fast Algorithm for the Simplified Theory of Rolling Contact. In: Vehicle System Dynamics 11, 1, pp. 1–13.

Kolbe, Thomas (2015): Das Radprofil S1002 ist kein Verschleißprofil mehr … 14. Internationale Schienenfahrzeugtagung Dresden (unpubl.).

Metzger, Max (2015): Einflüsse von Kraftwirkungen an Schienenfahrzeugen auf die Ausschöpfung der Sicherheit gegen Entgleisen. Diplomarbeit. Potsdam: Universität Potsdam. Institut für Physik.

Metzger, Max (2018): Radprofiloptimierung - eine epistemische Herausforderung. In: Tagungsband zur 16. Internationalen Schienenfahrzeugtagung Dresden. Hamburg: DVV, pp. 179–180.

Polach, Oldrich (1990). Matematické Modelování Adhezní Vazby Kola a Kolejnice (Mathematische Modellierung der Kraftschlusskopplung von Rad und Schiene). In: Dynamika Kolejových Vozidel a Železničních Tratí, pp. 91–96.

Approaching a Feminist Actor-Network Theory

Ingo Bednarek

1. Introduction

The concept of New Media describes a major change in technologies and their social uses from analog to digital media. Key terms characterizing this change are interactivity, hypertextuality, and virtuality. They are characterized by new images of the flexible, the flowing, and differentiation in process; gendered images of transformation. Not only the use of media platforms (such as social networks, online forums, etc.) is gendered, but also their content. The process of gendering is already effective in the technical devices used to access these platforms and during the development process of these devices. But in the public mass media discourse, media and their specific uses are mistaken almost exclusively for genderless and, supposedly, neutral objects, whereby the (re)producing properties of society and gender are lingering in hiding. For a more appropriate discussion of media transformation, new perspectives are, therefore, needed on the subject of media in order to decipher the novel images mentioned and take their effects seriously. The term technology is already defined by production methods that produce technology. Teresa de Lauretis emphasizes this meaning with her 1987 work "Technologies of Gender" in which she negotiates the construction and representation of gender. The sex-gender system, as De Lauretis calls it, is both a socio-cultural construct and a semiotic apparatus: a system of representation that significantly influences or represents the levels of meaning within a society (De Lauretis 1998). When De Lauretis developed her approach in the mid-1980s, it was probably not yet clear how much digital media would change all areas of life, in addition to the analog media she analyzed. Electronic, digital, and interactive media, which are summarized under the colloquially used term new media, have created new forms of construction and representation of gender. At the same time, this involves new demands on (media) scientific analyses. Many processes of gender (co)production are difficult to grasp. Considerations on the construction of gender in connection with information technologies are already taking place in the media-sociological discourse. However, current analyses are too often based on the tradition of feminist studies of social shaping, as noted, for example, by Vivian Lagesen (Lagesen 2012; Leach and Turner 2015) and are therefore insufficient for my project. The concept of social shaping describes how new technologies are not inevitably gendered in the way their producers develop them but only get charged with social meaning or become gendered by the users and their practices. While this alignment blurs the lines between making and using, the role or agency of the media (and technology) and their potential gender-producing properties are ignored (Lagesen 2012; Leach and Turner 2015; Pias 2004; Suchman 2007). Thus, my goal is to build on existing knowledge and analysis tools to expand the analysis capabilities of Actor-Network Theory. Because not only is agency ignored by media and technology, it is also difficult to grasp it using many previous theories and models. For example, Eileen Green and Carrie Singleton emphasized in 2013 that both social-gender interactions and gendered structural inequalities could be obscured by what they call the digital age. They emphasize that the connections of feminist theory, sociological ideas, and everyday digital experiences have to be explicitly strengthened to counteract potential obfuscation (Green and Singleton 2013: 36). The combination of ANT and feminist theories can be linked to ongoing arguments in German media studies on the connection between media technology and gender. In the "Gender & Medien-Reader" (Peters/Seier 2016b), published in 2016, the two editors draw a strong link between gender and media. They explain that the utopias of a post-gender world were still being worked on in the early 1990s. In this regard, a certain disillusionment has spread. Increasingly, they see this perspective being suppressed by the established critical Internet research, with its focus on control regimes, big data, and individualized self-expression. They write: "Not the computer or the Internet, but the software becomes an object of investigation as a technological artefact with an invisible gender history" (Peters/Seier 2016a: 16). Peters and Seier understand gender as constitutive of media thinking. They, therefore, emphasize the need for questioning where and how ideas about gender are affective in media and how, conversely, media structures gender stereotypes (Peters/Seier 2016a: 14). Criticism cannot be aimed at the establishing of critical Internet research in itself. Still, it must be noted that because of it another process has emerged, which carries the risk of hiding the role of gender in terms of media and technology.

2. Approaching a Feminist Actor-Network Theory

Actor-Network Theory (ANT) offers a perspective that allows the actions of human and non-human actors to be taken seriously in their interconnectedness. With its critique of the Enlightenment, which placed the human being at the center of the action, ANT and its many diverse approaches prove to be fruitful and central to my research project. Dualisms, such as micro- and macro-levels, human/nature, technology/human, and even, according to Donna Haraway, the separation of human/God, should be exploded as constructs of modernity. This theory, then, offers the opportunity to reformulate traditional questions of social order and, above all, questions of power and domination. Thus, we can gain new perspectives and insights (Belliger/Krieger 2006; Haraway 1995; Latour 2006a; 2006b; 2015; Saldanha 2003; Schüttpelz 2013). With its focus on the deconstruction of dualisms, ANT is very amenable to feminist considerations, even if this connection cannot be seamless. Working with ANT, the attempt to reject previous theories as structures of a constructed modernity risks also rejecting political theories and concepts that seem indispensable for a leftist, feminist point of view. Many current studies have already discussed the interplay between ANT, feminist theory and technology. However, most of the time the discussions tend to be limited to existing studies and lamenting the lack of updated research projects that could complement and negotiate the debates in practice. In the article "ANT and Politics: Working in and on the World" which is a conversation between Vicky Singleton and John Law, Singleton emphasizes that if we want to see gender, we will find it. It's just important to look for it (Law/Singleton 2013: 11). I wonder then, why gender rarely plays a crucial role in ANT studies. This suggests that ANT-inspired research itself shows a gender bias; a male one in which studies on exclusion, gender, and social discrimination cannot be found, at least not to my knowledge currently. It turns out that ANT basically has two problems: its actors and its networks, or rather its perspective on networks – even if it reads like a bad joke. The questions are which networks are selected and how to choose an entry point. These questions are directly related to the actors in the networks, the visible and invisible ones. Without feminist-motivated questions and without a feminist-transformed ANT that can decipher invisible elements in networks, new insights become difficult. Yet following the actors is precisely the strength of ANT. To do this, marginalized actors must be given a voice. Reflections on ANT and the possibility of making it productive for feminist research interests have taken place, especially (but not exclusively) in the English-speaking world. In addition, the question to what extent the application of ANT permits political positions, or whether it can be politically motivated itself, arises. It is, therefore, possible to form roughly two categories for reflecting on ANT: (1) the criticism of the apoliticism of ANT and, where appropriate, the attempt to politicize the same (Alcadipani/Hassard 2010; Bergermann 2016; Law/Singleton 2013, 2015; Star 2017). (2) The emphasis on the potential of power analysis regarding the production of gender from a feminist perspective (Bauer 2006; Bergermann 2016; Corrigan/Mills 2012; Holas 2011; Lagesen 2012; Law/Singleton 2013; Quinlan 2012; 2014; Star 2017).

Both are political concerns, but they differ in their reasoning. The political is often emphasized in terms of networks, while the feminist in terms of visible and invisible actors. A disparity between political claims and precise applications of ANT arises from two different views on ANT analyses that need to be merged: (1) If the researcher has a specific idea of society and its structures of inequality, the associated theories and perspectives threaten to influence one's view, or, in other words, affect the researchers neutrality and, therefore, their ability to actually follow the actors in the sense of ANT. With a politicized perspective, it seems harder to get involved in the actual actor network and the unknown. Hence Latour's demand to reject theories of modernity (Latour 2015). (2) Without theory and a concept of society, only the loud actors are visible in a network. Exclusion mechanisms, invisible parts in the construction and stabilization of networks would remain invisible in an analysis in that scenario. How the parts that make up the network even had the opportunity to become part of the network, while other parts can never belong to it, remains unclear. Possibility conditions – who receives the power to be visible, to silence others, or even to be able to join a network – cannot be captured without theory and a concept of society (Bauer 2006: 20; Bergermann 2016; Holas 2011; Star 2017: 2). When Vicky Singleton mentions that one has to be sensitive and attentive to the unexpected (Law/Singleton 2015), this is the necessary complement. Theoretical assumptions must not lead to blindness to the unexpected. According to Susan Leigh Star, incorporating experience is a crucial strength of feminist analysis. This can already have an effect at the beginning of research by allowing the choice of the experience of outcasts, non-users, and/or outsiders as the starting point for analysis. It describes perspective as a way to move from experience to analyzing the fact that this experience could have been different (Star 2017: 254). Referring to Fujimura, Star emphasizes that it is important to ask which human perspectives prevail in the construction of technologies and truths over others, and why, as well as why some human actors agree with the will of other actors, and why and how yet others oppose these role assignments (Star 2017: 245). Vivian Lagesen argues that it makes sense to look at how people construct themselves and their actions. In this context, she is interested in the role of technology. She writes: "The question is what ANT and Latour may offer in terms of analytical strategies to avoid binaries and essentialism, as well as dissolving asymmetries in the treatment of gender and technology" (Lagesen 2012: 447).

3. Outlook

Two perspectives can be deduced from the feminist intervention possibilities that I have analyzed up to now: (1) marginalization processes and visibility in networks, as well as their formation; (2) the specific question of the interplay of gender and technology and its mutual/reciprocal conditions of production. Central to this are the following assumptions and instructions: multiple marginality always accompanies multiple membership (Star 2017). The research entry point into an actor-network-analysis has to be deliberately chosen and justified, and the political and empirical implications of the decision have to be considered (Quinlan 2014). Here, the past and its interpretation as gendered knowledge can be understood as an actor in the network of actors, in order to create explanatory spaces for experiences of discrimination and/or marginalization (Corrigan/Mills 2012). According to Gitelman, the past can be extended as an actor as well as a factor in media and technology (Gitelman 2006), since she describes media as subjects that are always historical as well. Media technology itself then presents different (historically interpreted) knowledge structures that can decisively shape actor networks. From the combination of the concept of doing gender with ANT, it should become apparent which concrete parts of technology are inherent in the construction and production of gender (Lagesen 2012). The presented points are decisive influences on my project of the design of a feminist ANT. Acting as exemplars and imagining connections between ANT and feminist theories, these clues do not yet constitute a working research design for carrying out a gender-sensitive ANT analysis, but they do pave the way for such an important outcome.

References

Alcadipani, Rafael/Hassard, John (2010): Actor-Network Theory, Organizations and Critique: Towards a Politics of Organizing. In: Organization 17, 4, pp. 419–435.

Bauer, Robin (2006): Grundlagen der Wissenschaftstheorie und Wissenschaftsforschung. In: Ebeling, Smilla/Schmitz, Sigrid (eds.): Geschlechterforschung und Naturwissenschaften. VS Verlag für Sozialwissenschaften, pp. 247–280.

Belliger, Andréa/Krieger, David J. (2006): Einführung in die Akteur-Netzwerk-Theorie. In: Belliger, Andréa/Krieger, David J. (eds.): ANThology: Ein einführendes Handbuch zur Akteur-Netzwerk-Theorie. Bielefeld: Transcript, pp. 13–50.

Bergermann, Ulrike (2016): Kettenagenturen: Latours Fotografien, Brasilien 1991. In: Becker, Ilka et al. (eds.): Fotografisches Handeln: Das fotografische Dispositiv. Marburg: Jonas, pp. 161–181.

Corrigan, Lawrence T./Mills, Albert J. (2012): Men on Board: Actor-Network Theory, Feminism and Gendering the Past. In: Management & Organizational History 7, 3, pp. 251–265.

Gitelman, Lisa (2006): Always Already New: Media, History and the Data of Culture. Cambridge, Massachusetts: MIT Press.

Green, Eileen/Singleton, Carrie (2013): Gendering the Digital: The Impact of Gender and Technology Perspectives on the Sociological Imagination. In: Orton-Johnson, K./Prior N. (eds.): Digital Sociology. London: Palgrave Macmillan, pp. 34–50.

Haraway, Donna Jeanne (1995): Situiertes Wissen: Die Wissenschaftsfrage im Feminismus und das Privileg einer partialen Perspektive. In: Hammer, C./Stieß, I. (eds.): Die Neuerfindung der Natur: Primaten, Cyborgs und Frauen. Frankfurt am Main: Campus, pp. 73–97.

Holas, Katharina (2011): Technoscience: Akteur-Netzwerk-Theorien und feministische Akzentverschiebungen. In: Conradi, T. et al. (eds.): Strukturentstehung durch Verflechtung. Akteur-Netzwerk-Theorie(n) und Automatismen. München: Wilhelm Fink, pp. 297–312.

Lagesen, Vivian Anette (2012): Reassembling Gender: Actor-Network Theory (ANT) and the Making of the Technology in Gender. In: Social Studies of Science 42, 3, pp. 442–448.

Latour, Bruno (2006a): Drawing Things Together: Die Macht der unveränderlich mobilen Elemente. In: Belliger, Andréa/Krieger, David J. (eds.): ANThology: Ein einführendes Handbuch zur Akteur-Netzwerk-Theorie. Bielefeld: Transcript, pp. 259–307.

Latour, Bruno (2006b): Technik ist stabilisierte Gesellschaft. In: Belliger, Andréa/Krieger, David J. (eds.): ANThology: Ein einführendes Handbuch zur Akteur-Netzwerk-Theorie. Bielefeld: Transcript, pp. 369–397.

Latour, Bruno (2015): Wir sind nie modern gewesen: Versuch einer symmetrischen Anthropologie. Frankfurt am Main: Suhrkamp.

Law, John/Singleton, Vicky (2013): ANT and Politics: Working in and on the World. In: Qualitative Sociology 36, 4, pp. 485–502.

Law, John/Singleton, Vicky (2015): ANT, Multiplicity and Policy. In: HeterogeneitiesDOTnet: John Law's STS Web Page. Available at http://www.heterogenei

ties.net/publications/LawSingleton2014ANTMultiplicityPolicy.pdf, last accessed March 27, 2020.

Leach, Lori/Turner, Steven (2015): Computer Users Do Gender: The Co-Production of Gender and Communications Technology. In: SAGE Open. Available at https://doi.org/10.1177/2158244015604693, last accessed March 27, 2020.

Peters, Kathrin/Seier, Andrea (2016a): Gender & Medien: Einleitung. In: Peters, Kathrin/Seier, Andrea (eds.): Gender & Medien-Reader. Zürich/Berlin: Diaphanes, pp. 9–19.

Peters, Kathrin/Seier, Andrea (2016b): Gender & Medien-Reader. Zürich/Berlin: Diaphanes.

Pias, Claus (2004): Unruhe und Steuerung: Zum utopischen Potential der Kybernetik. In: Rüsen, J. et al. (eds.): Die Unruhe der Kultur: Potentiale des Utopischen. Weilerswist: Velbrück, pp. 301–326.

Quinlan, Andrea (2012): Imagining a Feminist Actor-Network Theory. In: International Journal of Actor-Network Theory and Technological Innovation 4, 2, pp. 1–9.

Quinlan, Andrea (2014): Studying DNA: Envisioning New Intersections between Feminist Methodologies and Actor-Network Theory. In: Tatnall, A. (ed.): Technological Advancements and the Impact of Actor-Network Theory. IGI Global, pp. 196–208.

Saldanha, Arun (2003): Actor-Network Theory and Critical Sociology: Review Essay. In: Critical Sociology 29, 3, pp. 419–432.

Schüttpelz, Erhard (2013): Elemente einer Akteur-Medien-Theorie. In: Schüttpelz, Erhard/Thielmann, Tristan (eds.): Akteur-Medien-Theorie. Bielefeld: Transcript, pp. 9–67.

Star, Susan Leigh (2017): Macht, Technik und die Phänomenologie von Konventionen: Gegen Zwiebeln allergisch sein (1990/91). In: Gießmann, Sebastian/Taha, Nadine (eds.): Grenzobjekte und Medienforschung. Bielefeld: Transcript, pp. 243–271.

Suchman, Lucille Alice (2007): Human-Machine Reconfigurations: Plans and Situated Actions. Cambridge: Cambridge University Press.

Theoretical Cross-Fertilization: Barad's Intra-Action and Cross-Cultural Studies

Yasemin Dayıoğlu-Yücel

1. Introduction

In 1994, German studies[1] Scholar Leslie Adelson published an article that proved to be as influential as it was timeless, for the predicaments described by her are still, or again, prevalent when discussing issues of cultural belonging in Germany and elsewhere today. As much as the 1990s – even if amidst rightwing attacks – set out hopeful notions of overcoming these conflicts, the recent rise of right-wing parties and renewed violence against people perceived as culturally foreign proves that a new intervention is needed.

This article's main aim is to exemplify how Karen Barad's theory of agential realism can be adopted to enrich theories of intercultural German studies, where traditionally the *inter* stands for exchanges between people of two cultural groups, while *intra* would refer to exchanges within the same cultural group. This differentiation already underscores the danger of essentializing that frequently accompanies attempts to foster respect for people of different cultural backgrounds. Barad's concept of intra-action offers a fruitful path out of this predicament. It also creates possibilities for including exchanges between humans and non-humans in cross-cultural studies, which so far have been unjustly overlooked, and helps to weaken the artificial walls built between the humanities (proclaimed as academic fields primarily engaging with humans) and the natural sciences (proclaimed as academic fields primarily exploring non-human objects).

---

1   German Studies is the term widely used for the study of German language, literature and cultures in the US and other English-speaking countries. Compared to *Germanistik*, as the study of German language and literature is referred to in Germany and German-speaking countries, the term German Studies encompasses more of a cultural studies approach and a wider range of interdisciplinary topics.

2. "Opposing Oppositions"

In her article with the telling title "Opposing Oppositions," Adelson makes a stand against opposing notions of Turkish vs. German and inquires what "methodological alternatives a multiculturally oriented German studies has to offer" to the asserted "shortcomings of intercultural Germanistik[2], historical constructions of both Turkish and German identity, and contemporary dilemmas of multicultural literary analysis" (Adelson 1994: 306). Adelson criticizes methods of "intercultural Germanistik" as reinforcing fixed poles, thus creating oppositions instead of pointing to the construction and fluidity of identity concepts:

> By stressing the communicability of difference and perpetuating a model that seeks to teach 'them' how to understand 'us,' interkulturelle Germanistik feigns interest in literary text and cultural context but effectively privileges author and reader as fixed poles in a supposed exchange of meaning. This leaves it helpless to account for the various ways in which culture is propelled by the ongoing production and displacement of unstable differences. Nor can it account for the historical-political functions to which such slippage attains. (Adelson 1994: 306)

Adelson cites David Bathrick's "permanent border action" as a "theoretical strategy concerned with questions of power and cultural representation" (Bathrick 1992: 322 cited in Adelson 1994: 306) and refers to Homi Bhabha's concept of hybridity, which at that time was able to offer scholarship a new framework for thinking out of binary oppositions and advanced the field of cultural studies. Bhabha famously describes his ideas through the image of the stairwell:

> The stairwell as liminal space, in-between the designations of identity, becomes the process of symbolic interaction, the connective tissue that constructs the difference between upper and lower, black and white. The hither and thither of the stairwell, the temporal movement and passage that it allows, prevents identities at either end of it from settling into primordial polarities. This interstitial passage between fixed identifications opens up the possibility of a cultural hybridity that entertains difference without an assumed or imposed hierarchy. (Bhabha 1994: 3–4)

Adopting Bhabha for the context of "Turkish-German relations," Adelson accentuates the "fundamental ambivalence of identity." She concludes: "This holds for the identity of a given 'self' as much as it does for the identity of a marginal 'other'." (Adelson 1994: 307) Texts, according to her, "are no longer seen as discrete cultural artifacts but as open-discursive processes infused with sociality[.] [C]ultural studies explore the production of culture as fundamentally hybrid, liminal, and performative" (ibid.: 306–307). Through her analysis of Sten Nadolny's novel "Selim oder die Gabe der

---

2   Adelson uses the term *Germanistik* to emphasize that she refers to the scholarship stemming from German-speaking countries.

Rede" (Nadolny 1990), Adelson shows how German and Turkish history are intertwined. An idea that she further explored in her article entitled "Touching Tales of Turks, Germans, and Jews: Cultural Alterity, Historical Narrative, and Literary Riddles for the 1990s" in which she turns her attention to shared and entangled pasts (Adelson 2000).

Although Adelson's intervention has been influential and undoubtedly made a difference in the field of Turkish-German studies, as much as Bhabha's concept of hybridity made a difference in the field of cultural studies, scholarship in the field of intercultural German studies, unfortunately, has not ceased to operate with oppositions. This might be attributed to the fact that binary thinking is too prevalent. Yet it might also indicate that concepts such as hybridity still rely on the poles they derive from. Even if those poles are delineated as hybrid in themselves, their hybridity is mostly described as a compound of two predecessors. This might be a simplifying misreading of Bhabha's original theory but it has been inscribed in the praxis of intercultural scholarship.[3]

Whereas Adelson's text from 1994 can hardly be criticized for inquiring about the "relationship" between "Turks and the German Past" (Adelson 1994: 321), from today's standpoint it rather has to be credited as a milestone that needs to be built on – as relationships still require at least two entities. Karen Barad's concept of intra-action offers a way of incorporating the potential of the concept of hybridity, while at the same time providing a vantage point from which to progress further. While ideas of performativity still play a role in Barad's work, Barad is less concerned with the shifting of identities or borders. In fact, pre-relational boundaries do not exist. The same is true of individual boundaries and agency: they are created in certain settings, and they are not only created discursively, but bodily. I will explore this further in staying with Adelson's topic of the Turkish guest worker, yet with a stronger focus on material implications.

3. Guests in the Machine[4]

Whereas Karen Barad's work has been well received in the field of feminist studies, it has not yet been applied to the field of intercultural studies with the

---

3   Cross-Cultural Studies is commonly used as the English equivalent of the German field of *Interkulturelle Studien*. In this article, I use the term *intercultural Germanistik* as Adelson in her programmatic article did. I mainly refer to scholarship that was produced in the context of *interkulturelle Literaturwissenschaft* (intercultural literary studies) or *interkulturelle Literaturdidaktik* (intercultural literary didactics/pedagogy).

4   I borrow this expression from Kerry Howley who uses it to describe the living conditions of guest workers in Singapore (Howley 2007).

important exception of a 2016 article by German studies scholar Margaret Littler (Littler 2016) which I will explore in more depth below. In the following, I will show how Barad's concept of agential realism initiates much-needed interventions in the field of intercultural studies. For a number of reasons, I will turn to the figure of the guest worker, more specifically the Turkish guest worker in Germany, as an example. First of all, the Turkish guest worker is a pivotal sociological and, by now, historical figure that has been widely depicted in literature and film, as it plays a central role in post-war Germany's debates around cultural belonging. Secondly, the figure of the guest worker represents a human as part of machinery. Thirdly, the figure of the guest worker cannot be interpreted in different fields without situating it in a wider discourse. I will illustrate how literature and literary studies (although the argument can be extended to the visual arts and their academic fields respectively) offer opportunities to question boundaries on a thematic as well as a structural level and how Barad's agential realism gives room for a range of interpretational approaches.

In 1975, the writer, artist, and art critic John Berger published the study "A Seventh Man." He writes:

Migrant workers do the most menial jobs. Their chances of promotion are exceedingly poor. When they work in gangs, it is arranged that they work together as foreigners. Equal working relationships to indigenous workers are kept to a minimum. The migrant workers have a different language, a different culture and different short term interests. They are immediately identifiable – not as individuals – but as a group (or a series of national groups). As a group they are at the bottom of every scale: wages, type of work, job security, housing, education, purchasing power. (Berger et al. 1975: 253)

As is obvious from the title and cover photograph[5], Berger restricts his study to the male guest worker. While male guest workers were the first to arrive in Germany, female guest workers followed shortly thereafter. They occupied an even lower rank than the male guest workers. Both male and female guest workers were first placed in gender-separated special hostels, where a number of them shared a room with bunk beds.[6] In her novel "The Bridge of the Golden Horn" (1998), renowned Turkish-German writer Emine Sevgi Özdamar puts the experiences of first generation female guest workers on the stage. It seems consequential (as an implicit acknowledgment of the short-comings of Berger's initial focus on male guest workers) that the foreword to the English translation was provided by John Berger, who describes Özdamar as an "irresistible, all-night story-teller" who "late in the morning wakes up telling another story" (Berger). Özdamar has frequently been cited for her

---

5   The photographs for the study were taken by Jean Mohr.
6   A very resourceful documentation of the Turkish guest worker migration has been published by Eryılmaz and Jamin 1998. DOMiD, the Documentation Centre and Museum of Migration in Germany, has been archiving objects that document migration to Germany in general (https://domid.org; last accessed April 29, 2020).

associations with the word *guest worker* through which the inherent contradiction in the term is blatantly brought to attention: "The word: 'guest worker.' I always see two people in front of me: one is a guest and sits there, and the other one is working."[7] (Özdamar 1993)

In her comprehensive analysis of "The Bridge of the Golden Horn", Margaret Littler was the first to link a cultural studies approach (influenced by Leslie Adelson's interventions[8]) with the work of Gilles Deleuze and situate it in a larger context of material studies for which Karen Barad's work has been influential. Littler's thorough reading of the novel and its aesthetics in the context of Deleuze's "Powers of the False" and machinic agency leads her to conclude that the novel's "non-representational aesthetics" (Littler 2016: 294) cannot be reduced to a "familiar narrative of migrant labour" (ibid.: 290). Rather, it opens up a "world's potential to become" (ibid.: 312). My reading of the novel in the context of human and machine builds on and profits from Littler's profound analysis (with a stronger emphasis on Barad's work) while differing from it in a number of ways:

Although my argument is embedded in the larger field of material studies, in which machinic agency plays an important part, my main focus here is narrow rather than broad, which is to engage with Barad's agential realism to enrich the field of intercultural literary studies as a way to explore potential interactions and intersections in both fields within German studies. What I specifically want to draw attention to is Barad's concept of intra-action as a border-making practice. Intercultural literary studies has focused on the connection of separate (cultural) entities that had not been connected before, while Barad (and material studies more generally) point us to the entanglements that have only artificially been separated in dualistic thinking. As Barad explains with reference to physics experiments, entities do not pre-exist, they are created in an apparatus that encompasses the experiment as much as the researcher. I want to go further than showing that humans and machines are entangled in an assemblage à la Deleuze (and Guattari). Though Littler seems to use these two terms interchangeably, insisting on the differences between the two is of vital importance in my approach. Last but not least, where Littler applies Deleuze's "Powers of the False" to describe Özdamar's narrative technique as non-representational, I use the term *poetic alterity* (*poetische Alterität*) as introduced by Norbert Mecklenburg. While there are overlaps between falsifying narration and poetic alterity, the former focuses on narration inspired by film, while the latter is established in the field of intercultural studies, thus enabling the cross-fertilization of intercultural studies and material studies.

---

7   My translation (Y.D-Y.) Original: "Das Wort 'Gastarbeiter': Ich liebe dieses Wort, ich sehe vor mir immer zwei Personen, eine sitzt da als Gast, und die andere arbeitet."
8   Littler's main point of reference is Adelson's 2005 study "The Turkish Turn in Contemporary German Literature" (2005).

The importance of poetic alterity in the context of intercultural literary studies has been repeatedly emphasized by Norbert Mecklenburg. According to Mecklenburg, poetic alterity finds its expression in any literary depiction that precludes a one-sided interpretation of a literary text and thus evokes several possible meanings. These can be (among others) voids, contradictory utterances that can be expressed through free indirect discourse, and utterances that are reminiscent of other utterances, such as unlabeled intertextual references.[9] All of the above can be applied to obtain humorous effects. While cultural alterity is represented on the thematic level of the text, poetic alterity is part of the particularly-literary structure of the text. The interplay of both forms of alterity in a literary text will enhance the likeliness of gaining intercultural competency through the study of literature. Mecklenburg devotes a chapter to interculturalism and humor in the texts of Özdamar, where he describes the "Bridge of the Golden Horn" as a *female picaresque novel* ("weiblicher Schelmenroman") (Mecklenburg 2008: 509).

In "The Bridge of the Golden Horn," Özdamar humorously describes how female guest workers spend their lives in the factory and the hostel. The hostel for female guest workers is referred to as *Frauenwohnheim* (hostel for women), but by spelling the word *Wohnheim* in a way that points to the articulation with a Turkish accent (*Wonaym*), it is being alienated. Alienation and humor are not only thematic but structural means through which literature creates polysemy. The English translation uses *hossel* instead of the correct *hostel*. The Turkish guest workers speak Turkish to each other, but they incorporate the German word *Wohnheim* as if it were a Turkish word. The *hossel* as well as the factory are gendered spaces. The working women are the majority, led by the German male *Herscher* and the Turkish male translator who also resides in the *hossel*. While harassment of the female guest workers is depicted elsewhere in the novel, female characters are still not shown as victims. On the contrary, the protagonist, a young girl who dreams of becoming a theater actress, regards losing her diamond, a metaphor for her virginity, as a means of becoming a good actress. Sexuality, thus, is not something that can be taken away from her, but something that empowers her to progress.

Power relations are also illustrated in a similarly humorous way:

"The factory boss's name was Herr Schering. Sherin, said the women, they also said Sher. Then they stuck Herr to Sher, so that some women called him Herschering or Herscher." (Özdamar 2007: 7) Here, a seemingly coincidental occurrence opens up a discursive field of power relations and exploitation. Calling the factory boss *Herscher* (which reads as *Herrscher*, the German word for *ruler* can be considered an act of mimicry in Bhabha's

---

9   Norbert Mecklenburg contextualizes the concept of poetic alterity in detail in his chapter on the relation between cultural and poetic alterity (Mecklenburg 2008: 213–237). He especially points out the relevance of Bakhtinian dialogism (ibid.: 229–230).

sense.[10] The language of the people in power is subverted through the means of the guest workers' language abilities in the majority language to call out the exploitative act while at the same time ridiculing the ones in power. This can be further exemplified through a close reading of the following sequence:

> We all worked in the radio factory, each one of us had to have a magnifying glass in our right eye while we were working. Even when we came back to the *hossel* in the evening, we looked at one another or the potatoes we were peeling with our right eye. A button came off, the women sewed the button on again with a wide-open right eye. The left eye always narrowed and remained half shut. We also slept with the left eye a little screwed up, and at five o'clock in the morning, when we were looking for our trousers or skirts in the semi-darkness, I saw that, like me, the other women were looking only with their right eye. (Özdamar 2007: 6–7)

In this description of the work done by the guest workers in the factory and its effect on their lives outside the factory, three aspects stand out. The fact that the guest workers continue using their right eye in their leisure time shows that the magnifying glass used in the radio factory has been inscribed on their bodies. The material magnifying glass might be left at the factory, but the impact it has on their bodies continues to affect them beyond working hours in a bodily and thus also material way. This quote also proves the inseparable entanglement of the labor force and means of production. Humor again is applied as an aesthetic device that creates distance and thus invites the (skilled) reader to delve deeper into the issues depicted here. Littler also points to the entanglement depicted in this scene when she writes that "the novel obscures the determinate distinction between the worker's body and the apparatuses deployed, presenting them as entangled, relational phenomena across which different agencies are dispersed" (Littler 2016: 293) and references the "parodic elements" through which a "'truthful' representation" is rendered obsolete (ibid.: 294). I would, however, suggest that these humorous depictions can be seen as a form of poetic alterity, something I will come back to later in more detail.

One could argue that the image of the female guest workers with their magnifying glasses inscribed on their bodies represents an assemblage as defined by Deleuze and Guattari. In "Two Regimes of Madness," Deleuze and Guattari explain their understanding of an assemblage:

> There are two ways to suppress or attenuate the distinction between nature and culture. The first is to liken animal behavior to human behavior (Lorenz tried it, with disquieting political implications). But what we are saying is that the idea of assemblages can replace the idea of behavior, and thus with respect to the idea of assemblage, the nature-culture distinction no longer matters. In a certain way, behavior is still a contour. But an

---

10   Bhabha dedicates a chapter in his seminal study "The Location of Culture" to his concept of mimicry. "Of Mimicry and Man. The ambivalence of colonial discourse" in Bhabha 1994.

assemblage is first and foremost what keeps very heterogeneous elements together: e.g. a sound, a gesture, a position, etc., both natural and artificial elements. (Deleuze 2006: 179)

The assemblage of guest worker and magnifying glass blends together the means of production and the labor force as well as the inanimate object and the human body. In Levi Bryant's paraphrase of Deleuze and Guattari's understanding of assemblage, objects that are in one way or the other visible are juxtaposed to sensations. Bryant stresses that assemblages can contain only objects, but not only sensations.

Assemblages are composed of heterogeneous elements or objects that enter into relations with one another. These objects are not all of the same type. Thus you have physical objects, happenings, events, and so on, but you also have signs, utterances, and so on. While there are assemblages that are composed entirely of bodies, there are no assemblages composed entirely of signs and utterances. (Bryant 2009)

4. Setting Out for Intra-Active Intercultural Studies

The magnifying glass on the women's eyes clearly encompasses bodily objects, behavior, and also sensations. In Bryant's paraphrase as well as in Deleuze and Guattari's original, the expression "heterogeneous elements" is being used. Bryant also writes about "elements and objects that enter into relations with one another," which can be appropriated to Adelson's quest for the relationship between Turks and the German past (cf. Adelson 1994: 321). This is why Barad's use of the term apparatus offers a much more precise description of the sort of inseparable entanglements that are depicted in the scene from "The Bridge of the Golden Horn." The magnifying glass is inscribed into the materiality of the bodies of the female guest workers, turning them to labor force and means of production at the same time. It is not a metaphor; it has an impact on their material bodies. Thus, what is depicted here is not mere discourse in the Foucauldian sense. Interestingly enough, Foucault's notion of *dispositif* has been translated as apparatus. Yet, Barad distinguishes her position from Foucault's:

The closest that Foucault comes to explicating this crucial relationship between discursive and nondiscursive practices is through his notion of *dispositif*, usually translated as *apparatus*. Foucault explains that dispositif is "a thoroughly heterogeneous ensemble consisting of discourses, institutions, architectural forms, regulatory decisions, laws, administrative measures, scientific statements, philosophical, moral and philanthropic propositions – in short, the said as much as the unsaid" (Foucault 1980: 194 cited in Barad 2007: 63).

So how exactly does Barad's notion differ from an assemblage or a *dispositive*? Barad describes her understanding of apparatus by distinguishing six sub-items:

(1) apparatuses are specific material-discursive practices (they are not merely laboratory setups that embody human concepts and take measurements); (2) apparatuses produce differences that matter-they are boundary-making practices that are formative of matter and meaning, productive of, and part of, the phenomena produced; (3) apparatuses are material configurations/dynamic reconfigurings of the world; (4) apparatuses are themselves phenomena (constituted and dynamically reconstituted as part of the ongoing intra-activity of the world); (5) apparatuses have no intrinsic boundaries but are open-ended practices; and (6) apparatuses are not located in the world but are material configurations or reconfigurings of the world that re(con)figure spatiality and temporality as well as (the traditional notion of) dynamics (i.e., they do not exist as static structures, nor do they merely unfold or evolve in space and time). (Barad 2007: 146)

From the elaborate definition of her use of the term *apparatus*, one item particularly stands out: "apparatuses are boundary-making practices." Looking at intercultural encounters through that lens, one can state that boundaries, and thus binary oppositions, don't pre-exist. They are created in a certain moment, set-up, or entangled timespace. It might not be possible to generally rid ourselves of binary thinking. But it is possible to learn to think in a way that sees these binary oppositions emerging out of densely entangled situations that encompass materiality, discourse, and interpretation. However, Barad goes further than stating that apparatuses partake in boundary-making practices. In her concept of agential realism, individual objects do not pre-exist and neither does individual agency.

Interpreting the scene in the novel "The Bridge of the Golden Horn" from a cultural studies perspective, we might focus on binary oppositions and how they are challenged, for instance in focusing our attention on a Turkish girl in German culture and how she is influenced by it. We might rightly interpret the girl's sexual liberalism as proof of the hybrid culture within Turkey, thus deconstructing cultural stereotypes.[11] We might focus on how 1968 was a global movement that happened in Turkey as well as in Germany.[12] We might also consider the girl's encounters in Germany and with Germans as an endeavor to understand the other or the foreigner.

As elaborated above, many of the concepts applied in cultural studies, such as hybridity, liminality, and alterity, theoretically still need two sources from which the place in-between can derive. Boundaries such as colonialist and colonized exist but get blurred and questioned through mimicry. The role of the material world can be buried under conceptual thinking. Thus, one could argue that the colonialized engaging in mimicry only challenges the

---

11   Both done by McGowan 2000.
12   As done by Schonfield 2015.

colonizer without actually changing anything about power relations. Barad offers a way out of this predicament without dismissing power relations.

As Adelson pointed out, intercultural studies in the German context especially have been pre-occupied with the notion of overcoming foreignness through an understanding of the culturally *other*. Werner Wintersteiner, one of the experts in the field, published a programmatic study with the title "Transcultural Literary Education" in 2006 (Wintersteiner 2006). As the quote below indicates, the parameters have slightly changed since Adelson's critical intervention:

> One of the concerns of literary didactics should be to disclose, to appreciate and to sustain the otherness of the other as it is expressed in the literary text (and in the discursive field it is attributed to) while at the same time seeking communalities and connectivities and thus overcoming the foreignness of the other at certain points in time. (Wintersteiner 2006: 187)[13]

Wintersteiner does not ask for an all-encompassing understanding of the cultural "other." On the contrary, he urges us to accept the "otherness of the other." Yet, the search for communalities and temporary overcoming of "foreignness" are still goals in his approach. Kaspar Spinner, a renowned scholar in the field of literary didactics, describes every kind of literature, not only inter-cultural literature, as "a medium for developing the understanding of the foreign." According to him, "a fundamental goal of literary education should be to promote the overcoming of egocentrism, the practicing of empathy and the ability to connect differing modes of experience with each other." (Spinner 1999: 600)[14] As desirable as these goals are, they – again – focus on encounters. They also bear the danger of neglecting the aesthetic value and structural characteristics of literature. Coming from Wintersteiner's school, Nicola Mitterer published a study in which she operates within the philosopher Bernhard Waldenfels' phenomenology of the foreign and calls for a responsive literary didactics (Mitterer 2016). This approach allows for the acceptance of "radical foreignness" (Waldenfels 2006) and is much closer to recent theoretical developments in the course of the material turn and subfields like object-oriented ontology. For instance, Mitterer refers to Wintersteiner's thought that every encounter with a literary text is an encounter with something foreign (Wintersteiner 2006: 187). Mitterer's responsive literary didactics could thus be extended to interrogating encounters between

---

13 My translation Y.D-Y. Original: "Es geht ihr [der transkulturellen Literaturdidaktik] darum, die Andersheit des Anderen, wie sie im literarischen Text (und dem Diskursfeld, dem es verpflichtet ist) zum Ausdruck kommt, herauszuarbeiten, wertzuschätzen und zu erhalten, zugleich aber auch darum, Gemeinsames und Verbindendes zu finden und somit die Fremdheit des Anderen punktuell zu überwinden."

14 (My translation Y.D-Y.) Original: "Literatur ist [...] auch ein Medium für die Entfaltung von Fremdverstehen. Daraus ergibt sich als ein grundlegendes Ziel für den Literaturunterricht eine Förderung der Überwindung von Egozentrik, der Einübung in Empathie und die Fähigkeit, verschiedene Erfahrungsweisen miteinander in Beziehung zu setzen."

humans and non-humans. Whereas Mitterer is still engaged with encounters and relationships, Barad's agential realism opens further possibilities to include exchanges between humans and non-humans in cross-cultural studies, which so far have been unjustly overlooked, and helps to weaken the artificial walls build between the humanities (proclaimed as academic fields primarily engaging with humans) and the natural sciences (proclaimed as academic fields primarily exploring non-human objects).

How then should literary didactics informed by agential realism operate? If we tie these explorations back to the magnifying glass scene, agential realism directs our sight to entanglements rather than encounters. These entanglements incorporate humans and other living beings as much as non-humans and discourses. Rather than deconstructing ideas of polarity as overlooking the inherent fluidity of individual and collective identities, agential realism focuses on the act of boundary-making itself. But what are the specifically literary means that correspond with an agential realistic approach? Humor has always been a means to challenge those in power through its ambiguity. Thus, one could argue that humor oversteps boundaries. This would in certain ways be in accordance with Bhabha's concept of mimicry. Shifting the focus to boundary-making practices, I would, however, argue that the means of humor, of polysemy, and more generally poetic alterity as explained above (Mecklenburg 2008) applied in "The Bridge of the Golden Horn," operate as literary devices that uncover these boundary-making practices, that point to the moment, the timespace of boundary making, and that have material and discursive implications. Thus, they point to more than just deconstructing fixed identities etc. – one could argue that they show that boundaries do not pre-exist, because, to stay with the example of "The Bridge of the Golden Horn," Turkish guest workers do not pre-exist. They are created in a certain timespace.

What Spinner assigns to the literary medium, can of course be extended to the medium of film. One movie that has indeed succeeded in creating understanding of the older generation of Turkish guest workers through entangling pasts and presents in a different way, is the comedy drama "Almanya." Sisters Yasemin and Nesrin Şamdereli's comedy drama "Almanya" was released in 2011, the year of the 50th anniversary of Turkish guest worker migration to Germany. It depicts the couple Hüseyin and Fatma Yılmaz, who moved to Germany in the 1960s. Their four children now have families of their own. As the youngest grandchild, Cenk, cannot find an answer to the question of whether he is German or Turkish (his mother is of German descent, while his father moved to Germany as a child), grandfather Hüseyin decides to take the whole family on a trip to their home village. The movie employs various comical devices that – in spite of their distancing effect – create empathy for the characters. For instance, at the beginning of the movie, everything that is being said in Turkish is being rendered as High German, while the Germans speak gibberish. Thus the perspective of the Turkish guest workers who don't speak German yet can be comprehended by the audience. Other comical scenes encompass the nightmare Hüseyin has before he is supposed to become naturalized, in which he is asked to eat pork twice a week and spend his summer vacation on Mallorca every second year. When Hüseyin dies on the trip to Turkey, past and present blend into each other in a moving scene in which the protagonists encounter their younger selves. In the foreword to "Meeting the Universe Halfway," Barad explains her understanding of intra-action in a broader context that I have here tried to exemplify with examples from Özdamar's "The Bridge of the Golden Horn" and to some extent the Şamdereli sisters' "Almanya":

> This book is about entanglements. To be entangled is not simply to be intertwined with another, as in the joining of separate entities, but to lack an independent, self-contained existence. Existence is not an individual affair. Individuals do not preexist their interactions; rather, individuals emerge through and as part of their entangled intra-relating. Which is not to say that emergence happens once and for all, as an event or as a process that takes place according to some external measure of space and of time, but rather that time and space, like matter and meaning, come into existence, are iteratively reconfigured through each intra-action, thereby making it impossible to differentiate in any absolute sense between creation and renewal, beginning and returning, continuity and discontinuity, here and there, past and future. (Barad 2007: ix)

The movie "Almanya" does not merely (re)enact, but plays with binary oppositions. Yet, humor and humoristic aesthetic devices do not only question the existence and validity of boundaries, but they also serve as tools that foreground boundary-making practices. Thus, they point to material circumstances while still being embedded in a discursive field. The Yılmaz family was not a guest worker family before they came to Germany. "Existence is not an individual affair." (Barad 2007: ix)

References

Adelson, Leslie A. (1994): Opposing Oppositions: Turkish-German Questions in Contemporary German Studies. In: German Studies Review 17, 2, pp. 305–330. DOI: 10.2307/1432472.

Adelson, Leslie A. (2000): Touching Tales of Turks, Germans, and Jews: Cultural Alterity, Historical Narrative, and Literary Riddles for the 1990s. In: New German Critique 80, pp. 93–124.

Adelson, Leslie A. (2005): The Turkish Turn in Contemporary German Literature: Toward a New Critical Grammar of Migration. New York: Palgrave Macmillan (Studies in European Culture and History).

Barad, Karen (2007): Meeting the Universe Halfway: Quantum Physics and the Entanglement of Matter and Meaning. Durham/London: Duke University Press.

Bathrick, David (1992): Cultural Studies. In: Gibaldi, Joseph (ed.): Introduction to Scholarship in the Modern Languages and Literatures. New York: MLA of America, pp. 320–340.

Berger, John (2007): About Badness. In: Özdamar, Emine Sevgi: The Bridge of the Golden Horn. London: Serpent's Tail, pp. ix–xi.

Berger, John et al. (1975): A Seventh Man. Harmondsworth: Penguin.

Bhabha, Homi K. (1994): The Location of Culture. London/New York: Routledge.

Bryant, Levi (2009): Deleuze on Assemblages. Available at https://larvalsubjects. wordpress.com/2009/10/08/deleuze-on-assemblages/, last accessed May 1, 2020.

Deleuze, Gilles (2006): Two Regimes of Madness. Cambridge: MIT Press.

Eryılmaz, Aytaç/Jamin, Mathilde (eds.) (1998): Fremde Heimat: Eine Geschichte der Einwanderung aus der Türkei. Yaban, Sılan olur. Türkiye'den Almanya'ya Göçün Tarihi. Katalog zur Ausstellung. Essen: Klartext-Verlag.

Foucault, Michel (1980): Power/Knowledge: Selected Interviews and Other Writings, 1972–1977. New York: Pantheon Books.

Howley, Kerry (2007): Guests in the Machine. In: Reason. Available at https://reason. com/2007/12/17/guests-in-the-machine/, last accessed April 1, 2020.

Littler, Margaret (2016): Machinic Agency and the Powers of the False in Emine Sevgi Özdamar's Die Brücke vom Goldenen Horn (1998). In: Oxford German Studies 45, 3, pp. 290–307. DOI: 10.1080/00787191.2016.1208420.

McGowan, Moray (2000): 'The Bridge of the Golden Horn': Istanbul, Europe and the 'Fractured Gaze from the West' in Turkish Writing in Germany. In: Hollis, Andy (ed.): Beyond Boundaries: Textual Representations of European Identity. Amsterdam/Atlanta, Ga.: Rodopi (Yearbook of European Studies = Annuaire d'études Européennes 15).

Mecklenburg, Norbert (2008): Das Mädchen aus der Fremde: Germanistik als inter-kulturelle Literaturwissenschaft. München: Ludicium.

Mitterer, Nicola (2016): Das Fremde in der Literatur: Zur Grundlegung einer respon-siven Literaturdidaktik. Bielefeld: Transcript.

Nadolny, Sten (1990): Selim oder die Gabe der Rede. München: Piper.

Özdamar, Emine S. (1993): Schwarzauge und sein Esel. In: Die Zeit. Available at https://www.zeit.de/1993/09/schwarzauge-und-sein-esel, last accessed January 4, 2020.

Özdamar, Emine S. (2007): The Bridge of the Golden Horn. London: Serpent's Tail.

Schonfield, Ernest (2015): 1968 and Transnational History in Emine Sevgi Özdamar's Die Brücke vom Goldenen Horn. In: German Life and Letters 68, 1, pp. 66–87. DOI: 10.1111/glal.12069.

Spinner, Kaspar H. (1999): Lese- und literaturdidaktische Konzepte. In: Bodo Franzmann/Georg Jäger (eds.): Handbuch Lesen. Berlin/Boston: De Gruyter Saur, pp. 593–601.

Waldenfels, Bernhard (2006): Grundmotive einer Phänomenologie des Fremden. Frankfurt am Main: Suhrkamp.

Wintersteiner, Werner (2006): Transkulturelle literarische Bildung: Die 'Poetik der Verschiedenheit' in der literaturdidaktischen Praxis. Innsbruck: Studien Verlag.

Acknowledgements

I would like to thank the anonymous reviewer and the editors for their valuable feedback on previous versions of this article.

Artificial Intelligence * Bodies as Artefacts

I-Algorithm-Dataset: Mapping the Solutions to Gender Bias in AI[1]

Galit Wellner

1. Introduction

The translation of a profession's name frequently reveals a stereotypical approach. The classical example is the *nurse and doctor* duo, where the former is frequently referred to as female and the later as male. In some languages the stereotypes are embedded in the sentence or in the words, especially in languages that gender artifacts' names and adjectives. For example, in Hebrew the words designating the profession of a nurse, doctor, teacher, or soldier vary according to the gender of the person who practices these professions. Translating a simple sentence like *I am a teacher* from English to Hebrew requires the translator to decide whether the *I* is male or female and change the word *teacher* accordingly. Another example is Turkish, where the third person is gender-neutral, and so the translation to English requires a similar decision, albeit from the opposite direction.

When the translation becomes automated these problems demand a systematic solution. Moreover, translation algorithms are expected to be neutral and impartial. They are not supposed to be biased by stereotypes. But gendered languages, phrases, and words lead the algorithms to make tough decisions. In November 2017, *Quartz Magazine* reported an interesting experiment that translated a list of professions from Turkish to English (Sonnad 2017). When framed in the neutral third person, the original Turkish sentences bear no clues as to the gender of the practitioner. The act of translation to English requires the algorithm to decide if the third person is *he* or *she*. In the test, Google Translate's algorithm assigned gender to the various professions, so that a soldier and a doctor were male (e.g. *he is a soldier*), while a teacher and a nurse were female. It was more surprising when the algorithm referred to a translator and a student as male, although in many countries the numbers of female practitioners are higher for these occupations. The test further tried

---

1   This chapter is based on my articles "Feminist AI: Can We Expect Our AI Systems to Become Feminist?" (Wellner/Rothman 2020) and "When AI Is Gender-biased: Some Philosophical Implications on AI in Everyday Life of Women" (Wellner 2020).

adjectives such as *strong, hard working, very beautiful,* and *old.* All were assigned to males. By contrast, *lazy, beautiful,* and *optimistic* were assigned to females. The adjective *old* is of special interest in this context, as statistically the majority of older adults are women. The translation algorithms presumably work according to statistics. The question is which statistics are taken into account.

Artificial Intelligence (AI) algorithms were introduced to computerized translation in an effort to improve the automation of these processes. AI can be defined as "a growing resource of interactive, autonomous, self-learning agency, which enables computational artifacts to perform tasks that otherwise would require human intelligence to be executed successfully" (Taddeo/Floridi 2018: 751). Unlike previous methods of automating translation, AI-based translation has, presumably, less human involvement in the process. The role of humans is mostly in the preparatory stages. In the case of AI algorithms that are based on the concept of machine learning, datasets are needed in order to build the neural networks that will later decide on real-world cases.

How did AI-based translation become gender biased? The common explanation points to the translation algorithms' training datasets. Computer scientists Aylin Caliskan, Joanna Bryson, and Nara Arvind (2017) reviewed the popular datasets with which AI algorithms are trained. Based on these datasets, the algorithms statistically assess which word is more likely to appear next to others. The researchers found that female names are more frequently associated with family than career words, compared to male names. Similarly, words indicating females, like *woman* and *girl*, are more associated with the arts than with mathematics or science, again compared against male-associated words. This method of word proximity does not just reveal the source of gender bias: it also reveals that words related to old people's names, as well as African American names, are more likely to appear next to attributes like *unpleasant*. There are biases in many dimensions.

The researchers asserted that "all implicit human biases are reflected in the statistical properties of language" (Caliskan et al. 2017: 185). They explained that machine learning algorithms are biased because the texts they are trained with are implicitly biased. Put differently, the datasets are biased because the spoken languages are biased. Their argument combines linguistic and statistical reasoning: "before providing an explicit or institutional explanation for why individuals make prejudiced decisions, one must show that it was not a simple outcome of unthinking reproduction of statistical regularities absorbed with language" (ibid.). Caliskan, Bryson, and Arvind regard the linguistic explanation as primordial. In their view, biases are practically inscribed into the words and sentences of the training datasets.

It is not only translation algorithms that are biased. This phenomenon exists in other applications of AI as well, such as gig-economy platforms. In these platforms, algorithms match service providers with customers and in some of them they even determine the price of the service. An article headline that describes Uber phrases this situation as follows: "when your boss is an Uber algorithm." (Simonite 2015) It is the algorithm that decides, instead of a flesh and blood human boss, who gets a customer (and hence an opportunity to earn money), when, where, and – in the case of Uber – also for how much. Arianne Barzilay and Anat Ben-David (2016) examined the revenues generated through gig-economy platforms. Their empirical findings revealed that women in general worked for more hours *on the platform*, but their average per-hour income was only two thirds of that of men. Another research found that women sellers received fewer bids and lower final prices on eBay than did equally qualified male sellers of the exact same product (Kricheli-Katz/Regev 2016). On average, women sellers received 80 cents for every dollar a man received when selling the identical new product and 97 cents when selling the same used product.

In order to find a solution for the gender bias problem in AI algorithms, we first need to understand the causes. Caliskan et al. argue that it is rooted in the dataset. Others, however, point to the algorithm and the implicit biases of those who designed and programmed it (e.g., O'Neil 2016). In this chapter, I map the various solutions into three categories according to their primary focus: humans who are involved in the process (designers, developers, data scientists or users), the algorithms, and the dataset. This classification is based on a formula originally developed in a branch of philosophy of technology known as postphenomenology. The formula is:

I – technology – world

The formula examines our relations to technologies and how these relations mediate the world for us. The first section of this chapter provides an overview of the classical formula and its permutations in order to provide a basis for the discussion on its adaptation to AI algorithms. The next section deals with the adaptation of the formula to AI in the form of:

I – algorithm – dataset

The section sketches some preliminary insights into our relations with AI algorithms. It is mostly descriptive, though it attempts to critically examine the relations imposed by some developers and corporations. The last section maps the major solutions proposed in recent years to the gender bias problem in AI algorithms. The solutions are grouped into five categories, following the I-algorithm-dataset logic but in reverse order: one for the dataset, two for algorithms, and two for humans.

2. A Short Introduction to Postphenomenology

The relationships between AI algorithms, datasets, and users are complex. Previous generations of technologies were also considered complex, and some theories tackled this complexity, modeled it and unpacked it. One of them is postphenomenology. It is a branch of philosophy of technology that studies the relations between people, their technologies, and the surrounding world. It was originally developed by Don Ihde in the late 1970s and remains applicable to contemporary technologies, such as the AI algorithms discussed here.

In the 1980s and 1990s, when digital technologies were mostly a personal computer at home, we saw the rise of what I term a *classical postphenomenology*. This is the period when Ihde developed the formula "I-technology-world" and its permutations with dashes, arrows and parentheses (Ihde 1990: 86). Basically, the formula represents how we experience the world through the mediating role of technologies. The *technology* element in the middle denotes that technology mediates the world for the *I*. The mediation can happen in more than one way:

2.1   Embodiment Relations

Some technologies change our body scheme and lead us to behave as if the technology is a part of our body. Think of parking a car or riding a bicycle: when using these technologies, the driver knows if she and her vehicle can pass through a narrow passage. An experienced driver senses the vehicle and detects its malfunctioning on a bodily level. Other technologies extend the bodily senses and facilitate seeing or hearing more than what is possible to see or hear with biological organs. For example, eyeglasses allow the wearer to bypass some difficulties in seeing; a cell phone enables the user to hear what an interlocutor says, even if that person is located thousands of kilometers away, far outside the normal reach of biological hearing. These are embodiment relations, and the permutation represents them as:

(I – technology) → world

2.2   Hermeneutic Relations

Sometimes the technology is perceived to be part of the world, and the user experiences the world through the technology. Here the classical example is a thermometer attached to a window, telling us – via our reading of its scale –

how cold it is outside. These are hermeneutic relations, and they are represented by the following permutation:

I → (technology – world)

The reading of the world is never neutral. Reading always involves interpretation, and that is why these relations are termed *hermeneutic*. Thus, geographical maps, for instance, do not represent the world in a neutral way, as there is always some form of translation involved. The popular *Mercator* projection does not represent the world exactly as it is. It manages to preserve the shape of geographical objects but not their size. Those located near the equator are geometrically smaller than those located near the poles. Consequently, the continent of Africa looks in the map as if it is a large as Greenland, although in practice it is much larger.

Hermeneutic relations are not mutually exclusive and can be combined. When looking through a radio telescope at remote stars and planets, the observer can *see* a black hole which cannot be seen with bare eyes. It is important to understand (i.e., to *read*) the colors assigned to the black hole as they may indicate some additional information.

2.3   Alterity Relations

And sometimes we refer to the technology as a quasi-other, maintaining a certain dialog with it, as we do with ATMs, voice menus of automatic answering systems, or the more updated example – virtual assistants and smart speakers. These are alterity relations, represented as:

I → technology – (world)

In many digital technologies, such as computers and cell phones, the screen functions as a quasi-face with which one interacts (Wellner 2014).

2.4   Background Relations

The last relation that Ihde formulates is background relations, where the technology "withdraws" to the background (Ihde 2010: 46) and we don't pay attention to it, as in the air-conditioner in the room, the chair, and the window. The permutation is:

I → (technology –) world

2.5   Cyborg Intentionality

The next stage can be located in the first decade of the 21st century, with the emergence of the cellphone (which evolved into the smartphone) as a ubiquitous everyday technology. The cellphone accelerated the distribution of human capabilities between users and technologies, so that memories, for example, can reside in our brain or in a device like the cellphone. Against this background arises the notion of technological intentionality. In postphenomenology it is not only humans who have intentionality, but also technologies. The postphenomenological notion of technological intentionality designates the ability of technologies to form intentions, so that they direct the users to do things that could hardly be done without such technologies. Peter-Paul Verbeek explains: "even though artifacts evidently cannot form intentions entirely on their own [...] because of their lack of consciousness, their mediating roles cannot be entirely reduced to the intentions of their designers and users either" (Verbeek 2008b: 95).

This new form of human intentionality that operates with the technological is termed by Verbeek "cyborg intentionality,"[2] and offers a frame for new types of relations beyond Ihde's four types. In these relations, technological intentionality operates together with human intentionality. Whereas Ihde's four relations model a "mediated intentionality" (Verbeek 2008a: 390) in which technologies mediate the world for the users, cyborg intentionality is a new set of relations in which the technologies demonstrate some freedom in the relations. Verbeek denotes additional types of cyborg intentionality:

Hybrid intentionality denotes a situation in which the human and the technological intentionality form a new entity. They are merged together, as in the cases of implanted microchips, antidepressant pills, or pacemakers. While in embodiment relations the human and the technology were linked by a dash, here they are linked (or better, fused) by a slash:

(I / technology) → world

Composite intentionality refers to situations in which the technological intentionality is added to the human intentionality. Verbeek demonstrates this relation with the radio telescope that constructs reality by showing the invisible radiation of an astronomic phenomenon. The scheme's permutation is based on Ihde's hermeneutic relations, so that the first arrow already exists and the second arrow replaces the dash between technology and the world:

I → (technology → world)

---

2   Thereby quoting the title of Verbeek's (2008a) "Cyborg Intentionality: Rethinking the Phenomenology of Human-Technology Relations."

This is a unique situation because "rather than putting these intentionalities in the service of human relations to the world – as is the case in Ihde's hermeneutic relations – they explore technological intentionalities as relevant in themselves" (Verbeek 2008a: 393).

In his book "Moralizing Technology" (2011), Verbeek ties these two types of relations together into a new kind of intentionality:

Rather than being "derived" from human agents, this intentionality comes about in associations between humans and nonhumans. For that reason, it could best be called "hybrid intentionality" or "composite intentionality." (Verbeek 2011: 58)

2.6   Reversing the Arrow of Intentionality

The introduction of AI algorithms poses a new type of intentionality and hence a new kind of relation. Composite intentionality is being pushed to its limits as some intentionality continues to flow from the *I* to the *technology* (as in the original permutation for hermeneutic relations), and some flows from the *technology* to the *world*.

What does it mean that the intentionality flows *to* the world? The example of a navigation app can clarify that. Basically, the app provides alerts in real time on traffic jams, and the driver still maintains her intentionality. A deeper look reveals that the app's technological intentionality shapes the traffic as the algorithm directs more and more drivers into a quiet street in order to bypass a traffic jam, thereby creating a new one (Wellner 2018). An interesting development occurs when the driver gives up her intentionality, lets the navigation app decide for her which route to follow, and then blindly obeys its instructions. Sometimes she realizes, often too late, that due to a bug she keeps going in loops. Or that the app selects a much longer route just to save (theoretically) a minute or two. This is the third stage of the evolution of postphenomenology as a theory that is sensitive to the here-and-now. It is radically different from the previous two because the arrow of intentionality is reversed so that it points *to* the human rather than *from* it:

I ← technology → world

In this permutation, the human intentionality "withdraws" (Ihde 2010: 46) and the technological intentionality takes over, so to speak. The technological intentionality decides and changes the world and directs the human user. It is the same logic that determines a loan's rate or decides on a driving route. In these cases, the human intentionality is consigned to an inferior position. The algorithms jeopardize human intentionality.

The more intelligent the apps, the more intentional they become (Wellner 2018), which is in line with Taddeo & Floridi's claim that AI is "a new form of agency" (ibid.: 751). In postphenomenological terms, AI algorithms possess an *enhanced intentionality* compared to previous generations of technologies.

The changes in the postphenomenological formula can be described as changes in the arrow of intentionality: in the classical permutations of the postphenomenological formula, the arrow always goes *from* the human to the technology or the world: in embodiment relations, the arrow goes from the combo (*I – technology*) to the *world*; in hermeneutic, alterity, and background relations the arrow departs directly from the *I* towards the *technology* and/or the *world*. Human intentionality dictates the relations. Technologies and the world are relevant as long as there is a human who perceives them. The introduction of AI transforms human intentionality and reverses the arrow, as detailed in the next section.

3. Postphenomenological Algorithmic Relations

In the realm of AI, the world is represented by data, organized as a *dataset*. The algorithms operate on the dataset and they are guided by the developers' belief that the dataset reflects the real world. Consequently, the postphenomenological formula can be adjusted to AI technologies and practices by replacing the *world* with *dataset*, and *technology* with the narrower term *algorithm*. The result is a new permutation that is built on the principles of the original one:

I – algorithm – dataset

Simply replacing the words is not sufficient. Entering the new realm of AI changes the relations, as the intentionality is distributed differently. This section describes the new relations one can find for algorithms, which are parallel to the classical postphenomenological relations of embodiment, hermeneutics, alterity, and background.

3.1 The Algorithmic Bodily Relations

The first type, corresponding to embodiment relations, is *algorithmic bodily relations*. It refers to algorithms that follow the human body in order to construct its representation in the form of data. In both forms of the postphenomenological formula, the *technology* element extends the body of the *I* (the human user): in embodiment relations what is extended is the biological body scheme (i.e. riding bicycles) or the senses (i.e. wearing eyeglasses); in algorithmic bodily relations, the extension is performed on the digital representation of the human body. For instance, the process of face recognition can be described as a relation between a user (or better – her face), an algorithm that analyzes an image of her face taken by a camera, and a dataset on which the algorithm was trained. The algorithm extends the face by adding a name to it, but the user has a limited knowledge of the results. The permutation for algorithmic bodily relations is:

(I ← algorithm) → dataset

This permutation depicts the ways in which such algorithms shape behaviors and practices and how users find themselves subjugated to those algorithms. In the case of entering a country or a facility that is controlled by face recognition algorithms, when one's entrance is blocked, he or she cannot continue through the gate or the door. This dominant position of the algorithm is represented by the reversal of the left arrow that now points *to* the human, rather than *from* the human as in the classical embodiment relations. The second arrow that points to the dataset reveals that the results of the algorithmic analysis are fed back into the dataset in order to improve the next rounds.

Another example is an algorithm that analyzes the user's typing speed in order to determine the user's mood. The results of the detection serve as a parameter in the offering of certain content to reinforce or mitigate that mood. Such systems are used by investment banks to curb brokers' activity in case of drastic events in the stock markets. The employees are *subordinated* to the algorithm's analysis and the related content, hence the arrow that points *to* the user. Although the user's body is digitally extended, often s/he cannot internalize this extension.

Embodiment relations as well as the new algorithmic bodily relations model the ways in which a technology relates to the human body and how the human body adjusts to the technology. The body is also a major topic in gender studies, especially as one of the main sites of gender bias and discrimination. Obviously, the female body is different from the male body, and AI algorithms need to be sensitive to such differences, or ignore them when they are not relevant (Michelfelder et al. 2017). Most algorithms, however, are designed under an assumption of neutrality that prevents them from taking the difference into account. To go back to the example of face recognition, feminist philosophy of technology would highlight the very low success rates in recognizing female faces compared to male faces. This kind of analysis would also show that those algorithms can identify *white faces* very well, but are much less successful in recognizing the faces of people of other colors. The combination of the two biases leads to higher error rates in recognizing darker-skinned females – 34.7%, compared to 0.8% in the case of lighter-skinned males (Buolamwini/Gebru 2018).

3.2   Maximum Opacity

The second type, analogous to hermeneutic relations, refers to situations in which algorithms actively shape the users' worldview as they interact with them. Just like in hermeneutic relations, where the technology and the world are taken as one unit, here the algorithm and the dataset are operating together. The permutation of the formula is:

I ← (algorithm – dataset)

These relations model the algorithmic translation as described in the opening paragraphs of this chapter. Examining the relations of users with translation algorithms from the perspective of gender bias reveals a worldview according to which the world is ruled by men and for them. In some cases, attempts to use the female variations of a word are classified as mistakes. This type of relation also applies to search results whose content and order match a hidden agenda. For example, *Wired Magazine* reported how Facebook's algorithm tends to show pictures of women in bathing suits, and interprets a query such as "photos of my male friends" as a typo for "female friends" (Matsakis 2019). Moreover, when "Wired" ran the query "photos of my male friends," it did not bring up pictures of male friends, but rather male dogs and a few male-themed cartoons. A Facebook spokesperson defined this as a bug to be fixed. Wired Magazine did not blame the algorithm but rather the dataset, and indirectly – the users who type sexist search queries.

It is difficult to examine the algorithm itself for two reasons. First, the algorithm is considered a trade secret of the companies that developed it. We can guess that they take our searching, browsing, and reading histories into account, as well as the IP address from which we enter the Internet, the device that we use for access (e.g. the model of the cellphone or laptop), and the preferences of our Facebook friends. Another reason for the opacity lies in the process of machine learning in which the algorithm is trained with a specific dataset. The training process is so obscure that even the developers of the algorithms do not always understand how the algorithm reached a certain decision. This process renders the dataset inseparable from the algorithm.

This type of relation is termed *maximum opacity* after our inability to know how algorithms reach decisions. The algorithms and the dataset form one entity that remains obscure. Because of this inability to separate algorithm from dataset, the dataset is frequently criticized for its gender bias. Take for instance job advertisement: These systems have been accused of showing women and minorities relatively low paid jobs, compared to young men, mostly of lighter skin. Is it the fault of the algorithm? Or is it the dataset that is biased?

Ali et al. (2019) interrogated Facebook's ad delivery mechanisms by creating eleven job ads. Each ad contained a different text and images while the target audience was set to be the same for all the ads. For each job, they created five variations with diverse pictures of potential employees differing in gender and race (four in total) and a neutral one with no human being depicted. They found that "our five ads for positions in the lumber industry deliver to over 90% men and to over 70% white users in aggregate, while our five ads for janitors deliver to over 65% women and over 75% black users in aggregate" (ibid.: 20). Again, the parameters for the campaign were identical for all ads. These results mean that the bias is in the algorithm.

In both cases (photo search and ad placement) Facebook is responsible for the algorithm as well as for the dataset, thereby fitting into the *algorithmic hermeneutic* relations where the two elements form a unit that interacts with the user. The relations are opaque because of Facebook's policy against the transparency of its algorithms and datasets, as well as because of the process of machine learning.

3.3   *"Her"*

The third type, parallel to alterity relations, represents the algorithmic quasi-other, i.e. those algorithms that communicate in a natural language. In its extreme form, this kind of relation aims at producing a dialogue that resembles a human-to-human interaction, which is the goal of designers of robots and chatbots. This category also encompasses other forms of interaction with algorithms, such as the *auto-complete* feature that complements the user's typing with suggestions. What unites these algorithms is their intention to directly communicate with the user, and hence the permutation is:

I ← algorithm (– dataset)

The gender biases in this category can be very visible, as in the case of voice assistants that are given female names – Siri, Cortana, etc. Not only are they given female names, but their voices are also frequently programmed to sound like those of females. From the first *hello*, the setting is clear, and the user expects a dialogue with an obedient female.

A less dialogue-like interaction is offered by *auto-complete* features. Take for example Gmail's Smart Compose that automatically proposes an answer to an email. Users discovered that when they typed "I am meeting an investor next week," the Smart Compose algorithm suggested as a possible follow-up question: "Do you want to meet *him*?" and did not offer "her" as an option (Dave 2018). The company explained that most investors are male, so statistically the proposed answer may fit most cases. The problem is that these emails are fed back into the system and would reinforce this answer, even though the number of female investors is actually rising. The way the company handled this bias was by temporarily deactivating the Smart Compose feature in gender-related references. Consequently, when a user types in a sentence regarding a meeting next week, the algorithm will not make any suggestion. Gmail's solution does not deal directly with the way the algorithm decides, but rather tweaks the output side. One may wonder why the Smart Compose algorithm itself was not modified, or why it does not present several options as part of the dialog with the user.

3.4 Background Collection

Lastly, the algorithmic relations that correspond to the classical background relations are termed *background collection*. Like the original background relations where the *world* gains our attention, here what is important is the dataset itself. The algorithms that maintain background collection can be those that analyze the user's browsing history, as well as medical algorithms that diagnose cancer based on huge databases of x-rays and other imaging outputs. The permutation here can be:

(I ←) algorithm → dataset

The user is the least important element in the transaction and hence s/he is the one placed in parentheses, while in the classical permutation, it was the technology. This permutation accentuates the shift of intentionality and its distribution patterns. Whereas in the original relations the human intentionality was dominant, in the realm of AI, the algorithmic intentionality is more dominant.

The gender biased example here is an algorithm developed for Amazon's Human Resources department to automate the reading and filtering of candidates' CVs. The AI algorithm automatically scored the incoming CVs based on a dataset of the CVs of employees who were hired in the last ten years. It turned out that the system did not recommend women candidates for software development jobs. The explanation was that the training dataset included a majority of men, thereby reflecting the company's employment history, and so the algorithm concluded that the ideal candidate is a man. *Reuters* reported that Amazon abandoned the project (Dastin 2018). The relevant relation to model this situation is background collection because the candidates had no idea why they were rejected. Their reduced intentionality is modeled in the permutation by putting the "I" inside the parentheses. Unlike *classical* background relations where the user notices the technology when it does not operate properly, in background collection her position does not enable her to notice if the algorithm operates properly.

In gig economy platforms, such as Uber and AirBnB, the customer is considered of importance – the car's passenger or the guest at the apartment. But there are other users who are of lesser importance. These are the service providers: the car's driver, the homeowner. In these newly formed markets, the platforms had the potential to avoid the existing gender bias that is reflected in legacy datasets. They could have provided equal opportunities for women as drivers or as homeowners. Surprisingly, they duplicated the salary differences and unjust distribution of opportunities. In these platforms, women receive fewer orders and their income is lower than that of men (see Fisman/Luca 2016 and the references there; see also Barzilay/Ben-David 2016). It also happens in less controlling platforms such as eBay (Kricheli-Katz/Regev 2016), where women sellers received a smaller number of bids and lower final prices than did equally qualified male sellers of the exact same product.

4. Solutions

There are numerous solutions to algorithmic gender bias. These solutions can be organized according to the formula *I-algorithm-dataset*. For the sake of simplicity, the review of solutions starts from the dataset, then proceeds to the algorithm, and ends with the human actor, which may be the user, the designer, or the developer. The solutions are collected into five groups: one for the dataset, two for the algorithm, and two for the human actor.

4.1   Dataset: No gender please!

The first group of solutions is relatively simple. It involves removing any reference to gender in the dataset or ignoring it. This solution is implemented by music streaming services for music personalization. Shazam does not rely on users' gender or race to determine personal taste because "demographics discriminate" (Prey 2018). Instead of identity, the algorithm looks for behavioral models. This solution separates the question of the user from the question of the dataset. It is applicable when the service is personalized, so that the users might be discriminated against by their gender or race. It will not solve the problem of biased translation.

Other solutions allow the gender field to remain in the dataset, but use it selectively. Fisman and Luca (2016) propose that calculating and displaying the gender in the initial stages of the process may mean "too much information." Practically, they recommend that system designers limit the requests for bias-sensitive data on gender and race, such as pictures of hosts in service platforms like AirBnB and Uber. They advise that such data is provided only after the transaction has been confirmed.

Critics argue that avoiding gender by excluding this field from the dataset might not help, because the algorithms are likely to find an alternative parameter and take that one into account. This happened, for example, when race was omitted for mortgage calculations, but the algorithm took instead the zip code which may represent neighborhoods comprised of certain racial and ethnic majorities (O'Neil 2016).

4.2   Transparent Algorithms

One of the more popular solutions is transparency, according to which the algorithm should *explain* how it reached a certain conclusion. But "simply releasing all the parameters of a model won't provide much insight into how it works" (Courtland 2018: 360). Therefore, IBM recommends that AI algorithms reveal: which factors weighted the decision in one direction or another; the confidence in the recommendation; and the factors behind that confidence (Lomas 2018). The rationale is that if we know how the algorithm reached a conclusion then we can identify the bias (cf. Zerilli et al. 2019).

Just showing the considerations behind the scenes does not cure bias, and additional actions are required, probably by the users or the operators. In the case of the translation algorithms mentioned in the introduction, transparency can be followed by the presentation of the gendered variations of professions' names.

Another aspect of transparency relates to the ways the data was collected and annotated (Zou/Schiebinger 2018). This solution requires a new profession, *data curators* who would supply a kind of *nutrition labels* for datasets (ibid.: 325–326).

O'Neil (2016) calls for a more radical transparency that involves the developers and mathematicians who designed the algorithm. She advises they should reveal their guiding logic and expose the choices they made from the beginning of the research. Her example is an AI system in the education management sphere that points to excellent vs. underperforming teachers. O'Neil shows that pupils' grades cannot be taken as the main parameter, as it leads to the constant laying off of teachers working in the lowest ranking schools, even if the teachers did a great job. Those teachers are eventually hired by private schools, and the public systems remains weak. Revealing the logic of the AI system could have saved the education system resources and effectively assisted the weaker students. It is important to remember that transparency is a first step that needs to be followed by additional actions.

4.3   Anti-bias Algorithms

A third kind of solution is to develop non-discriminating algorithms that should resist the *built-in* biases of the datasets (see Zou/Schiebinger 2018). One variation of this kind of solution entails the developers defining in advance which bias they wish to avoid. Another variation requires that the developers identify *sensitive attributes* and avoid dependence on such attributes. However, biases and sensitivities are usually revealed after the system is operative, so the proposed variations work *ex post factum*, usually after some damage has been caused. One way of revealing biases and sensitivities is ensuring they surface at early stages of the development. This is the rationale behind the recommendation to involve various groups in the development teams (e.g. Feenberg 2002; Verbeek 2011). This solution can be affective for algorithms and datasets.

Another suggestion by Zou and Schiebinger (2018) is to develop a supervising algorithm that can identify biases and then alter the dataset. Once there is an algorithm that can detect gender bias, it can serve as a kind of *moral compass* to the other systems. It can function as a feature in the algorithm or become part of a set of algorithms, like those known as Generative Adversarial Network (GAN), where one algorithm provides feedback to the other. This solution delegates the handling of the gender bias to an algorithm. However, human involvement is still needed to identify the bias and the necessary strategies to bypass it in an ethical way.

4.4   Human Involvement

A fourth kind of solution is to deepen the cooperation between humans and algorithms. Fisman and Luca (2016: 95) suggest asking: "Should your algorithms be discrimination-aware?" They urge designers to plan the user experience through the lenses of potential biases, because "Thus far many algorithm designers have ignored factors such as race and gender and just hoped for the best. But in many cases the probability that an algorithm will unintentionally achieve equality is essentially zero" (ibid.). This strategy should involve self-scrutiny practices in the companies developing algorithms, so that they "proactively monitor and respond to such problems" (ibid.).

Human involvement is necessary because deep learning algorithms cannot acquire abstract ideas like gender or race (Marcus 2018). The technique of machine learning can recognize patterns in huge amounts of data, mostly based on word proximity as shown by Caliskan et al. (2017), but the reasoning and meaning extraction are human. Therefore, intelligence must combine both tasks – identify the pattern (by the algorithm) and understand its meaning (by a human supervisor).

Human involvement can also be applied at the usage phase by involving the users in the detection of gender biases (Feenberg 2017). A simple example of such an involvement can be evidenced in navigation apps that allow their users to examine alternative routes rather than blindly following the route selected by the algorithm. Once the user sees the alternatives and chooses, the arrow of intentionality is reversed again. However, not all AI algorithms provide alternatives, and many function as *black boxes* that produce just one output, like an interest rate or the price of an insurance policy's premium (O'Neil 2016). A true dialog between users and AI algorithms necessitates a certain level of *un-black-boxing* and the provisioning of alternatives by the algorithm.

4.5   Educating the Algorithms

The last solution moves from *teaching* to *educating*. If the concept of *machine learning* is based on a certain mode of teaching, this type of solution calls for an educational paradigm. Educating in this context means to teach AI algorithms to be gender-neutral or take gender into account when needed (Michelfelder et al. 2017).

One challenge for the education of algorithms is teaching them to overcome the gender biases in their training dataset. Specifically, can they be trained to identify biases, just as they can be trained to identify faces, animals, plants etc.? What is the difference between *deciphering* a photograph (i.e. understanding what it includes) and identifying a gender bias in a dataset? The difficulty lies in the different treatments for each learning process: Whereas a picture includes objects or persons that can be identified or not, biases are less *identifiable*. In other words, the question of bias cannot always be answered simply by a yes or a no. We can assess whether a person, animal, or object have been successfully pinpointed by an algorithm, but when it comes to discrimination, answers among humans tend to be confusing. Courtland (2018) demonstrates this complexity by a thought experiment on a group of persons characterized, *inter alia*, by a high rate of arrests. Presenting members of that group as at risk at higher rates seems to be fair. When this presentation is done by an algorithm, such a presentation might be classified as unethical. Avoiding the *false positive* becomes a more complicated challenge, where a member of the group is considered dangerous just because he or she belongs to the group. Courtland explains that some theorists regard the *false positive* as a price that should be paid in the name of efficiency and safety. This thought experiment exposes the difficulties in classifying a certain grouping as biased.

5. Summary and Conclusions

Understanding AI entails the understanding of the relations algorithms have with their users, on one hand, and the training dataset on the other. Postphenomenology offers a theoretical basis to begin asking questions about these relations. Employing this theory on AI algorithms demands adjusting the terminology and the relations to the new landscape of AI, where the world is no more than a digital representation of reality and where the human intentionality is distributed among – and sometime even fully delegated to – the technology.

The problem of gender bias in AI algorithms has many facets, from the translation of professions and assigning meaning to adjectives, to credit allocation and access to job opportunities. Gender bias can take many forms, and this chapter described four of them: the algorithmic bodily relations, maximum opacity, "Her," and background collection. In all these algorithmic relations, the intentionality migrated – so to speak – to the side of the algorithm. This migration contrasts with the classical relations, in which the intentionality is a human property. In the realm of AI, intentionality is no longer uniquely human.

In the last section, five strategies to avoid gender bias were detailed. They were classified according to dataset, algorithm, and user/developer categories. Dealing with the dataset, the solution assessed the possibility of a dataset with no reference to gender as a means to combat gender bias. The next two solutions belong to the algorithm category, one dealing with transparent algorithms which reveal the parameters that led them to a certain conclusion, and the other involves the development of algorithms that avoid biases. The last two solutions belong to the human category, one calling for more human involvement in the automated processes, and the other positions the humans as educators of AI, and not only as trainers. The solutions can be combined in order to tackle gender bias more effectively and more ethically.

To conclude, AI's enhanced intentionality calls for new relations between humans and technologies, in which we may expect a higher sophistication from these technologies. In order to combat gender bias, we can recall a basic feminist understanding – visibility matters. Users and developers should be aware of the possibility of gender and racial biases, and try to avoid them, bypass them, or exterminate them altogether.

References

Ali, Muhammad et al. (2019): Discrimination through Optimization: How Facebook's Ad Delivery Can Lead to Biased Outcomes. In: Proceedings of the ACM on Human-Computer Interaction 3, 199, pp. 1–30.

Barzilay, Arianne Renan/Ben-David, Anat (2016): Platform Inequality: Gender in the Gig-Economy. In: Seton Hall L. Rev. 47, pp. 393–431.

Buolamwini, Joy/Gebru, Timnit (2018): Gender Shades: Intersectional Accuracy Disparities in Commercial Gender Classification. In: Proceedings of Machine Learning Research 81, pp. 1–15.

Caliskan, Aylin et al. (2017): Semantics Derived Automatically from Language Corpora Contain Human-Like Biases. In: Science 356, 6334, pp. 183–186.

Courtland, Rachel (2018): The Bias Detective. In: Nature 558, pp. 357–360.

Dastin, Jeffrey (2018): Amazon Scraps Secret AI Recruiting Tool that Showed Bias Against Women. In: Reuters. Available at https://www.reuters.com/article/us-amazon-com-jobs-automation-insight/amazon-scraps-secret-ai-recruiting-tool-that-showed-bias-against-women-idUSKCN1MK08G, last accessed September 14, 2020.

Dave, Paresh (2018): Fearful of Bias, Google Blocks Gender-Based Pronouns from New AI Tool. In: Reuters. Available at https://www.reuters.com/article/us-alphabet-google-ai-gender/fearful-of-bias-google-blocks-gender-based-pronouns-from-new-ai-tool-idUSKCN1NW0EF, last accessed December 28, 2019.

Feenberg, Andrew (2002): Transforming Technology: A Critical Theory Revisited. New York: Oxford University Press.

Feenberg, Andrew (2017): Technosystem: The Social Life of Reason. Cambridge, MA/London, UK: Harvard University Press.

Fisman, Ray/Luca, Michael (2016): Fixing Discrimination in Online Marketplaces. Harvard Business Review 94, 12, pp. 88–95.

Ihde, Don (1990): Technology and the Lifeworld: From Garden to Earth. Bloomington and Indianapolis: Indiana University Press.

Ihde, Don (2010): Heidegger's Technologies: Postphenomenological Perspectives. New York: Fordham University Press.

Kricheli-Katz, Tamar/Regev, Tali (2016): How Many Cents on the Dollar? Women and Men in Product Markets. In: Science Advances 2, 2, pp. 1–8.

Lomas, Natasha (2018): IBM Launches Cloud Tool to Detect AI Bias and Explain Automated Decisions. In: Tech Crunch. Available at https://techcrunch.com/2018/09/19/ibm-launches-cloud-tool-to-detect-ai-bias-and-explain-automated-decisions/?guccounter=1, last accessed September 14, 2020.

Marcus, Gary (2018): The Deepest Problem with Deep Learning. In: Medium. Available at https://medium.com/@GaryMarcus/the-deepest-problem-with-deep-learning-91c5991f5695, last accessed September 14, 2020.

Matsakis, Louise (2019): A 'Sexist' Search Bug Says More About Us Than Facebook. In: Wired. Available at https://www.wired.com/story/facebook-female-friends-photo-search-bug/, last accessed December 1, 2019.

Michelfelder, Diane P. et al. (2017): Designing Differently: Toward a Methodology for an Ethics of Feminist Technology Design. In: Hansson, Sven Ove (ed.): The

Ethics of Technology: Methods and Approaches. London and New York: Rowman and Littlefield, pp. 193–218.

O'Neil, Cathy (2016): Weapons of Math Destruction: How Big Data Increases Inequality and Threatens Democracy. New York: Broadway Books.

Prey, Robert (2018): Nothing Personal: Algorithmic Individuation on Music Streaming Platforms. In: Media, Culture & Society 40, 7, pp. 1086–1100.

Sonnad, Nikhil (2017): Google Translate's Gender Bias Pairs "He" with "Hardworking" and "She" with "Lazy, and Other Examples. In: Quartz. Available at https://qz.com/1141122/google-translates-gender-bias-pairs-he-with-hardworking -and-she-with-lazy-and-other-examples/, last accessed September 14, 2020.

Simonite, Tom (2015): When Your Boss Is an Uber Algorithm. In: MIT Technology Review. Available at https://www.technologyreview.com/2015/12/01/247388/ when-your-boss-is-an-uber-algorithm/, last accessed September 14, 2020.

Taddeo, Mariarosaria/Floridi, Luciano (2018): How AI Can be a Force for Good. In: Science 361, 6404, pp. 751–752.

Verbeek, Peter-Paul (2008a): Cyborg Intentionality: Rethinking the Phenomenology of Human-Technology Relations. In: Phenomenology and Cognitive Science 7, pp. 387–395.

Verbeek, Peter-Paul (2008b): Morality in Design: Design Ethics and the Morality of Technological Artifacts. In: Vermaas, Pieter E. et al. (eds.): Philosophy and Design: From Engineering to Architecture. Dordrecht: Springer, pp. 91–103.

Verbeek, Peter-Paul (2011): Moralizing Technology: Understanding and Designing the Morality of Things. Chicago: The University of Chicago Press.

Wellner, Galit (2014): The Quasi-Face of the Cell Phone: Rethinking Alterity and Screens. In: Human Studies 37, 3, pp. 299–316.

Wellner, Galit (2018): From Cellphones to Machine Learning: A Shift in the Role of the User in Algorithmic Writing. In: Romele, Alberto/Terrone, Enrico (eds.): Towards a Philosophy of Digital Media. Cham: Palgrave MacMillan, pp. 205–224.

Wellner, Galit (2018): Posthuman Imagination: From Modernity to Augmented Reality. In: Journal of Posthuman Studies 2, 1, pp. 45–66.

Wellner, Galit (2020): When AI Is Gender-Biased: Some Philosophical Implications on AI in Everyday Life of Women. In: Humana.Mente – Journal of Philosophical Studies 13, 37, pp. 127–150.

Wellner, Galit/Rothman, Tiran (2020): Feminist AI: Can We Expect Our AI Systems to Become Feminist? In: Philosophy & Technology 33, 2, pp. 191–205.

Zerilli, John et al. (2019): Transparency in Algorithmic and Human Decision-Making: Is There a Double Standard? In: Philosophy & Technology 32, 4, pp. 661–683.

Zou, James/Schiebinger, Londa (2018): AI Can be Sexist and Racist – it's Time to Make it Fair. In: Nature 559, pp. 324–326.

Reconfigurations of the Turing Test: Unraveling CAPTCHA

Thomas Nyckel

1. Introduction

For quite a long time now, internet users have been having to solve certain tasks, be it to decipher distorted text images by retyping them or to detect cars and fire hydrants in pictures. Solved correctly, those CAPTCHAs grant access to the webservices they guard, like email providers or databases. Accordingly, if one is unsuccessful in solving the task, access to the resource in question is denied – an experience that can be quite unnerving. CAPTCHAs are put in place to prevent (ro)bots from misusing such webservices, and in order to do that they necessarily have to discriminate between algorithmic programs and human users. CAPTCHAs, therefore, present tasks that only human beings are expected to solve in an appropriate timespan. In this paper, I want to give a short overview of the development of this digital practice of differentiation and unravel some threads involved in the CAPTCHA phenomenon and the production of subjects within it.

2. CAPTCHA as Turing Test

Introduced by a group of computer scientists around Luis von Ahn in 2000 (von Ahn et al. 2003: 297), the acronym CAPTCHA stands for *Completely Automated Public Turing test to tell Computers and Humans Apart*. Hence CAPTCHAs are a form of Turing test – an experiment proposed by the mathematician and computer pioneer Alan M. Turing in the year 1950 under the term *imitation game* to replace the question *Can machines think?* with something more practical. In this Turing test, a human person is asked to discern between a digital machine and another human being, solely on the basis of communicating with both of them by text. The difficulty arises from the fact that the digital machine is programmed to *imitate* human conversations by responding to any possible topic, from the weather to poetry, in the same manner one would expect human persons to respond. Turing then suggests that if the human judge in this experiment is only able to discern correctly between machine and human person in 70% of iterations of such tests, the machine in question is to be regarded as intelligent and thinking (Turing 1950).[1]

As N. Katherine Hayles brought up in the "Prologue" of her classic book "How We Became Posthuman" (Hayles 1999: xi–xiv), this test – which has indeed become a benchmark for AI – constitutes nothing less than "the inaugural moment of the computer age" (Hayles 1999: xi). For her, it has never been the machine alone that was (con)tested in the Turing test. Instead, it was the liberal humanist subject, which, on the one hand, echoes throughout Turing's test, and, on the other hand, starts to crumble in the light of the very same testing concept: The figure of the detached observer with the safety of distance turns into a precarious category in this cybernetic circuit. This is because of the mere possibility of being wrong about who one is having such a convincingly human conversation with – *man* or machine.[2] This Turing test, however, seems to get reconfigured in various ways when it comes to CAPTCHA.[3]

3. Beyond the Turing Test

The most obvious change from Turing test to CAPTCHA is that in this *automated* Turing test – a term introduced by Naor (1996) to grasp the concept of CAPTCHA avant la lettre – it is no longer a human interrogator that has to discern between human person and machinic imposter. In CAPTCHA, this

---

1   To understand Turing's imitation, it is good to remember that Turing's paper starts with a version of the imitation game in which the judging person has to discern between a male and female person. Although Turing's first biographer, Andrew Hodges, dismissed this earlier version as a "red herring" (Hodges 1983: 415), strong cases were made for the importance of this gendered version for a comprehensive understanding of the implications of Turing's ideas (Bath 2002; Bergermann 2018; Draude 2011; Hayles 1999; Heintz 1993). Moreover, Turing's work indicates that his use of imitation also stems from the concept of the universal Turing machine, designed to imitate or mimic any other (discrete or digital) machine. This intertwining of questions of gender or identity formation and the notion of mechanical processes in Turing's imitation seems worthy of further study, particularly when *read through one another* (Barad 2007: 71) with the work of Judith Butler.
2   As Clemens Apprich reminds from a media scientific standpoint, questions of who speaks are particularly central to the analysis of paranoia, especially in Lacanian psychoanalysis (Apprich 2018: 32).
3   I use the term *reconfiguration* in this paper to indicate the openness and ongoing changes of the CAPTCHA phenomenon by referencing Lucy Suchman (Suchman 2007) and Karen Barad (Barad 2007). I do not follow the implications of Barad's agential realism here comprehensively, but this contribution is shot through with her *wor(l)dings and thoughts*.

position is occupied by another digital machine, ordered to allocate the tested subjects into dualistic categories like human or non-human, user or (ro)bot, legitimate or non-legitimate, harmless or harmful. Correspondingly, the possibilities for *having a conversation* are drastically narrowed down: Instead of discussing freely chosen topics, a CAPTCHA offers only one particular task that resembles an intelligence test.[4] Accordingly, as one could be inclined to presume, in automated Turing tests the (con)testing of the human subject manifests much more explicitly.

One of the instances indicating this, is the start of the reCAPTCHA service in 2007, six years after the first patent for CAPTCHA was granted (Lillibridge et al. 2001). Created by another team around Luis von Ahn, it introduced changes: Instead of presenting random text, reCAPTCHA was using scanned words which had been proven unrecognizable by contemporary programs for optical character recognition. As envisaged, CAPTCHAs started to harness the power of human brain cycles (Havel 2015) by roping in millions of users every single day to help – knowingly or not – recognize the illegible words from scanned documents like the "New York Times" archive (von Ahn et al. 2008).

In 2009, Google adopted reCAPTCHA to digitize its book stock (Havel 2015). In 2012, reCAPTCHAs presenting graphics of street numbers launched. The data gained from users soon after that launch were fed into advancing AI systems, particularly in the field of machine learning. While, on the one hand, this was designed to work to improve the data for Google's services, on the other hand, it has led to the training of new algorithms able to solve exactly those CAPTCHAs the data stemmed from (O'Malley 2018). Interestingly enough, Naor's very first conception of automated Turing tests already expected them to spark such advancements in the field of AI (Naor 1996: 3); an expectation taken up by Naor's successors even before the feedback circle between CAPTCHAs and machine learning was closed: "A CAPTCHA implies a win-win situation: either the CAPTCHA is not broken and there is a way to differentiate humans from computers, or the CAPTCHA is broken and a useful AI problem is solved." (von Ahn et al. 2004: 60)

So, what could still have been regarded as a figure of the potent anthropos rising above the machines through his abilities to solve CAPTCHAs, turned not only into a free labor resource, but also started to deliver the data propelling its own erosion. This erosion of the detached humanist subject becomes all the more apparent in the needs and dependences of crowdworkers in various locations and situations, solving CAPTCHAs at large scales for differing clients, as underground services do not solely rely on algorithmic tools for

---

4   Resembling such intelligence tasks, CAPTCHAs demand similar *basic* abilities of the subjects using them, i.e. the ability to see or hear. In fact, the question of how to include persons without certain abilities, e.g. by using sound CAPTCHAs is addressed in many technical texts (for example already in Lillibridge et al. 2001).

hacking CAPTCHAs, but resort on crowdwork just as much, which turns out to be cheaper than maintaining the software otherwise needed (Thomas et al. 2015: 11). While the incorporation of the free human labor of *legit* users has been legally justified – a class-action lawsuit against Google alleging fraud through the use of CAPTCHA was dismissed in 2016 (Kravets 2016) – the abuse of other kinds of invisible labor *shot through* the CAPTCHA phenomenon seems to be regarded as a threat to be addressed.

Indeed, newer CAPTCHAs no longer demand from the user to solve tests for human abilities, and it would seem, therefore, that data of that kind would no longer be necessary for the training of AI. Such newer CAPTCHAs, like Google's NoCAPTCHA, only present a simple checkbox that has to be clicked, or no task at all, but work unnoticed in the background. It is not human abilities that are tested anymore, but instead the data the user has created, and creates, are tracked: Digital traces like browser preferences, cookies, the IP address, and the movements of the mouse constitute what is called (among other things) advanced risk analysis techniques (Pohlmann 2015): a data body for the evaluation of its status as human or non-human, and the potential threat it poses. As the source code and information about what data are surveyed remain a business secret and are not publicly available (Kuketz 2017), it would, strictly speaking, no longer be appropriate to talk about this new form of CAPTCHA as such, because these tests originally were designed to be *public*: "'Public' means that means that [sic] commented source code is made available to anyone who wants it [...]. Following the [...] definition, a program that can generate and grade tests that distinguish humans from computers, but whose code or data are private, is not a CAPTCHA." (Li/Shum 2003: 34)[5] But still, as CAPTCHA is not an all-or-nothing affair, it would be quite wrong to assume that these definitional problems imply that CAPTCHA at large has ceased to exist.

4. Conclusion

There is not one single thread following a more or less linear progress, as the technological advancements might indicate, but many different intertwining threads. CAPTCHAs that are officially broken, and thus should be obsolete for the protection from (ro)bots, do not vanish from the world wide web but can still be encountered on various actively used sites, forming a dispersed sociotope of different strands, rather than a family of linear descendants. So, it seems that the artificially closed and isolated experimental situation in

---

5   It would arguably be appropriate to drop the term *public* and speak of CATCHA, instead of CAPTCHA.

Turing's imitation game has opened up in a multitude of ways, and changes through its entanglements with other phenomena and with the world's needs and turbulences. The question of what is human and what isn't is thus, of course, not definitely answered by CAPTCHAs. Nonetheless, it is precisely the issues at stake with this question of who or what is rightfully human and who or what is not, that point to the CAPTCHA phenomenon as possibly providing a very suitable case for examination: Not only may it be possible here to analyze how digital practices change over time, but also what hierarchies, exclusions, and invisibilities digital societies can bring forth on global scales, and how subjectivities are made, destabilized, and treated within those societies. Furthermore, this analysis could provide further ideas for how digital methods are (and could be) used to coproduce and deal with what is regarded as a threat and has to be kept out at certain times, and what limitations, false certainties, and consequences the use of digital methods for such tasks might bear.

References

von Ahn, Luis et al. (2003): CAPTCHA: Using Hard AI Problems for Security. In: Biham, E. (ed.) Advances in Cryptology – Eurocrypt 2003, pp. 294–311.

von Ahn, Luis et al. (2004): Telling Humans and Computers Apart Automatically. In: Communications of the ACM, 2004, 47 (2), pp. 57–60.

von Ahn, Luis et al. (2008): ReCAPTCHA: Human-Based Character Recognition via Web Security Measures. In: Science, 2008, 321 (5895), pp. 1465–1468.

Apprich, Clemens (2018): Secret Agents. A Psychoanalytic Critique of Artificial Intelligence and Machine Learning. In: Digital Culture and Society 4 (1), pp. 29–44.

Barad, Karen (2007): Meeting the Universe Halfway. Quantum Physics and the Entanglement of Matter and Meaning. Durham/London: Duke University Press.

Bath, Corinna (2002): Was können uns Turing-Tests von Avataren sagen? Performative Aspekte virtueller Verkörperungen im Zeitalter der Technoscience. In: Epp, A. et al. (eds.): Technik und Identität. Paper zur Tagung vom 07.06.–08.06.2001 an der Universität Bielefeld. Bielefeld, pp. 79–99.

Bergermann, Ulrike (2018): Biodrag. Turing-Test, KI-Kino und Testosteron. In: Engemann, C./Sudmann, A. (eds.): Machine Learning. Medien, Infrastrukturen und Technologien der Künstlichen Intelligenz. Digitale Gesellschaft, Band 14. Bielefeld: Transcript, pp. 339–364.

Draude, Claude (2011): Intermediaries: Reflections on Virtual Humans, Gender, and the Uncanny Valley. In: AI and Society, 2011, 26 (4), pp. 319-327.

Havel, John (2015): ReCAPTCHA: The Genius Who's Tricking the World into Doing His Work. The Hustle. Available at https://thehustle.co/the-genius-whos-tricking-the-world-into-doing-his-work-recaptcha, last accessed January 7, 2018.

Hayles, N. Katherine (1999): How We Became Posthuman: Virtual Bodies in Cybernetics, Literature, and Informatics. Chicago/London: University of Chicago Press.

Heintz, Bettina (1993): Die Herrschaft der Regel: Zur Grundlagengeschichte des Computers. Frankfurt/New York: Campus.

Hodges, Andrew (1983): Alan Turing: The Enigma. London/UK: Burnett Books.

Kravets, David (2016): Judge tosses proposed class action accusing Google of CAPTCHA fraud. In: Ars Technica. Available at https://arstechnica.com/tech-policy/2016/02/judge-tosses-proposed-class-action-accusing-google-of-captcha-fraud/, last accessed June 4, 2020.

Kuketz, Mike (2017): Google: No CAPTCHA reCAPTCHA Datenstaubsauger. In: Kuketz IT-Security. Available at https://www.kuketz-blog.de/google-no-captcha-recaptcha-datenstaubsauger/, last accessed April 10, 2019.

Li, Shujun/Shum, Heung-Yeung (2003): Secure Human-Computer Identification against Peeping Attacks (SecHCI): A Survey. Available at http://www.hooklee.com/Papers/SecHCI-Survey.pdf., last accessed June 4, 2019.

Lillibridge, Mark D. et al. (2001): Method for selectively restricting access to computer systems. Patent US 6,195,698 B1.

Naor, Moni (1996): Verification of a human in the loop or Identification via the Turing Test. Available at http://www.wisdom.weizmann.ac.il/~naor/PAPERS/human.pdf, last accessed October 4, 2019.

O'Malley, James (2018): Captcha if you can: how you've been training AI for years without realising it. In: Techradar. Available at https://www.techradar.com/ news/captcha-if-you-can-how-youve-been-training-ai-for-years-without-realising -it, last accessed April 9, 2019.

Pohlmann, Jan (2015): Captcha Usability: Probleme und Alternativen. In: UsabilityBlog. Available at https://www.usabilityblog.de/captcha-usability-probleme-und-alternativen/, last accessed September 19, 2019.

Suchman, Lucy (2007): Human-Machine Reconfigurations. Plans and Situated Actions. 2nd Edition. Cambridge et al.: Cambridge University Press.

Thomas, Kurt/Bursztein, Elie (2015): New research: The Underground Market Fueling for Profit Abuse. In: Google Security Blog. Available at https://security. googleblog.com/2015/09/new-research-underground-market-fueling.html, last accessed September 23, 2019.

Thomas, Kurt et al. (2015): Framing Dependencies Introduced by Underground Commoditization, pp. 1–24. Available at http://static.googleusercontent.com/ media/research.google.com/en/us/pubs/archive/43798.pdf, last accessed February 2, 2020.

Turing, Alan (1950): Computing Machinery and Intelligence. In: Mind: A Quarterly Review of Psychology and Philosophy, 1950, LIX (236), pp. 433–460.

The Metaphysical Machine as a New Method of Education in Philosophy

Evgeny Zakablukovskiy

1. Introduction

Before we address the concept of a *Metaphysical Machine*, we might need to make a problem statement. Do we have to state an existing philosophical problem right at the beginning or can we assume that a problem may be considered as a meta-problem, e.g. by raising questions like, how and where does the problem appear, what conditions should we create to induce this process, or what are the roles of human and machine here? Modern philosophy assumes the following rule: the categories of truth and falsity should be applied not only to *solutions*, but also to the *problems* themselves. We need to "condemn false problems and reconcile truth and creation at the level of problems" (Deleuze 1997: 3). F. Nietzsche, H. Bergson, A. Badiou, Q. Meillassoux, L. R. Bryant and others would probably agree as well. This means that philosophical problems are fundamentally *inventable*: the true problem is not what was discovered or was found as a pre-existent reality, but what endows *something non-existent* with *existence* in the process of invention. Thus, the problem statement is an excess that might not exist; therefore, it is extremely difficult to demonstrate the relevance of a philosophical problem (in the modern academic sense). On the other hand, the inventability of a problem links the problem to a solution, since both involve an invention. H. Bergson once wrote that "the stating and solving of the problem are here very close to being equivalent; the truly great problems are set forth only when they are solved" (Bergson 1934: 59).

This rule is often overlooked when it comes to such an important and acute topic as Artificial Intelligence. In this interdisciplinary field, many issues intersect: technology, automation, machine learning, education, etc. N. Bostrom's simulation argument is a perfect example of this omission: the philosopher proves that AI almost certainly already *exists*, simulating our reality following the instructions of the so-called posthumans (Bostrom 2003). In his recent monograph, Nick Bostrom goes further and considers AI action options *depending on its (AI's) own goals*, taking into account the simulation hypothesis (Bostrom 2014: 134). However, most issues regarding AI's role in politics, military affairs, or education are debated as if AI already exists or, in any case, as if we know what it actually is.

The opposite approach, assuming the inventability condition, is conceptualized differently. It takes into account the factors of contingency, temporality, and the special structures of time, affective disposition, and learning, which is especially important for us. In this paper, I will focus on the latter aspect by stating a problem within the framework of discussions about AI. I will also outline the suggested technical solution to this problem. However, I will also take into account the context of modern philosophical, educational, and engineering discussions regarding our topic by elaborating on the elements of philosophical artificial intelligence in the context of education in philosophy.

The idea of a *Metaphysical Machine* has matured in the philosophical environment of Minin University in the background of automating and digitalizing education – processes that are developing very actively indeed. Thinking philosophically about education presupposes the presence of invention. G. Deleuze, while writing on the problem of learning, gives the example of swimming (Deleuze 2001: 23). This lets him identify three dimensions in education: a *meeting*, an *experiment*, and an *invention*. A *meeting* suggests that you cannot learn – in this case, learning to swim – without affective participation, that is, without trying to swim *on land*. The important thing is that this is a meeting with something that one had never met before. In the case of swimming, it is the deep waters that require the *invention* of swimming. The *experiment* assumes that during a meeting we do not have a *ready and tested* version of our attitude towards the meeting; we do not know how to swim yet, we must try out the possible options of our actions, rejecting those that do not match what we meet. We *paddle* – but in such a way that the desired movements gradually match the ability to swim. An *invention* involves the emergence of something new, the discovery of a perspective that has not yet existed (we are floating). All three elements were important to our work; swimming is impossible without water and without floundering.

We started from the following pressing problems in philosophical education:

A. The prevailing use of traditional educational methods and tools, in particular when studying the history of philosophy. As a result, a *meeting* with philosophical tradition – in the abovementioned sense – does not occur.

B. Outdated formats of student self-work. There is a mismatch between the dynamic thinking process development and the static material available on philosophical tradition.

C. Easy access to ICT has led us to a huge increase in the volume of available material, both on the history of philosophy and on the modern philosophical thought. In fact, nowadays, a young philosopher learns to swim in an ocean with huge waves right from the start. This problem assumes not only a *human dimension* – let's call it an *athletic* one – but also a *technical solution*. We would like to automate a large number of routine operations that are needed for the development of modern philosophical information space. Please note that we do not contrast automation and creativity. The fact is that, in addition to simplifying and accelerating the solution of many educational and research tasks, the automation of specific aspects of education assumes a *contingent meeting area*.

D. STS and the object-oriented ontology demonstrate a relatively independent, and even *thinking life* of technical objects (cf. Bryant 2014: 79; Harman 2009: 226; Latour 2018: 47–64). However, the question of technical objects' participation in the area of philosophy is barely being tackled in practice – we cannot witness a *meeting* with the *technical background* of thought. Paraphrasing Latour, we may say that the philosophical *parliament of things* does not exist and its existence is not even on the agenda. This means that philosophy, which has repeatedly questioned anthropocentrism *in theory*, remains anthropocentric *in practice*. Meanwhile, we assume that the world of technical objects may grant us a discovery of *pre-socratic cosmos of elements*, potentially full of philosophical inventions.

2. Methodology

These problems were collectively worked out with undergraduate and graduate students, as well as the faculty of Minin University's Department of Philosophy. We were looking for solutions and, in parallel, the functions of a metaphysical machine. We are well aware that this was the *paddling* stage, but it was a necessity. Thus, the author conceptualized and drove a creative session by inviting a selected group of professors and philosophy students at various stages of their studies to meet offline, while trying to maintain the teams' gender balance. The *Initiation* stage included mutual agreement on the session rules, plan, and objectives followed by a short author's intro to group dynamics using the diverge-and-converge concept, known in design thinking (Norman 2013), as well as B. Tuckman's model of group development (Tuckman 1965). The *Diverge* stage applied an original *sticky note storming* method, where the whole group silently generated ideas on what a metaphysical machine might do (one idea per sticky note) and then put them onto a specially prepared room wall. At the *Converge* stage, the group (divided into three teams) used the *How-Now-Wow* matrix to select ideas and organize their thoughts collaboratively. This tool is pretty widely known and helps cluster ideas based on their originality and the ease of implementation. The *Presentation* phase offered group members the opportunity to present their ideas and answer questions in order to deepen mutual understanding. Finally, the *Selection* stage was used to vote on the best ideas that could then be transferred to the technical team for implementation.

3. Results

3.1   Philosophical Functions of a Metaphysical Machine

So, a *Metaphysical Machine* in our understanding is a digital environment, the functionality of which can be structured and clustered according to the following groups of problems: Automating Routine Operations (Group I); Generating Matter for Philosophical Processing (Group II); Life, or The System Contingency (Group III):

3.1.1   Group I – Automating Routine Operations

This group of functions includes:

A Live Concept Database – this one implies the presence of encyclopedic information in our Metaphysical Machine. One of the main features of this database is the lack of linear structure. Multifunctional search would be possible: by personalities, by directions, by key and marginal concepts, by word frequency, even by geographical parameters (cf. Deleuze and Guattari 2009: 82–108). We may search by the non-philosophical context – for example, aesthetic, political, social. Hybrid search is also possible. In essence, this function represents both the ultimate structuring and the ultimate randomization of search: the first aspect increases speed, accuracy, and relevance of search, the second one allows generating unpredictable *search mixtures*. In addition, the possibility of interacting with the material (editing, deleting, filtering, annotating, tagging, etc.) would make such a database of concepts a dynamic one.

A *Concept Searcher* is a tool necessary for achieving a high degree of effectiveness in a live database. It enables searching and filtering necessary information. Ideally, each word in a living-concept database should have the properties of a hyperlink, connecting each database dot with all other dots. The search is designed to simplify user orientation in this data array and provide an opportunity to assemble search results. This assembly may look like a name or term index, listing the texts (and maybe even fragments) where the term occurs.

An *Annotator* allows the user to simplify and speed up the process of writing abstracts or summaries, and therefore, speed up the process of filtering and digesting information. The annotator acts as a text compressor, revealing the required conceptual trajectory in those texts, and it can be customized.

3.1.2   Group II – Generating Matter (ὕλη) for Philosophical Processing

This group of functions would include:

A *Multifunctional Combinational Mixer* (the students kept calling it a *grinder*). Many modern philosophical studies assume that "things can be creative" (Shaviro 2015). Today, this function of machine *phylum* is actively used in art. We keep talking about the hypoaesthetics of spam poetry; automatic generation of headlines and science fiction stories; poetry and painting by artificial neural networks. However, the philosophical, hypo-conceptual potential of such a function has not yet been evaluated and, most importantly, not yet tested. A combinatorial mixer is basically a text generator, from which, of course, you cannot demand any high conceptual level. However, being contingent, it forms *hypo-conceptual mixtures* that can be used as material for philosophical creativity.

We can further specify the work of a combinatorial mixer through the following functions:

Topic Generator: can *focus* both on current philosophical *trends* as well as create unpredictable assemblies.

Virtual Opponent: a function of philosophical artificial intelligence that could enter into a dialogue with the user in a quasi-natural language. Its*objective would be to help novice philosophers in their work, suggesting acceptable and already implemented ways to solve a particular problem. For those who have been good at creating their own philosophical texts and projects, the service could help find problem areas in their work or provide an opposite point of view.

Fabricator/Fabulist/Fiction Generator: In one of his articles, S. Shaviro used M. McLuhan's metaphor of rear-view-mirrorism. In order to create something new, it is not enough to focus on the former, but it is necessary to discover a dimension of the future through the invention of a *fiction*. A fiction cannot be extrapolated from what is already known, as it assumes maximum invention contingency. This means less breaking up with the present or the past, but instead actually implementing alternative extrapolations (Shaviro 2007). A fiction suggests that, not only the new is invented, but the old is open to re-invention by implying as liberal an attitude as possible towards tradition. In the context of a possible metaphysical machine's functions, this could mean generating, not only texts, but *trajectories* of how the texts are built up in the context of philosophical tradition. In essence, the definition of philosophy should in a sense be *reinvented* by every philosopher (cf. Deleuze, Nietzsche or Heidegger). Now, in order to reinvent the definition of *philosophy, meetings with non-philosophy* are needed, which would allow one to redefine the very trajectory of the philosophical movement in the tradition of thought. This presupposes that we see philosophical tradition, not in the form of a tree structure, but as a *rhizome* – a decentralized network with an infinitely variable set of *distribution routes*. Hypothetically, this function of rhizomorphization and redefinition of the historical and philosophical trajectory can be mechanized.

3.1.3   Group III – Life, or The System Contingency

Let's start with a more or less realistic and end with almost fantastic options.

A *Universal Communicator,* in our case, serves to arrange and direct collective work. The Communicator focuses on identifying common ground between the interests and goals of different groups of researchers, establishing feedback across different concepts and offering a range of common problems.

A *Radical Gamifier,* in the most common sense, would embrace all the possibilities and functions of a Metaphysical Machine that could be called upon to diversify users' work, entertain them, or even *complicate* their work.

A *Concept Aesthetizer* would make it possible to implement that correlation of philosophy and art, to which the majority of philosophers, from Plato to Badiou, attached great importance. As A. Badiou puts is, philosophy "has clung to language, to literature, to *writing* just as to the last possible representatives of an a priori determination of experience, or to the preserved place of a clearing of Being" (Badiou 1999: 58). The Aesthetizer can be specified through increasing the complexity of functions and tasks: schematizing of concepts, metaphorical transferring of a concept to a holistic aesthetic image, or even constructing a digital concept body.

Finally, the most experimental and debated idea at creative sessions was the proposal to create so-called *Artificial Forms of Hypo-philosophical Life*. Presumably, a certain artificial form of philosophical life may emerge out of the work of all three groups of functions. In any case, some space must be provided for this artificial life.

These were the experimental results of our *paddling* at creative sessions within the *Metaphysical Machine* project. Their importance lies, not only in a certain abstract accumulation of experience, but also in the attempt to respond to a real request of the philosophical community.

3.2   Technical Solution

Of course, the projective idea of a *Metaphysical Machine* should not remain an arbitrarily deeply elaborated concept. The very *swimming* of this concept (that is, the invention itself) must be carried out, tested, and confirmed materially and technically. It is the technical scenario that would allow us to filter most of the development options offered during creative sessions.

In collaboration with a potential supplier, the following technical solution was developed for *selected functions* of a metaphysical machine. Based on the basic services offered by a special platform, the team is planning to create an interactive digital tool that would facilitate the understanding of selected philosophical systems. The result would be achieved through a dialogue process between the student/researcher and the machine. The dialogue will be carried out in quasi-natural language with special expressive means in the context of a reference system for philosophical characters' ontologies.

More specifically, we plan to build a hardware and software toolset that would allow the student/researcher to do the following: start a meaningful dialogue with the machine in quasi-natural language; launch a virtual debate between two Metaphysical Machines; and, finally, organize a *court trial* – a debate between two philosophical personae with the participation of an *arbiter*, who will also be a virtual character.

Through specifying the concept, developing implementation scenarios technically, as well as making changes to the platform, we can start designing the metaphysical machine. The process involves a preliminary processing of texts that the machine has to digest.

The digital platform client will initially include the following functions: text filtering using the algorithms of stop word removal (cf. Silva/Ribeiro 2003); providing text description in form of a keyword list as a result of stemming procedures (cf. Lennon et al. 1981); building and visualizing semantic networks of texts based on a keyword list; analysis of isomorphism and other characteristics of network graphs (cf. Goldberg 1982). Then the user can evaluate the list of keywords and words contained in the text according to the frequency principle, based on a tag cloud. Based on the match results, a digraph will be constructed that reflects links between the keywords. By analyzing the archive with the help of special tools, the user will be able to see which texts are almost certainly talking about the things that one describes with the help of identifiers independently entered. Extracting information from the corpus of texts involves, first of all, clustering texts by subject, identifying new text subjects, searching for texts of similar subjects, and creating a hierarchical text catalog (Malik 2010). Based on the work results, the user will be able to assess the formation of directories (adding or deleting texts from the archive) by the system according to the double hierarchy principle (most frequent keywords vs. degree of keywords' proximity).

Descriptor keywords are generated by the system at this stage. The graphical interface of the catalogs is presented as a *forest*, with *branches* along the horizontal hierarchy and *trunks* along the vertical one. Newly downloaded texts are cataloged automatically. The user will be able to transfer between *forests* depending on the clustering method. The strength of semantic communication is reflected in the *branch length* and the *trunk height*. The user can use the *planting* mode, where it would be possible to simultaneously catalog the texts of *trees* belonging to different *forests*, for a comparative assessment of texts that lack common features.

Further, it will be possible to create an individual ontology of a specific philosopher. We will be able to assess relations between ontology objects; to form the description of (a philosopher's) character based on unique ontological relationships; to determine a specific author's writing style and classify texts by style (Hmelev 2000: 115–126).

As a result, the user will receive a dialogue system with the ability to replenish the archive, a text interface in the form of a Q&A command line that produces detailed answers to questions. An answer can be presented in text form, as a link (if it is in the database), a graph, or a list. At this stage, the user will be able to verify the system's quality and offer appropriate adjustments. As the project progresses, the model will be improved using various artificial intelligence algorithms, and the functions of *debate* and *trial* will be implemented.

At this point we need to address the hermeneutical issue of translated texts that are fed into the machine. The team was originally going to start the pilot project with one Russian philosopher (Vladimir Solovyov, 1853–1900). This would enable us to avoid issues with translation and copyright, but even there some terms needed explanations (e.g. *Godmanhood*) – those could have been embedded as URLs to encyclopedic/dictionary sources. With translated texts the issue of style classification may become severe, so one-language systems may be preferred at this stage, as they would be more valid (when the source texts are written in the same original language). In any case, these points should be a matter for further discussion between philosophers, attorneys, software engineers, and linguists.

4. Discussion

While presenting the preliminary research results at the Interdisciplinary Conference on the Relations of Humans, Machines and Gender (run in October 2019 in Braunschweig, Germany) the author was asked whether the project included any intentions to avoid/mitigate the gender gap. A gender gap is the disproportionate absence of women in a discipline or workforce compared to the gender proportion in the pool of potential members (Thompson 2017). Regarding our project, we may assume the gender gap may be understood as a) disproportional absence of women in the project team and/or in the pool of stakeholders and b) disproportional absence of women in the pool of authors and/or titles that are used to *feed* into the machine. Such potential disproportions are relatively easy to avoid/mitigate, by making the gender gap avoidance/mitigation and equal number of male and female project team members one of the project's strategic objectives; appointing a woman as project co-manager; and balancing male and female authors in the pool of sources.

Another issue we need to tackle may be using gender-neutral language. That also may be considered one of the project's objectives by applying, for example, the ASA rules to ensure "avoidance of language reflecting bias or stereotyping on the basis of gender, race, ethnicity, disabilities, sexual orientation, family status, religion, or other personal characteristics" (ASA 2010). So, unless gendered terms are specific to data or demographic analysis, we should commit to using non-gendered terms in our project-related papers, presentations, charts, etc.

A final issue (which is much harder to solve) may be the gendered terms used by selected authors, whose works we may use to *teach* the machine. The author considers manually *correcting* gendered terms in, say, Plato's works, so that our *Metaphysical Machine* starts talking to us in gender-neutral Plato language, a dubious approach. However, we may apply specific algorithms that may search and replace gendered terms in the machine's *own* texts (e.g. mankind → humankind, boy → child).

5. Conclusion

We described our experimental virtual *swimming* into the problematic sea of philosophical artificial intelligence, pedagogy of machine learning, modern philosophy, and pedagogy of technology. Given the philosophical, conceptual, gender, engineering, and technical dimensions of the problems stated, we can now proceed to the formulation of some intermediate conclusions.

The *Metaphysical Machine* as a modern anthropological and technical, philosophical and educational model, is not only conceivable, but also fundamentally feasible in the form of a specific technical object. The successful existence and functioning of the *Metaphysical Machine* are strictly temporalized, that is, it cannot appear instantly, but involves an intense period of *learning time*. Machine learning and educational relationships between a person and a machine (software product) also involve the discovery and study of a whole unknown field of *machine pedagogy*.

We need to pay attention and avoid/mitigate the gender gap in philosophy, in whichever way it appears: be it the specific project logistics, working rules/style, staffing, *raw material* selection, or the more general approach in terms of avoiding gendered terms in the texts that the machine produces.

A significant proportion of *contingent areas* that inevitably would emerge during the project implementation phase represent the informed risks that make the project viable. Without these, a metaphysical machine would become another interactive electronic encyclopedia that could not be anything but a rear-view mirror.

References

American Sociological Association (2010): American Sociological Association Style Guide. 4th ed. Washington, DC: American Sociological Association.

Badiou, Alain (1999): Manifesto for Philosophy. Albany: State University of New York Press.

Bergson, Henri (1934): La Pensée et le Mouvant [The Though and the Shift]: Essais et Conférences. Paris: Librairie Félix Alcan.

Bostrom, Nick (2003): Are You Living in a Computer Simulation? In: Philosophical Quarterly 53, 211, pp. 243–255.

Bostrom, Nick (2014): Superintelligence: Paths, Dangers, Strategies. Oxford: Oxford University Press.

Bryant, Levi R. (2014): Onto-Cartography: An Ontology of Machines and Media. Edinburgh: University Press.

Deleuze, Gilles (1997): Le Bergsonisme [Bergsonism]. Paris: Quadrige/PUF.

Deleuze, Gilles (2001): Difference and Repetition. London: Continuum.

Deleuze, Gilles/Guattari, Felix (2009): Qu'est-ce que la Philosophie? Paris: Les Éditions de Minuit.

Goldberg, Mark (1982): A Nonfactorial Algorithm for Testing Isomorphism of Two Graphs. In: Discrete Applied Mathematics, pp. 229–236.

Harman, Graham (2009): Prince of Networks: Bruno Latour and Metaphysics. Melbourne: Re.press.

Hmelev, Dmitri (2000): Raspoznavanie Avtora Teksta s Ispolzovaniem Cepej A. A. Markova [Recognizing the Text Author Using Markov Chains]. In: Vestnik MGU 9, 2, pp. 115–126.

Latour, Bruno (2018): Esquisse d'un Parlement des Choses. In: Écologie & Politique 1, 56, pp. 47–64.

Lennon, Martin et al. (1981): An Evaluation of Some Conflation Algorithms for Information Retrieval. In: Journal of Information Science 3, 4, pp. 177–183.

Malik, Hassan (2010): Improving Hierarchical SVMS by Hierarchy Flattening and Lazy Classification. In: Proc. ECIR Large-Scale Hierarchical Classification Workshop.

Norman, Don (2013): The Design of Everyday Things: Revised and Expanded Edition. New York: Basic Books.

Shaviro, Steven (2007): Sex + Love With Robots: The Pinocchio Theory. Available at http://www.shaviro.com/Blog/?p=614, last accessed July 24, 2020.

Shaviro, Steven (2015): Discognition. London: Repeater Books.

Silva, Catarina/Ribeiro, Bernardete (2003): The Importance of Stop Word Removal on Recall Values in Text Categorization. In: 816 Neural Networks (IEEE). Proceedings of the International Joint Conference 3, pp. 1661–1666.

Thompson, Morgan (2017): Explanations of the Gender Gap in Philosophy. In: Philosophy Compass 12, 3.

Tuckman, Bruce (1965): Developmental Sequence in Small Groups. Psychological Bulletin 63, pp. 384–399.

Biohacking and Orthorexia as Methods of Self-Optimization and Technologies of the Self, Examined through the Perspective of Gender Studies and Science and Technology Studies

Anja Trittelvitz

1. Introduction

Citius, altius, fortius! How can I get fitter, healthier, (almost) immortal? The desire to do the impossible, to halt the ticking clock of life, is as old as humanity itself. But under the name *biohacking*, this desire has been revived in the last few years, supported by current technological developments.

Do you start your day with a so-called bulletproof coffee[1] next to a variety of upscale dietary supplements, after an ice-cold shower, a meditation session and fasting till midday to feel energized? Then you might be a fan of biohacking. Biohackers do not only want to look younger, better: they want to crack, hack, biology. They measure their bodies: they know how much REM sleep they need in order to work most efficiently, how many calories and nutritional value their food has to ensure an optimal supply, and they won't leave their homes without a wearable for self-tracking (which shows pulse and calories burnt next to kilometers run). The market fulfills the desire for self-monitoring, observation, and profiling – and demands it at the same time: Strong is the new skinny! Physical health is the new form of bodily capital that can be transformed into economic capital.

In the past, so-called biohackers were mostly academic do-it-yourself biologists who were interested in exploring the world outside academia and the body. This gave rise to the quantified self movement that uses biohacking as primarily direct physical changes (with the help of technology) to optimize the biohacker's own body. Nowadays, personality development (*mindhacking*) and certain forms of nutrition (*food-hacking*) are also subsumed under the generic term biohacking and marketed accordingly.

As this optimizing trend is on the rise predominantly in the food sector, and (interdisciplinary) food studies are still underrepresented in the German-

---

1   250 ml brewed coffee mixed with 2 tb ghee and 2 tb coconut oil.

speaking academic world, I will focus on the providers, users, and forms of food-hacking.[2] Here I am specifically interested in *clean eating*[3] with its heavy users (on social media), and its implementation in the related current food trends.

2. *You Are What You Eat* – Identity Generation Through Enhanced Alimentary Behavior

Biohacking startups with (self-proclaimed) experts propagate food-hacking through a pure, *healthy* nutrition – especially paleo, clean, vegan[4], or ayurvedic. Clean eating is included in all of them: the (in the western society *rediscovered*) detoxing ayurvedic nutrition is called *mother of clean eating* for example, while the *paleolithic* nutrition, free from grain, legumes, and dairy products, is considered to be a stricter form, in addition to a variant of a clean, vegan diet free of animal *products*[5]. In all those approaches, industrially manufactured food, additives, or sugar are taboo. Its target group is the broad mass with its disposable income, who yearns for a more energized and toned body in the challenging everyday (work)life.

Through social media, these new types of living and nutrition are getting more coverage than before and various nutrition topics permeate the popular cultural context: Styled photos of food (also known as *food porn*) are presented on the digital platform Instagram, modern cooking shows have been (re-)established in the mass medium of television, and moderate, *healthy* food is promoted in formats such as "The Biggest Loser" or "Germany's Next Top Model." Terms like *detoxing* or *slow food* are taking root (in contrast to *convenience* and *fast food*) and so-called *challenges* for a sugar-free, intestinal optimizing, or keto[6] lifestyle arise (often in connection with sports) alongside workshops, webinars, and other events.

---

2   In my dissertation I only refer to living spaces that are among the so-called welfare states (most people living there are not threatened by starvation and can occupy themselves with food-hacking) and that are linguistically accessible to me. That means I can make use of sources from the German- and Anglo-American-speaking parts (and appropriate translations).

3   A modern form of whole and functional food including exotic superfoods.

4   In this case I do not refer to people who choose to live vegan out of moral/ethical motivations but out of (supposed) healthy living/enhancement motivations.

5   Vegans do not consider/use body parts of dead or secretions of living animals as products. Considering non-human animals as usable works in an omnivorous society that regards the consumption and use of certain animal species to be ethically justifiable (see *Carnism* according to Melanie Joy).

6   The ketogenic diet is a carbohydrate-limited, protein and energy-balanced, high-fat form of nutrition, which imitates the metabolism of starvation.

120

In my dissertation project, I am putting my gender glasses on and carrying out a (historical and contemporary) discourse-analytical classification of the food-hacking phenomenon, including a closer look at the psycho-socio-cultural meaning of nutrition through the ages and the biographical identity generation through eating behaviors:

> Food habits – how we produce, procure, prepare, and consume food – represent powerful systems of symbols whose associations are closely held [...] by nearly everyone. Looking at people's relationships with food can speak volumes about the people – their beliefs, their passions, their background knowledge and assumptions, and their personalities. [...] Food can tell the stories of migration, assimilation or resistance, changes over time, and personal and group identity. (Miller/Deutsch 2009: 7–8)

Food intake represents a communication situation and is socially effective, creating individual and collective identities. So, eating culture is not just what we eat, but also what we think and feel, with whom we eat, and it reflects what we and others expect from ourselves. In that context we are influenced by various factors, such as status, religion, habits, taboos, and our immediate environment.

3. Can *Clean* Food Be a Sin? Confessional Culture and Self-Thematization in Virtual Alimentary Communities

The cyberspace as a special, pseudo neutral (non-)room plays a notable role in information spreading and community building, including the culture of identification and self-presentation online. What role do different technologies (that are independent from time and space), like wearables, apps, and social media networks, play in the agents' identity generation? "[G]ender relations can be thought of as materialized in technology, and gendered identities and discourses as produced simultaneously with technologies" (Wajcman 2007: 293). What requirements for technology (e.g. the Internet of Things) arise in this context?

(Online) communities form around (pure/clean) eating habits as a (quasi-religious[7]) lifestyle and individuals tend to define themselves through those practices. This can go far enough that people develop eating problems, such as the so-called *orthorexia nervosa*, a form of *pathologically*[8] too healthy nutrition.

---

7   Even the proselytizing can be observed, as devotees are not necessarily under psychological strain and are exceedingly convinced of their way of living.

8   I don't want to fuel any pathologization in this context. Orthorexia nervosa can be associated with great stress to those affected, but is currently not yet classified as an eating disorder in the ICD10 / DSM5.

Jean Anthelme Brillat-Savarin is considered the founder of gastrosophy, the science of good food, in the 18th century. However, what counts as good, healthy food varies depending on culture and time (cf. Hüttl 2020). In 1990, the first circumscription of allegedly healthy and beneficial (not-)eating habits that could be described as orthorexia nervosa (according to current knowledge) took place. It was intended for protection against diseases, performance enhancement, and acted as a symbol of youth and beauty (cf. Barthels 2014: 9–10). In 1997, Steven Bratman described this phenomenon as a new variation of known eating disorders – but not necessarily pathological. He thought that the oversupply of food demanded a selection, based on individual preferences and ideologies. Depending on its specific manifestation, orthorexia can act like other known eating disorders. Affected people are limited in their food choices and thereby maybe even undernourished (as nothing available might be good enough). They spend many hours a day in planning and preparing their meals and suffer from obsessive ruminations around food-related topics. Eating (out) with friends or colleagues? Hardly possible. Additionally, the (socially accepted) expressed wish to lose weight could be used to mask an ascetic-orthorexic diet inside a peer group (cf. Barthels 2014: 70). *Lapses* lead to feelings of guilt, failure, and loss of control that are nowadays shared, or rather *confessed*, on social media with others of the ingroup. Through their wide dissemination, these restrictive diets seem so *normal* that people seek help (too) late, or after developing a second eating disorder, such as anorexia or bulimia nervosa. Nonetheless, it is important to mention that starting to eat *clean* might also replace a preexisting (worse) eating disorder (cf. Klotter 2015: 41).

Research on orthorexia has become of increasing scientific interest in recent years, especially in psychology, but is still limited. In particular, the direct connection to self-selected (online) communities does not seem to be sufficiently researched.

What are the motivations of the convinced supporters of a strictly clean diet? How are they doing, especially those who meet the criteria for orthorexia and/or are suffering? Which (other) biohacking (self-)technologies do they use and what are the characteristics of the exchange in online communities?

4. Optimally Disciplined for the Neoliberal Market: Health as Economic Capital

I am also interested in finding out how this challenging self-optimization (especially in/through communities and technologies online) comes about. In order to answer this, I am taking a look at the phenomenon of self-discipline, as in Zygmunt Bauman's post-panopticism, leading back to Michel Foucault.

Foucault describes the increasing surveillance and control mechanisms in the development of western society from the 18th century up to capitalism, where the interest in one's own body and the resulting social conformity of individuals arose. The individual disciplines themselves by matching their behavior to the given normative ways of living, until the norms are internalized and transformed into self-constraints – as opposed to external constraints, which were needed in the beginning. Bauman places panopticism in the context of postmodernism and emphasizes the influence of the current (communication) technologies that are independent of time and location, like the ones we find in cyberspace. (Post-)panopticism served the increase in efficiency and marketisation – the former at least is also the wish of today's biohackers. To what extent might self-optimization also have an emancipatory effect, in addition to the disciplining one?

Apart from the volume of market sales, and maybe the advantages from (and for) health insurance companies, people who (pretend to) live according to these ideal conceptions earn money by putting themselves and their products on the market: advertising through blogs, YouTube channels, Instagram accounts, or podcasts, in which they teach others how to live as efficiently and *well* as they do. *This* meal prep-box, *this* e-book, *this* diet course – they all promise a healthier and fitter life. Additionally, many also promote ways to inner happiness and fulfilment (often combined with yoga) camouflaged as essential self-care.

Being more energetic and productive is also promised through minimalist lifestyle trends (most of them urban), paired with the wellbeing Scandinvian lifestyle trends *lagom* and *hygge*. A central aspect of those involves a conscious and slowed down handling of food and the constitution of a happy life through it. The food-hacker's kitchen transforms into a place where do-it-yourself and technology are strongly connected: food, as natural as possible, is being processed with the help of cutting-edge technology. The juicer, the high-powered blender, and the spiralizer have become must-have devices. In this context, the naturalness of the country life with its *pure*, handmade products is becoming more and more idealized and purity-based ideologies are represented (like in certain clean diets).[9]

---

9   Dystopic examples of *clean*/vegan nutrition restrictions in fictional narratives can even be found in contemporary German popular literature, like Christian Kracht's "Imperium" (2012) in the form of *cocovorism* or in Theresa Hannig's "Die Optimierer" (2017) in the form of *synth-meat*.

5. Method Selection, Approach, and the Author's Position

In my dissertation I make use of mostly qualitative research strategies in addition to the rather subordinate quantitative methods listed here. These are an evaluation of online content (e.g. appearances/interactions on social media platforms, newsletters, websites, videos, and podcasts), participant observation, and expert/user interviews with selected partners. I am aware of the difficulties in questioning people about their bodies, which they always carry with them and where they often do not immediately know the background of their own behavior. Here the body is both object and subject.

I attended a rash of various on- and offline events (like fairs, seminars, and lectures) in the German biohacking community (of which I made observation records), established contacts all over Germany, collected a lot of field documents (e.g. advertising/information material and seminar content) and the influencers' (electronic) books for interpretation. In my interpretation, I also pay attention to forms of discrimination[10] that might be (re-)produced here.

In my research so far, the leading characters in Germany show themselves to the outside as mostly *white*, able-bodied, skinny, fit, and *cis-gendered*. The majority of supporters seem to be (young) females, people who have vegetarian or vegan lifestyles, and people who have already tried a dietary change (cf. Barthels 2014: 52, 55). As a veggie with diet experience, I have a longstanding personal (and scientific) passion for food. I share the desire for self-optimization and also struggle with the finiteness of life. I am a heavy user of social media, own a wearable for self-tracking and pay for an app for weight management. Consequently, I speak not from an outsider's perspective, but with the necessary distance.

---

10 Images of femininity are for example already staged closer to a healthier/veggie diet while meat as a symbol of power is rather associated with masculinity.

References

Barthels, Friederike (2014): Orthorektisches Ernährungsverhalten: Psychologische Untersuchungen zu einem neuen Störungsbild. Diss. Düsseldorf: Heinrich-Heine-Universität Düsseldorf/Department of Experimental Psychology.

Bauman, Zygmunt/Lyon, David (2013): Liquid Surveillance: A Conversation. Cambridge: Polity Press.

Foucault, Michel (1994): Überwachen und Strafen: Die Geburt des Gefängnisses. Übersetzt von Walter Seitter. 17. Aufl. Suhrkamp: Frankfurt am Main.

Hüttl, Tina (2020): Ernährung als Statussymbol: Du bist, was du isst. Available at https://www.deutschlandfunkkultur.de/ernaehrung-als-statussymbol-du-bist-was-du-isst.976.de.html?dram:article_id=471820, last accessed June 2, 2020.

Klotter, Christoph et al. (2015): Gesund, gesünder, Orthorexia nervosa: Modekrankheit oder Störungsbild? Eine wissenschaftliche Diskussion. Wiesbaden: Springer.

Miller, Jeff/Deutsch, Jonathan (2009): Food Studies: An Introduction to Research Methods. Oxford: Berg.

Wajcman, Judy (2007): From Women and Technology to Gendered Technoscience. In: Information, Community and Society 10, 3, pp. 287–298.

"[...] You Are a Nobody After This Kind of Surgery." On the Fragility of the Cis-Male Gendered Body

Myriam Raboldt

> Henceforth, I will use the nomenclature cis- and trans, with the understanding that these two biopolitical gender statuses are technically produced. (Preciado 2013: 127)

1. Introduction

Through a wide range of medical-technological artefacts and practices, such as plastic surgery, hormone therapy, testicle, penile, or breast implants, the gendered body can be constructed, enhanced and repaired. For this argument, and taking into account Preciado's claim in the initial quote, I want to take a closer look at the cis-male body, which can be seen as the "quasi gender- and sex-less normative body" (Wöllmann 2005: 140, translation by the author), whose scientific objectification and medicalization is still considered a desideratum.[1] But what happens when the matter of course gets fractured, the self-evident is no longer evident? My foci are fractures of materials and functions critical to a hegemonic masculinity[2] whose self-perception is significantly bound to virility, lust, and performance. How does this image of one's self falter when testicles or penises get injured, even amputated, or become so-called dysfunctional? How do the affected men cope, what does medical science offer as treatments, and how does the fractured norm get repaired? How do these technologies in turn shape the gendered body and social normative expectations on sex, gender, and sexuality?

---

1   Hence, I want to refrain from taking trans*-bodies into focus, as is often done when looking at the construction of gendered/sexed bodies. By focusing explicitly on the norm instead, I am trying to not let it be the unmarked category that has the power to see without being seen, as said by Haraway (1988).
2   For the concept of hegemonic masculinities see Connell (2005).

2. Route

Before elaborating more on my dissertation project, I want to take you along on the journey of how I got there, because it is as much a part of my research process as anything else. During my master's degree in History of Science and Technology, I worked on a joint research project that was based on a huge historical collection of prostheses at the German Hygiene-Museum in Dresden. Our first conference focused on the First World War and the mass supply of artificial limbs to amputee soldiers. From the beginning, I was interested in how this attempt to recreate the national work force could also be framed as an attempt to recreate a certain type of hegemonic masculinity that is bound to performance, intactness, strength, and independence. Through these lenses, I studied the research literature available and soon wondered what had happened to those who lost their genitals and, by assumption, their virility during the war. A statement by the German historian Sabine Kienitz concurs with my own analysis: Kienitz (1999: 65, translation by the author) calls these kinds of injuries "the taboo and unwritten chapter of the First World War."

At the same time, I thought about this issue from a gender-theoretical perspective: Making use of the concept of Doing Gender, which technologies we use and how is part of our everyday gender performance.[3] But other than bicycles, cars, or razors,[4] there is something special about penile, breast, or testicle implants: Through those artefacts, the material construction of gendered bodies is possible.[5] So, via these two threads – the amputees of the First World War and the theoretical exploration of the scope of the concept of Doing Gender through technology – I began researching the question of genital prosthetics. Since I couldn't find much in the historical literature, I searched for physical historical penile prostheses myself and contacted collections, archives, institutes, and other researchers. The findings were scarce. I felt I had stumbled into some mysterious research gap and I decided to take a closer look at the fractured cis-male body in my dissertation project.

---

3   For the concept of *doing gender* see West/Zimmerman (1987; 2009) and for using this concept from an STS-perspective see Kienitz (2010).
4   See for example Van Oost (2003).
5   The interesting yet ambivalent point here is that, the same practice that is used as an instrument to reproduce hegemonial norms, has the potential to actually deconstruct or infiltrate the binary heteronormative matrix.

3. Change of Course: From Doing Sex to Losing Sex

As part of the interdisciplinary PhD program KoMMa.G, I planned to inter-rogate the construction of cis-masculinity in terms of materializing bodily processes and functions through medical-technological practices, such as implants, hormone therapies and other active pharmaceutical substances, as well as plastic surgery; hence analyzing the *Doing Sex* through technologies. Apart from existing literature and medical expertise, I planned to gather ma-terial and data by conducting qualitative interviews with affected people.

In this undertaking, I stumbled again. My research process meanders into dead ends and is crisscrossed by a lot of irritation, laughter, awkwardness, silences, and embarrassed faces. The injured or missing (cis-gendered) penis seems to be an unspeakable taboo with a continuous presence at least from "the castrated of the war" (Kienitz 1999, translation by the author) until today.

Soon I decided to shift my focus from Doing Sex through medical-technological artefacts and practices, by taking a step back and looking pri-marily at the *losses* that cis-men with injured, amputated, or so-called dysfunctional genitals experience:

How do they feel about it? What are their coping strategies? What exactly is it that they bemoan? How does it change their sexual life? How does it affect their gender identity? Also: How do they feel the medical-industrial complex has treated them? Which roles – if any at all – do technologies, such as implants, prostheses, and sex toys play in overcoming the losses? And finally: Can a revision of the phallocentric cis-male identity and sexuality be brought to the fore?

With reference to Annie Potts (2014: 149) I suggest that the deconstruc-tion of the synecdochial relationship between cis-masculinity and the penis, as well as a reconfiguration of the relation between the penis and the phallus, go hand in hand with overcoming "hierarchical pairings such as hard/soft, penetrator/penetratee, outside/inside, active/passive, dominant/submissive, mind/body, and masculine/feminine" – hence, "a transformation at the level of signification, or meaning."

4. Field Access

To find my interview partners I contacted different networks such as the Men's Health Foundation (Stiftung Männergesundheit) and searched for self-help groups and similar organizations. When that wasn't very fruitful, I managed to find a clinic in Germany that has set up a database for patients with penile cancer. One of the doctors contacted over 40 patients and asked if they would be willing to give an interview, but all of them declined. On the website of the database itself the word "taboo" is used, but, interestingly, it is justified through the "relatively low number of cases."[6] What the clinic refers to as a relatively *low* number is actually around 800 cases of penile cancer in Germany per year[7] and my assumption here is that this taboo is not only linked to this relatively low number, but to the organ affected by the cancer itself. Finally, I found my first interview partner because he brought his experience with testicular cancer and amputation onto the stage, being a director and actor. Another interview partner, who recently had a penile fracture, contacted me through my poster at a conference. His main request, however, was not to take part in an interview (which he kindly did do after all), but, since he couldn't find any self-help groups or decent physicians himself, he was hoping to get information from me.

These examples show the particularities of my research's empirical field: Unlike other contexts, such as the trans* or inter* community, within my field self-help groups and support infrastructures are very rare and not easy to find: a *community* – if any – is mainly limited to anonymous online fora. Without this kind of strong infrastructure there are also no gatekeepers to gain access through. A scholar I contacted, who is a member of a research group working with psychoanalytical methods, commented on my problems with access: "Your observation that it is hard finding a narrative approach into the fragility of masculinity is not surprising. There is very strong resistance."

5. Creative Workarounds

It seemed I needed to either give up on my project, reshape it again, or get creative. I chose the latter and posted my call in an online forum in a thread on penile amputations,[8] but this time I also offered anonymous chat interviews. This got me at least a few replies, though only two have resulted in actual chat interviews so far: one man with a penile amputation and one who described himself as impotent. Both conversations required tenacity on my part and asking questions more and more directly, which seemed to help the interviewees formulate certain aspects more clearly. Both stated they have never spoken to anyone about their problems before.

---

6   See Peniskarzinomregister der Universitätsmedizin Rostock [Data Base for Penile Cancer].
7   Database query at the German Centre for Cancer Registry Data.
8   Interestingly, most posts in that thread were from men who wanted to get rid of their genitals (without wanting a transition process) and could not find a willing surgeon.

After these interviews and my experiences in this research process, the feeling that there might be something between the lines, something latent, grew. This brought me to an interpretation method called *deep hermeneutics,* at the suggestion of a scholar of psychoanalysis. The main idea is that through psychoanalytic concepts, such as *scenic understanding,* the analysis of the material is done by letting a group of scholars or people discuss it. Within this discussion, the latent themes of the material shift in that group discussion, which later becomes subject to interpretation itself. Conducting anonymous chat interviews and using this psychoanalytical method to grasp what was latent in the material were ways of trying – with various degrees of success – to tackle the silence.

6. Gaps

By then, an additional question had entered my research universe like a bright star: Why is it so hard to write and speak about the broken cis-male body? With this, my project moved from being an analysis of empirical data alone, to a meta-reflection on the process itself. Since the empirical data kept rather quiet and my search movements into different directions always led into silences or dead ends down the path, the main trope of my research process became a gap or a void, the grasping-into-the-nothing.

I suggest approaching this gap through the following analytical dimensions:

The first is the actual research object itself: the material or functional loss of cis-male genitals, a nothing where something had been, a no more or no longer there. This material or functional loss leads into the second void and analytical dimension, in the form of the silence of the men affected, as I demonstrated in the above paragraph. But it is not just that there is silence on an individual level and therefore no self-organized community infrastructure. This silence is closely connected to the fact that there is no normalized speaking about the missing or injured penis or testicles, no discourse on a societal level. For example, compared to breast cancer, there is not much of a public discourse about testicular cancer, not to mention penile amputations; no awareness-raising celebrities, no charity runs, and not much literature. This absence of public discourse I see as the third gap and analytical dimension: "On a societal level you are a nobody after this kind of surgery," as the interviewee who had had his penis amputated brings to bear.

This discoursive gap is again linked to the silent voids in research, in collections, in archives that I stumbled upon when doing research about the First World War amputees. The questions arising here are: What is actually research-able and what is not, whose stories can be told by archival material, and therefore sediment into discourse, and whose stories do not? Handling these gaps sometimes involves challenging the boundaries of traditional scientific methods and the self-perception of certain scientific fields.[9]

One example from my historical research: During the search for historical objects, I found a penile prosthesis in the storage of the Museum of Technology in Vienna. Because the artifact was without provenance, to my then history of technology professor it was a useless object. Stubbornly and resolutely, I included it into my master's thesis anyway and saw the missing provenance as part of what the object can actually tell us.

Finally, after all gaps mentioned so far, there is this kind of meta-gap, that reaching-into-the-nothingness that seems to arise when finally trying to grasp the norm itself, when trying to see and talk about the fragility of a norm.

7. Tackling Taboos

I argue that we need to see gaps, missing parts, and links – in research, in archives, in discourse and in speech, as silence, as the unspeakable – as evidence instead of dismissing or ignoring them. Whitespace characters are a useful analogy: Something that looks like a blank space in a document isn't actually a *nothing*, but lines of code that also take up storage space. Discovering these hidden lines of code can be achieved by a queering of methodologies and scholarship that is informed by queer-feminist theory, memory, and critique, and a creative handling of silences, absences and shattered material. It needs bold adjustments of methods and therefore criticizing and questioning so-called good science in general.

---

9   Learn more about these boundaries with Gieryn (1999).

References

Connell, Raewyn (2005): Masculinities. 2. ed. Cambridge: Polity Press.

German Centre for Cancer Registry Data. Available at https://www.krebsdaten.de, last accessed April 9, 2020.

Gieryn, Thomas F. (1999): Cultural Boundaries of Science: Credibility on the Line. Chicago: University of Chicago Press.

Haraway, Donna (1988): Situated Knowledges: The Science Question in Feminism and the Privilege of Partial Perspective. In: Feminist Studies 14, 3, pp. 575–599.

Kienitz, Sabine (1999): Die Kastrierten des Krieges: Körperbilder und Männlichkeits-konstruktionen im und nach dem Ersten Weltkrieg. In: Zeitschrift für Volkskunde 95, pp. 63–82.

Kienitz, Sabine (2010): Prothesen-Körper: Anmerkungen zu einer kulturwissenschaft-lichen Technikforschung. In: Zeitschrift für Volkskunde 106, pp. 137–162.

Peniskarzinomregister der Universitätsmedizin Rostock [Data Base for Penile Cancer]. Available at https://urologie.med.uni-rostock.de/forschung-und-lehre/peniskarzinomregister, last accessed April 9, 2020.

Potts, Annie (2014): The Science/Fiction of Sex: Feminist Deconstruction and the Vocabularies of Heterosex. London: Routledge.

Preciado, Paul B. (2013): Testo Junkie: Sex, Drugs, and Biopolitics in the Pharmaco-pornographic Era. New York, NY: The Feminist Press at CUNY.

Van Oost, Ellen (2003): Materialized Gender: How Shavers Configure the Users' Femininity and Masculinity. In: Oudshoorn, Nelly/Pinch, Trevor (eds.): How Users Matter: The Co-Construction of Users and Technology. Cambridge/London: MIT, pp. 193–208.

West, Candace/Zimmerman, Don H. (1987): Doing Gender. In: Gender and Society 1, pp. 125–151.

West, Candace/Zimmerman, Don. H. (2009): Accounting for Doing Gender. In: Gender and Society 23, 1, pp. 12–22.

Wöllmann, Torsten (2005): Die Neuerfindung des Männerkörpers: Zur androlo-gischen Reorganisation des Apparats der körperlichen Produktion. In: Bath, Corinna et al. (eds.): Materialität denken. Bielefeld: Transcript, pp. 139–163.

Humans and Machines in Everyday Life

The Win-Win Competition/Cooperation of Humans and Non-Humans

Cecile K. M. Crutzen

We need to move from a vision of a world of separateness and hierarchy to one of multiplicity and creativity. This is an approach in which objects aren't shown according to a pre-existing category but rather according to their potential to ensnare the audience in a web of interpretative implications. (Clémentine Deliss, Design Museum Gent, Exhibition "Object Stories," 2018)

1. Introduction

Cyber-Physical Systems are the entanglement of humans and non-humans: their agency (the ability to act) constitutes a changing world. They are *phenomena*, integrating computation, networking, and physical, biological, and chemical processes so that non-humans and humans are not separable. In those systems, technology is and will be outside and inside human bodies as prosthesis and enhancement of human and non-human bodies.

Humans have created several worlds where people are experimenting with the enhancement or even redesign and improvement of the human species. Elite sport is one of these worlds. In its rooms of agency (parts of worlds where (intra-)acting is possible) design and use of technology are not mutually opposed but intertwined in the ongoing intra-actions of humans and non-humans. The agency of design is integrated into the agency of the becoming of the use of the ready-made acting.

The ready-made acting is the produced technology which is offered to users.

Rooms of agency can be critically transformative[1] if they are reliable in the sense of the German word *Verlässlichkeit*, which has a dual meaning of being trustworthy and of being able to let go. Awareness of the kinds of doings taking place in these rooms is crucial. However, actors in these rooms are not always visible to themselves and others. Physical, mental, and methodological invisibility will restrict the possibilities for change. Awareness of

---

1   The transformative rooms focused in this paper are both *critical and transformative* and *critically transformative*. Hence the interchangeable use of these terms.

and sensitivity to the becomings of humans and non-humans will be needed to establish an ethics of responsibility regarding agency and the possibilities of change. Diffractional methods can change the patterns of visibility and invisibility, showing the potential of critical transformation.

An important discussion nowadays is the ontological and epistemological relationship between human and non-human actors. Should we maintain the dualism between human and non-human actors? Technology brings non-human actors into the world. The ontological recognition of these actors, their capacity to act, and their complexity is more urgent than ever. The inclusion of non-human actors in gender analysis can save us from a dualism in which avatars, robots, cyborgs, ambient intelligence, and other manifestations of simulated humanity are seen as basically oppositional to humans.

In critical, transformative rooms, technology can *kick back* and open up the possibilities of many genders and design possibilities in use, as gender analysis opens up the possibilities of intervention in the power constructions of technology; making the gendered aspects of design and design-in-use visible. In the future, humans should engage with non-humans through a reliable (*verlässliche*) win-win competition and an even better win-win cooperation.

2. Who Are the Winners?

Journalists and researchers still discuss computers, robots, and artificial intelligence as if they were the opponents of humans in a competition, which implies that it is apparently known in advance that humans are bound to lose. There are a lot of articles written on how non-humans will take over routine, manual, and even cognitive work. The daily routines of humans will change, influenced by artificial intelligence's takeover of work and decision-making and the routine cognitive work of humans has already begun to decline.

Computers now replace humans in work such as entering data, searching documents, and writing formal reports. Driving a car is already partly taken over by built-in artificially intelligent assistant systems. In the past, many competitions have been organized between people and computers. The most famous examples are the Turing test and the chess competition between the IBM supercomputer Deep Blue and Garry Kasparov. In cases where specific competencies were involved, the comparison between the computer and the human has often been in favor of artificial intelligence. "AI is better at detecting skin cancer. The CNN Neural Network missed fewer melanomas than the dermatologists" (Haenssle 2018: 1839) and "Programs can now provide even routine step-by-step legal and financial advice: the nation's top lawyers lost recently in a competition with computers on the interpretation of contracts by computers" (Chin 2018) to provide just two of many recent examples.

As Haraway has already said in her cyborg manifesto, a lot of labor will be translated into robotics, artificial intelligence, and decision algorithms. Sex life, sex, and gender will be subjects for genetic engineering, reproductive technology, and information technology (Haraway 1991: 165). Due to technological developments, new non-human actors will be continuously created, while humans and society will have to worry about whether they should intra-act with those actors or not.

In philosophy, computer science, and gender studies, one of the most discussed questions at the moment is, what the ontological and epistemological relationship between humans and non-humans is and what will it become. Should we maintain that dualism between human and machine, which is still being shaped by the questions of who is smarter and who will function better? Human and non-human actors both have agency skills[2]: every technological product presents ready-made actions that can either be carried out autonomously or in cooperation with people and institutions that integrate these actions into the design of their own activities.

Ontological and epistemological recognition of these non-human actors, their capacity to act, and their complexity is more urgent than ever. Humans already live in cyber-physical systems. In these systems knowing and being are no longer separated. Humans intra-act with non-humans and vice versa in a continuous flow of agency. The question is, how can we transform the predicted and feared win-lose competition into a win-win competition and, going further, into win-win cooperation between humans and non-humans.

3. Humans, Machines, and Their Similarities

People are increasingly discussed and dealt with as input-output machines. Quantifying values and improving those that are economically valuable is part of the routines of a capitalist society. In areas as diverse as economics, entertainment, military, and especially elite sports, human performance is now controlled in a technical way that closely resembles the control and processing of a machine: from input to output (Crutzen 2016; 2018).

On the other hand, the development, design, and use of machines are often based on the competencies and characteristics of people. By adopting the notion of machine learning, designers intend to create machines that will perform as humans or even better, achieved through building machines with sufficient computational resources, through offering training examples from

---

2   With agency I mean the ability to act. It is a skill to have that kind of abilities.

real-world data, and through designing specific algorithms and tools for learning processes. Just like humans, machines can improve their performance through learning by doing, inferring patterns, and hypothesis testing. It is no longer necessary to program long and complicated rules for a machine's specific operations in advance. Instead, programmers can equip them with flexible mechanisms that facilitate machines' adaptation to their task environment. At the core of these learning processes are artificial neural networks, inspired by the networks of neurons in the human brain (Petropoulus 2017).

The human body treated like a machine is infiltrated and inextricably linked with technology. Artificially produced organic and non-organic replacements will become more and more available to poorly-functioning body parts. The breeding of human organs in animals is already possible and, in the future, these could be used as parts of technological equipment. The similarity and connectedness of people and technology will increase and the reification and instrumentation of people will continue. Both the machine and the human are already measured in terms of their input and output values. Their processes and methods will be analyzed and subjected to technical control (Crutzen 2016; Geertsema 2006: 295–296). Biotechnology and communication sciences will blur the difference between machine and organism. The intended redesign of the human body, and more broadly the human species, designated by the obscuring term *enhancement technologies* will lead us to trans-humanism.

4. Elite Sport as a Microcosm of Risk

Technological interventions on the body are moving on from curing disease to improving and optimizing the self. Technology creates artificially-produced organic as well as non-organic spare parts, which can be manufactured with 3D printers, for example. In the scientifically manipulated construction and deconstruction of the body, the border between "nutritional supplement" and "medical treatment," between the therapy and artificial improvement of the body is blurred (Crutzen 2016: 42; Khushf 2005: 2). In elite sport, there is a tradition, not only of competition between athletes but also between the producers of technology: "Who can offer the best technology for improving sports performance, without being characterized as doping. Winning the Olympics in the cyborg era isn't just about running fast. It's about the interaction of medicine, diet, training practices, clothing and equipment manufacture, visualization and timekeeping." (Haraway in an interview with Kunzru 1997)

Elite sport can be described as an already trans-human world in which the human species is the object that is being redesigned. Andy Miah says in (2003): "Athletes have metamorphosed into super-humans, blurred suitably by the softening presentation of modern television. Athletes are ambassadors of trans-humanism, placed at the cutting edge of human boundaries of capability. The athlete's body is in a state of flux, continually transcending itself, and thus perpetuating trans-human ideas about the biophysics of humanity." According to Ivana Zagorac "The field of sport figures is a fascinating magnifying glass, which unveils entirely specific and intuitive ways of manipulating our fears of an altered future." It is a "microcosm of risks" in which humanity is trying to create "an illusion of control." (Zagorac 2008: 292)

In microcosms like elite sport, humans are experiencing the increasing need to deal with risks beyond our values and personal control. In elite sport, the experimental use and design of enhancement technologies can proceed, renegotiating the borders of physical normality under the justification of fair play. Athletes' use of technology to improve their performance is increasingly accepted and the replacement of entire body components will be allowed as soon as the performance of disabled athletes with high-tech replacement parts becomes better than that of non-disabled athletes. Now it is still being debated whether a disabled athlete may compete in a competition for able-bodied athletes. In the future, this could be the other way around: we will be discussing which parts of the body of a non-disabled athlete may be replaced. In elite sport, the *natural human* is disappearing.

However, designing the artificial-technoid human, abandoning the natural human, creates doubts and fears: fear of loss of identity, because technology touches on personality; doubts about self-worth, because we can no longer distinguish what is our real, own achievement and what has been achieved artificially; and finally, there is the fear that, despite all our efforts, humans will fail in a contest against artificial-technoid humans (Afram 2015). Nevertheless, humans experience a sense of progression in pushing the barriers of the body and the mind and transcending the limits of human abilities. The engagement with computer games shows us how all humans, and not only athletes, are eager to overcome their imperfections and be in competition with non-humans.

5. Cyber-Physical Systems

Living in cyber-physical systems (CPSs) will change the core characteristics of human nature. As Karen Barad said: "Machines will generate new life; life will be reworked. The nanoscale is the scale of life processes, and the combination of computational nanotechnology and bio-nanotechnology foretells the possibilities of neuron-electronic interfaces that use nano devices to join computers to the human nervous system. With one hand on a computer mouse and an eye to the future, not only do we make changes to configurations of individual atoms, but the very nature of who "we" are begins to shift. Our imaginations, bodies, desires, organizational structures of research and investment, and much more, quake with the expectation of the impending "nano-tsunami" that portends immense changes to life on earth and beyond." (Barad 2007: 363) The nanoscale changes happen slowly and almost unnoticed because people have already been used to invisible technology for a long time. Most CPS function invisibly in the background of human intra-actions.

The term *cyber-physical systems* refers to a new generation of systems with integrated computational and physical capabilities that interact with humans and non-humans through multiple new modalities. CPSs are integrations of computation, networking, and physical processes. They represent the further development of embedded systems; hardware and software embedded in devices whose principal mission is not computation, such as cars, toys, medical devices, and scientific instruments (Gupta et al. 2013). Embedded computers and networks monitor and control physical processes, with feedback loops where physical processes affect computations and vice versa. Sensors in the physical world will detect changes in the environment, providing information for the controllers in the cyber world. Actuators take physical input from the cyber world and turn that into physical actions (De et al. 2017; Lee 2015; Technopolis group 2016).

CPS are entanglements of humans and non-humans. Their agency constitutes a continuously changing world and they will be outside and inside human bodies as prostheses and enhancements. Brain signals will control physical objects. These intra-actions of humans and non-humans in the entanglements of our daily lives, at home and in our workplaces, will be present and unavoidable in a wide range of situations. Technology will increasingly cross the boundaries of our body and settle in our body. People will get used to it, just like we are already used to the (invisible) technology around us. Ambient intelligence in our environment means that the entire environment surrounding an individual has the potential to function as an interface. Our physical body's representations and movements will unconsciously become the cause of actions and interactions in our technological environment between devices inside and outside our bodies.

The definition of what is human and what is artificial, non-human, is becoming fluid. Understanding the impacts of the agency of CPSs and their ambient intelligence will be essential for the accountability and responsibility of humans and non-humans. People will have to determine and record in rules and legislation to what extent they want to be aware of the activities of the technology around them. Responsibility for intra-actions between technology and people will unavoidably be placed in the hands of those for whom these intra-actions are visible and transparent, while those to whom they are invisible will become increasingly dependent.

6. Invisibility in Cyber-Physical Systems

The term *invisibility* represents everything humans cannot or can only partly (re)cognize, directly or indirectly, using their senses: hearing, seeing, touching, smelling, and tasting, occasionally with the support of unveiling apparatuses. Visibility has always been an important subject in gender studies, such as when researching the circumstances of non-persons, invisible employees mostly women working in care and service. Their invisibility was and "is linked with power and status, differences between employer and employee." There are also circumstances "where the workers themselves are quite visible, yet the work they perform is invisible or relegated to a background of expectation." In gender studies we examine how to change such work that is "embedded under a general rubric of 'care' and usually taken-for granted into work that is legitimate, individuated and traceable across settings." (Star 1999: 15)

The visibility and visual abilities of artificial actors depend on the technical constraints of their construction. Both their field of vision and their visibility spectrum can differ from that of human actors because of their technical means and possibilities. Determined by implemented data models, processing functionality, connectivity, and the chosen sensors and actuators, the awareness of non-humans is different from that of humans. Invisibility can freeze the possibilities of change and transformation, because the potential responses of the invisible intelligence are uncertain, due to the wide dynamic in their spectrum. Neither feeling their presence nor seeing their full (inter-)action options, but only some designer-intended fractional output, makes it impossible to understand the complete arsenal of their functionality and it will also make it impossible to integrate the agency of design in the becoming-of-use of these artificially intelligent agents. This means that transformations will go in the direction of the obvious, stabilizing routines and biases that are always embedded in the design and use of technology and become invisible and frozen in the intra-actions of humans and non-humans. Physical invisibility is not the only cause of these hidden biases and frozen habits. Invisibility in general can be classified into "mental," "methodical" and "physical invisibility" (Crutzen/Hein 2009).

6.1 Physical Invisibility

Invisibility is important for the ethical significance of computers, according to James H. Moor: "Most of the time and under most conditions computer operations are invisible. One may be quite knowledgeable about the inputs and outputs of a computer and only dimly aware of the internal processing." (Moor 1985: 272) Nowadays the visibility of the inputs and outputs of CPS is limited. In the intra-action of humans and non-humans there are two irreversible major trends of physical invisibility.

One is the continued process of miniaturization, down to nanotechnological intelligent dust. The other is global wireless Internet access, which allows such mini devices to be included in almost any object of everyday life. The embedding, and therefore the invisibility, of artificial intelligence in daily aesthetic objects or infrastructure results in invisibility of agency in worlds where humans and non-humans are entangled. Technology resides in the periphery of our attention; actors are continuously whispering in our background, observing our daily behavior.

People become the objects of the ongoing conversations of artificial agents that are providing us with services, without demanding a conscious effort on our behalf or involving us in their inter-activities. These hidden devices are an invisible surveillance network that covers part of our public and private life. "The old sayings that 'the walls have ears' and 'if these walls could talk' have become the disturbing reality. The world is filled with all-knowing, all-reporting things." (Lucky 1999) New meanings of *home*, *intimacy*, *health*, *privacy*, *identity*, and *security* are constructed. Visible actions of people are preceded, guided, and followed by visible and invisible actions of artificially intelligent tools and environments – and their often anonymous providers (Crutzen/Hein 2009: 465, 479, 480, 492).

6.2 Mental Invisibility

In our interaction with tools and equipment, most technical products become mentally invisible; they are taken for granted when they become a natural part of daily life. Their evident and continuous availability causes their disappearance in the complexity of our environment. Weiser writes about the most profound technologies: "They weave themselves into the fabric of everyday life until they are indistinguishable from it." (Weiser 1991: 94)

As Berger and Luckmann said: "All human activity is subject to habitualization. Any action that is repeated frequently becomes cast into a pattern, which can then be reproduced with an economy of effort and which, ipso facto, is apprehended by its performer as that pattern. Habitualization further implies that the action in question may be performed again in the future in the same manner and with the same economical effort. This is true of non-social as well as of social activity." (Berger/Luckmann 1966: 70–71)

Mental invisibility is the invisibility of those habitual and routine actions, inter- and intra-actions, of which humans may not be or are not aware of. We create and nourish this invisibility. Dewey called these unreflective responses and actions "fixed habits," "routines": "They have a fixed hold upon us, instead of our having a free hold upon things […]. Habits are reduced to routine ways of acting, to which we are enslaved […]. Such routines put an end to the flexibility of acting of the individual." (Dewey 1916, Chapter 4). Routines are the frozen habits of actors, human and non-human. The meanings of sex and gender are also situated constructions; frozen in habits.

Life is a treadmill; Judith Butler's analysis of gender performativity is helpful here. According to her, it is a repetitive act that perpetually reproduces itself. "Sex is an ideal construct which is forcibly materialized through time. It is not a simple fact or static condition of the body, but a process whereby regulatory norms materialize 'sex' and achieve this materialization through a forcible reiteration of those norms" (Butler 1993: 1–2). It is difficult to jump off that treadmill of habitualization, it is hard to jump out of the gender expectations and get away from the habits of technology use. Letting go is difficult, and so, biases and habits embedded in technology are and will be spread by the unreflective design and use of technology. However, is there a kind of technology that should be mentally invisible?

Mental invisibility is not only and not always negative. Many things and tools that we use daily are mentally invisible. Humans need a high degree of obviousness in their living environment to handle daily life. More precisely, we love our environment, because human adaptation has been accompanied by many efforts to make it work for us. According to Naomi Scheman, it is impossible to know everything about the useful technologies in our environment: "It is impossible that we could all come to learn for ourselves what we would have to know for our cars to run, our bread to be baked, our illnesses to be cured, our roofs to keep the rain out, our currency to be stable, and our airplanes to fly." (Scheman 1993: 208) If human behavior could not be based partially on individual or collective routines and habits, life would become unlivable. Human actors would be forced to constantly and consciously decide about everything. Faced with the amount and complexity of those decisions, they would not be able to act anymore and would become completely isolated and conflict-ridden. They would be in a permanent state of despair; in the stress of constantly redesigning their environment.

6.3   Methodical Invisibility

In the eighties and nineties, work was often standardized, regulated, and embedded. The labor of workers was intended to become calculable and organized by computers and, therefore, be partly automated. For that computerization, work and workers had to be (re-)presented in models. These modeling methods were based on abstraction, such as generalization, classification, specialization, division, and separation. Abstractions are always simplified descriptions with a limited amount of accepted properties. Abstractions arise from the recognition of similarities between certain objects, situations, or processes in the real world and the decision to concentrate upon these similarities and to ignore, for the time being, the differences. They rely on the suppression of many other aspects of the world (Booch 1991: 39).

Researchers in gender studies, especially Susan Leigh Star, criticized the modeling methods used by computer sciences. According to Star, we are constantly wrestling with the properties of visible things: they are many, they are resistant to our attempts to change them, they clutter our landscape. In facing the tyranny of blind empiricism, however, we temper the clutter of the visible by creating invisibles: "Abstractions that will stand quietly, cleanly, and docilely for the noisome, messy actions and materials" (Star 1991: 82).

Standardization and classification are used to transform intra-action processes into regulated procedures to limit the ambiguity of meaning construction. Computer analysts and scientists make their models according to these principles of abstraction, thinking that abstraction can tame the complexity and ambiguity of the real world. Modeling methods embed these perspectives and views in the ready-made acting of artificial products, beforehand, which results in ignoring differences, ambiguity, and the situatedness of human and non-human acting (Crutzen 2009).

Modeling a domain changes it. The emerging models are not additions; they become actors that run after the reality of intra-action, but at the same time begin to play a role that changes other actors, human and non-human, as well as themselves. Their dynamic will change intra-actions in the domain they operate in. They create visibility and invisibility. An intangible dynamic reality cannot be controlled by static abstract models, so the choice of the *apparatus* of modeling and design will materially and immaterially influence its use and, consequently, also the design itself, because design and use are entangled (Crutzen 2013).

However, in the process of modeling the complexity of our dynamic worlds, abstractions are needed and unavoidable. According to Haraway, we can love our abstractions, which should be built with "our best calculations, mathematics, reasons." But each abstraction should "be able to break down, so richer and more responsive invention, speculation, speculation, proposing, and worlding can go on." (Haraway 2008: 93) Abstractions are not suitable as a one-to-one (re-)presentation of the "ways in which the world creates enduring patterns of difference by dynamically enfolding and unfolding itself." (Barad 2007: 176) Abstractions can give humans food for creative thought.

Another cause for methodical invisibility is the mental invisibility of producers and designers: "In order to implement a program which satisfies the specifications a programmer makes some value judgments about what is important and what is not. These values become embedded in the final product and may be invisible to someone who runs the program." (Moor 1985: 274) Mental invisibility hides the biases of our thinking and doing. Too often designers think that their perspective is free of biases and they are unaware of the preexisting biases that are present in their models and designs (I-methodology). Biases become embedded in the design and use of technology. Biases in computer systems are difficult to identify because of the widespread impact of these systems. They are "hidden in the code, difficult to pinpoint or explicate" (Friedman/Nissenbaum 1996: 331). If these biases are, or become, also mentally invisible in society, then users are not aware of them anymore and they become part of the users' habits. Biases in systems become frozen in the intra-actions of humans and non-humans. They are physically invisible and become mentally invisible in the design process of use. The "data that are used to train systems are already a product of the sociomaterial transformation of language and discourse and of intransparent practices of data processing" (Allhutter 2019: 342). The trained algorithm is no longer an algorithm in the true sense. It lacks not just universality, but also explicability and recordability, because the resulting software program, the code, cannot be traced back to its origins. No re-engineering is possible and the correctness of any kind of specification included in the training cannot be proved (Schinzel 2018: 7). The iterative use of training data will accumulate and strengthen the embedded biases and habits, it will make them mentally invisible and the algorithm will then choose a conservative outcome.

6.4   Diffraction and Visibility: Response-ability, Attentivity

Humans and non-humans live together in transformative rooms, where biases are present and invisible. Representation and reflection are not always the proper instruments to create visibility in the ongoing being of humans and non-humans. They "only displace the same elsewhere," according to Haraway (1997: 16, cfr. Geerts/Tuin 2016). We should look beyond reflection to create instruments that can handle dynamic processes. Diffraction refers to various phenomena that occur when waves encounter an obstacle or pass through slits. Sound waves, water waves, and electromagnetic waves, such as light, bend and intra-act with other waves, create troughs where they cancel each other out, and peaks where they amplify each other: that's what generates diffractive patterns (Truman 2019).

Haraway and Barad use diffraction as a metaphor for the effort of creating differences in the world, of being attentive to the production of patterns of difference. "We can understand diffraction patterns as patterns of difference that make a difference – to be the fundamental constituents that make up the world." (Barad 2007: 72) Diffraction patterns can be created by making slits so that we can leave and change the patterns of visibility and invisibility, brightness and darkness. Diffraction shows that the relation between visibility and invisibility is not dualistic. Invisibility is not always undesirable, as we have seen regarding mental and methodical invisibility. Abstractions can be used as interventions, according to Haraway, to show new possibilities for living. Mental invisibility is necessary to make our daily lives live-able. Visibility or transparency is also not always desirable, as the loss of privacy in social media shows. A dynamic balance between visibility and invisibility is necessary. According to Barad, diffraction patterns illuminate the indefinite nature of boundaries, displaying shadows in *light* regions and bright spots in *dark* regions. The relation of visibility to invisibility and use to design is a relation of *exteriority within*. With diffractive methods, we can create dynamic patterns of invisibility and visibility, changeable by varying the obstacles and slits. Diffractive patterns "reveal that there is light in darkness and darkness in light – they are fluid and provide an understanding of how binaries can be queered, and how differences exist both within and beyond boundaries." (Barad 2007: 71; Barad 2014: 171; Bozalek/Zembylas 2017: 115; Haraway 1997: 16, 34)

Response-ability means that we are able to respond to the patterns of visibility and invisibility created by humans and non-humans: "Ultimately, each practice must invent a manner of responding to the modes of mattering with which it is involved in a way that allows for the crafting of new contrasts, that is, of novelty and new habits of attention." As Savranski says, this is a "risky, inventive process of inheritance and creativity." Humans and non-humans can "contribute to assembling forms of problematic togetherness that show a 'concern' for the becoming of the world." (Savransky 2016) Attentivity is only the beginning of a response-ability for the becoming of the intra-acting world of humans and non-humans.

7. CPSs as Transformative Rooms

CPSs including the agency of humans and non-humans are transformative rooms, they are "phenomena" with a "dynamic process of intra-activity and materialization in the enactment of determinate causal structures with determinate boundaries, properties, meanings, and patterns of marks on bodies." These rooms do not need to have geometrical dimensions. They are spaces of change and possibilities for change: "This ongoing flow of agency through which causal structures are stabilised and destabilised [...] does not take place in space and time but happens in the making of spacetime itself." (Barad 2007: 140)

A microcosm like elite sport is a transformative room because humans and nonhumans intra-act in training and competitions. Tomorrow's road network as a part of public traffic is another example of a transformative room where humans and non-humans intra-act, where sensors and actuators become the senses and limbs for the flow of agency: Data exchange between sensors, actuators, and embedded algorithms will, in the future, control the flow of traffic. The oft-mentioned pros are the improvement of traffic flow, the reduction of pollution, and the ability for drivers to work or relax during transport. However, important negative consequences will also have to be solved, such as who is responsible and liable for crashes or who will be able to drive a car when people are used to automated driving. Automated driving will "change relations between humans and cars in a fundamental way, that affects the traditional connection of cars and driving with masculinity." "[D]riverless cars turn the active human driver into a passive passenger" and it is possible that "the structural-symbolic gender order will change when the human driver is (at least partially) replaced by a technological system." (Buchmüller et al. 2018: 166)

Rooms of agency like the future traffic system are always transformative because their internal dynamics affect the agents involved, mentally and materially. Some of the changes in this CPS will be preprogrammed or suited to the adaptivity spectra of humans and non-humans, but some will be invisible or unexpected. The partly-automated mobility system will be a dynamic process of intra-activity and materialization. What the boundaries will be and how the system will be stabilized in the design and use of these traffic systems by humans and non-humans depends on the agential cuts, the modeling, and models: "what automated driving systems will mean in the future and how these systems will matter does not only result from engineering efforts [...] meaning and matter is rather an ongoing process of emerging socio-technical interpretations, stabilizations, and destabilizations by different actors who coproduce or co-materialize these artefacts" (Buchmüller et al. 2018: 167–168).

8. Use and Design in Critical Transformative Rooms

In transformative rooms, design and use activities always take place. "The world's effervescence, its exuberant creativeness, can never be contained or suspended. Agency never ends; it can never "run out."" (Barad 2007: 177) Design and use activities are always intertwined and entangled in the ongoing intra-actions of humans and non-humans. They are not mutually opposed or separated but belong to every intra-action of humans and non-humans. The agency of design is integrated into the agency of the becoming of the use of the ready-made acting of technology: "matter and meaning come into existence, are iteratively reconfigured through each intra-action, thereby making it impossible to differentiate in any absolute sense between creation and renewal, beginning and returning, continuity and discontinuity, here and there, past and future." (Barad 2007: ix)

Use activities are iterations of already-existing actions, the ready-made actions come into existence. Design activities are not only the doings of what we call designers. Design activities are those activities where new possibilities of change are opened up by humans and non-humans. Design happens when in agency the possibilities of change are changing. Design is possible if in the ready-made acting of humans and non-humans the possibility of changing the change is offered and can be used, if the frozenness of routine acting can be put on hold. Mental invisibility can be seen as a precondition for the acceptance, the stabilization of use, and the domestication of technology, but it should not be the frozen final state of human actors. This status of acceptance and domestication bears the risk of being frozen in a frame, in a limited scale of possible actions in specific situations. We will lose reliability.

According to Heidegger, reliability (*Verlässlichkeit*) and usability are connected; one could not exist without the other. He says: "The usefulness of the equipment is, however, only the necessary consequence of reliability. The former vibrates in the latter and would be nothing without it. The individual piece of equipment becomes worn out and used up. But also, customary usage itself falls into disuse, becomes ground down and merely habitual." (Heidegger 1960, 28; 2002: 15) Heidegger also noticed that tools become "normal" – mentally invisible. The word *Verlässlichkeit* has two meanings in German: *reliability* and the *ability to let go*. We lose reliability if the connection between humans and non-humans is frozen and we cannot get disconnected anymore, when we cannot change the routines in our actions. *Letting go* is a design activity, because new possibilities of change, of dynamism, can be opened. As humans, we have to find a balance between the frozenness of habits and routines and the despair of a forced continuous design. Rooms of agency can be critically transformative when they are reliable, trustworthy, and bear the potential to be left again. Critical transformativity means enabling the total spectrum of *Verlässlichkeit*; design and design-in-use are available options.

For instance: will the CPS *traffic*, based on artificial intelligence, be reliable if humans lose their ability to drive? Losing this ability does mean that in dangerous situations we cannot take over and drive the car ourselves anymore. Transformative rooms are critical if we can experiment with *Verlässlichkeit*, testing the full spectrum between trust and discard (Crutzen 2003). Ease of use stimulates laziness and forces us into routines, similarly to how humans have made an addiction of the use of mobile phones and social media. Electronic banking has become unavoidable in our society.

In the transformative room of elite sport, the athletes are forced into the use of technology, regardless of whether it is forbidden or not. The habit of winning is unavoidable and through it the athletes have lost the agency of design. The sponsoring industry, the sports institutions, and the media determine which technological means are allowed. The spectators are only passively present in this room, accepting and delegating the risks of the use of enhancement technologies to the athletes. If elite sport continues to pursue the goal of expanding the biological limits of humans, it will discover that it cannot do so without technological enhancement (Miah 2003).

This means that the question of whether doping is necessary or not is to be answered according to this goal. Doping has become routine in the redesign of humans, so the transformative room of elite sport is not critical anymore. Elite sport can only be critically transformative by giving the athletes personal responsibility for their bodies and the release of enhancement technologies, such as doping, into their power and disposal, under the condition that they are fully aware of all consequences and risks. Users of technology, in this case the athletes, are the designers of their body transformation and as such, they should have the right of self-determination in the way they want to change their own bodies. Such an approach would also open up the fair and individualized participation of all athletes in all competitions, regardless of gender, without having to exclude disabled people with high-tech prostheses, cyborgs with robotic applications, or anyone else as monsters or aliens (Crutzen 2016; 2018).

9. Verlässlichkeit, Diffraction and Response-ability

Awareness of the kinds of doings taking place in rooms of agency is crucial. However, as mentioned before, actors in these rooms are not always visible to themselves and others. Physical, mental, and methodological invisibility will restrict the possibilities for change. Reliability (*Verlässlichkeit*) can remain visible only if the process of repeated and established action can be interrupted.

Critical transformations can happen with diffractional methods, like interventions and obstructions creating unexpected events to disrupt the waves of norms, obviousness, and normality. These make the choosable differences visible and disrupt the mental and methodical invisibility of our routines. It is like metaphorically throwing stones into the smooth water of habitualization. For *Verlässlichkeit*, humans need to be attentive and response-able, aware of possible obstructions and responding by changing the ongoing transformations. Disruption and obstruction open up design in the use of technology. They are necessary for a awakening from the ease of our habits.

Bio-amazons like Dutee Chand, Caster Semeneya (N.N. 2010; N.N. 2020) and the disabled, physically challenged athletes have already created these interventions and obstructions in elite sport. They pull down the boundaries drawn by conservative supporters of the ideology of fairness and the strict enforcement of gender segregation. The diffractive use of enhancement technology and the performance of many different genders can make elite spot critically transformative.

Non-humans can also create *Verlässlichkeit* because they can kick back by not functioning as expected, or not functioning at all, or standing in the way. These obstructions can be seen as diffractional methods in which their functionality and iterative, frozen use can become visible again. They utter signs of not coping so that their use or the interaction with them can only be continued in a different, conscious way. Moor recognized the strengths of computers already in 1985, despite possible ethical dilemmas, e.g. concerning privacy: "the ability to locate hidden information and display it. Computers can make the invisible visible" (Moor 1985: 275).

Researchers, designers, producers, and users are responsible for the nature and purpose of analyzing and modeling, as well as the methods and materials used in the material design and production of technology (Irni 2010: 85). According to Barad, research and modeling are based on "the real consequences, interventions, creative possibilities, and responsibilities of intraacting within and as part of the world." It opens "the possibilities for change humans and non-humans still have." (Barad 2007: 37, 46) Responsibility is localized in the phenomena of design, where human and non-human actors meet: "Ethical agency is not an attribute of human beings, in this case technology designers and technology users, but enacted in and through the sociomaterial configuration of people and technology." (Velden: 42)

Out of that ethical agency and in cooperation between gender studies, social studies, and computer science, critical design methods (Bath 2014: 31–34) have been developed, such as participatory design, creating a more intimate view of workspaces and work practices, disembedding invisible work and non-persons, since how people work is not always apparent:

152

"Too often, assumptions are made as to how tasks are performed rather than unearthing the underlying work practices." (Suchman 1995)

In participatory design, the waves and vibrations of actions and materiality, emanating from several positions and roles – analysts, users, spectators – come together to make room for diffractional patrons for future use and design-in-use of technology. Diffractional methods in modeling and design constitute an alternative to mirroring and modeling with abstractions based on similarities. The focus of analysis should be on the finding and making of differences: "[...] identifying sameness seems to close off discussion. If we are intent on finding out what is the same about things, then our search ends when we achieve the goal." To focus on differences is to embark on limitless discovery. [...] Difference reveals further difference. Difference also opens up the possibility of dialectic, the revealing interplay between two entities [...]" (Coyne 1995: 195). So differences lead to "creativity rather than separation and lack." Difference is not oppositional to "sameness – but is also incorporated into the self as difference within and seen as a means of becoming." (Bozalek/Zembylas 2017: 115; referring to Barad 2014: 169, 171)

For example, "mind scripting" is such an "analytical tool to disclose and consciously decide on gendered assumptions that are otherwise unknowingly inscribed to artifacts." It is a tool to challenge and to reoccupy commonly-held beliefs and the values systems that they are based on (Allhutter 2012: 703). It can disrupt the mental invisibility of the participants in a process of production.

Materiality in the form of, for instance, "cultural probes" can function as diffraction slits. The diversity of probes and their combinations can create several diffractional patterns of the transformative room in which future technology will be an actor. Probes are interventions affecting future users "while eliciting informative responses," making users aware of their routines and future wishes and offering new perspectives on their everyday life. Developers can view the users "in new ways, opening new opportunities for design." (Gaver et al. 1999: 25; Maaß/Buchmüller 2018: 125)

Diffractional practices – the generation of diffraction patterns by metaphorically changing the diffraction slits – changing and combining methods and modes of design and use is the specific entanglement of use and design that is reliable. What was invisible could become visible and vice versa. It will be giving the design-in-use back to the actors in cyber-physical systems. These changes can only be made in the lively relations of becoming of which humans and non-humans are part. So response-ability cannot be formulated in "an abstract mode of a once-for-all response" (Savransky 2016). Every entanglement will call for differences in the responses to make *Verlässlichkeit* possible.

10. Conclusion: Humans, Non-humans, Gender, and Technology

Awareness of, sensitivity to, and attentivity to the becomings of humans and non-humans will be needed to establish an ethics of response-ability for the agency in critically transformative rooms and the possibilities of changing the change. Flexibility and response-ability in the design and use of humans and non-humans can be the conditions for a win-win competition and even better win-win cooperation, using and designing diffractional methods to look at the signs of the invisibilities of acting and explore the possibilities for a critical transformation: the possibilities of changing the change that humans and non-humans still have in cooperative non-hierarchical interrelation with others – humans or non-humans. They can experience "pleasure in these kinds of relationships, and especially for a feminist ethics of scientific research and innovation." (Ernst 2015: 7)

In critically transformative rooms, technology can *kick back* and open up the possibilities of many genders for humans and non-humans. Gender analysis, as has been done in the past, will open up possible interventions in the powerful co-constructions of technology and gender making the gendered aspects of design and use visible. The inclusion of non-human actors in gender analysis can save us from a dualism in which avatars, robots, ambient intelligence, and other manifestations of simulative humanity can be seen as fundamentally oppositional to humans. The deconstruction of that dualism will show us the network of dualism in which we have embedded the dualism of human and non-human. This involvement can explain to us the importance of differences in non-humans and the differences between humans and non-humans. Non-human actors can make us doubt the constructions of gender that are familiar in our society when we recognize them as fully-fledged partners in gender processes taking place particularly in the making of technology (Crutzen 2013: 317–318).

References

Afram, Elimada Patricia (2015): Sport als „Wettkampf der Götter!?" – Transhumanismus. Available at http://wiki.ifs-tud.de/biomechanik/aktuelle_themen/projekte_ss14/transhumanisten, last accessed October 23, 2020.

Allhutter, Doris (2012): Mind Scripting: A Method for Deconstructive Design. In: Science, Technology & Human Values 37, 6, pp. 684–707. DOI: 10.2307/234744 85.

Allhutter, Doris (2019): Of "Working Ontologists" and "High-Quality Human Components": The Politics of Semantic Infrastructures. In: Vertesi, J./Ribes, J. (eds.): DigitalSTS. A Field Guide for Science & Technology Studies. Princeton: Princeton UP, pp. 326–348.

Barad, Karen (2007): Meeting the Universe Halfway. Durham/London: Duke University Press.

Barad, Karen (2014): Diffracting Diffraction: Cutting Together-Apart. In: Parallax 20, 3, pp. 168–187.

Bath, Corinna (2014): Diffractive Design. In: Marsden, Nicola/Kempf, Ute (ed): GENDER-UseIT. HCI, Usability und UX unter Gendergesichtspunkten. Berlin: De Gruyter, pp. 27–36.

Berger, Peter L./Luckmann, Thomas (1966): The Social Construction of Reality: A Treatise in the Sociology of Knowledge. Garden City (New York): Anchor Books.

Booch, Grady (1991): Object Oriented Design, with Applications. Redwood City: Benjamin/Cummings.

Bozalek, Vivienne/Zembylas, Michalinos (2017): Diffraction or Reflection? Sketching the Contours of Two Methodologies in Educational Research. In: International Journal of Qualitative Studies in Education 30, 2, pp. 111–127.

Buchmüller, Sandra et al. (2018): To Whom Does the Driver's Seat Belong in the Future? A Case of Negotiation Between Gender Studies and Automotive Engineering. In: GenderIT '18: Proceedings of the 4th Conference on Gender & IT, pp. 165–174. Available at https://dl.acm.org/doi/10.1145/3196839.3196866, last accessed October 23, 2020.

Butler, Judith (1993): Bodies That Matter. London/New York: Routledge.

Chin, Monica (2018): An AI Just Beat Top Lawyers at Their Own Game. In: Mashable. Available at https://mashable.com/2018/02/26/ai-beats-humans-at-contracts, last accessed October 23, 2020.

Coyne, Richard (1995): Designing Information Technology in the Postmodern Age: From Method to Metaphor. Cambridge (MA): The MIT Press.

Crutzen, Cecile K. M. (2003): ICT-Representations as Transformative Critical Rooms. In: Kreutzner, Gabriele/Schelhowe, Heidi (eds.): Agents of Change: Virtuality, Gender, and the Challenge to the Traditional University. Opladen: Leske und Budrich, pp. 87–106.

Crutzen, Cecile K. M. (2009): The Disappearance of the (Human) Subject in Computer Science. In: Feminist Research Methods – An international Conference, February 4–6, 2009, Stockholm, Sweden. Available at http://citeseerx.ist.

psu.edu/viewdoc/download?doi=10.1.1.426.7161&rep=rep1&type=pdf, last accessed October 23, 2020.

Crutzen, Cecile K. M. (2013): Nicht-menschlich ist auch Gender. In: Informatik-Spektrum 36, 3, pp. 309–318.

Crutzen, Cecile K. M. (2016): Gender und Transhumanismus im Sport. In: FIfF-Kommunikation 3, 16, pp. 41–45.

Crutzen, Cecile K. M. (2018): The Critical Transformative Room "Elite Sport" as Phenomenon. In: GenderIT '18: Proceedings of the 4th Conference on Gender & IT, pp. 71–73.

Crutzen, Cecile K. M./Hein, Hans-Werner (2009): Invisibility and Visibility: The Shadows of Artificial Intelligence. In: Vallverdu, Jordi/Casacuberta, David (eds.): Handbook of Research on Synthetic Emotions and Sociable Robotics: New Applications in Affective Computing and Artificial Intelligence. IGI-Global, pp. 472–500.

De, Suparna et al. (2017): Cyber-Physical-Social Frameworks for Urban Big Data Systems: A Survey. In: Applied Sciences 7, 10, 1017. Available at https://www.mdpi.com/2076-3417/7/10/1017/pdf, last accessed October 23, 2020.

Dewey, John (1916): Education as Growth, Democracy and Education. Champaign, Ill: Project Gutenberg.

Ernst, Waltraud (2015): Responsibilities that Matter. Paper for the Conference on „Living in Technoscientific Worlds," December 3–5, 2015, University of Vienna.

Friedman, Batya/Nissenbaum, Helen (1996): Bias in Computer Systems. In: ACM, Transactions on Information Systems (TOIS) 14, 3, pp. 330–347.

Gaver, Bill et al. (1999): Design: Cultural Probes. In: Interactions 6, 1, pp. 21–29.

Geerts, Evelien/Tuin, Iris van der (2016): Diffraction & Reading Diffractively. Available at http://newmaterialism.eu/almanac/d/diffraction.html, last accessed October 23, 2020.

Geertsema, Henk G. (2006): Cyborg: Myth or Reality? In: Zygon 41, 2, pp. 289–328.

Gupta, Abhishek et al. (2013): Future of All Technologies – The Cloud and Cyber Physical Systems. In: International Journal of Enhanced Research in Science, Technology and Engineering 2, 2. Available at http://www.erpublications.com/uploaded_files/download/download_28_02_2013_20_24_26.pdf, last accessed September 8, 2020.

Haenssle, Holger A. et al. (2018): Man Against Machine: Diagnostic Performance of a Deep Learning Convolutional Neural Network for Dermoscopic Melanoma Recognition in Comparison to 58 Dermatologists. In: Annals of Oncology 29, 8, pp. 1836–1842. Available at https://doi.org/10.1093/annonc/mdy166, last accessed September 8, 2020.

Haraway, Donna (1991): A Cyborg Manifesto: Science, Technology, and Socialist-Feminism in the Late Twentieth Century. In: Simians, Cyborgs and Women: The Reinvention of Nature. New York/London: Routledge, pp. 149–181.

Haraway, Donna (1997): Modest_Witness@Second_Millenium.Female Man©_Meets _OncoMouseTM. New York/London: Routledge.

Haraway, Donna (2008): When Species Meet. Minneapolis: University of Minnesota Press.

Heidegger, Martin (1960) [1936]: Der Ursprung des Kunstwerkes. Stuttgart: Reclam.

Heidegger, Martin (2002): Off the beaten track. Cambridge (UK)/New York: Cambridge University Press.

Irni, Sari (2010): Ageing Apparatuses at Work, Transdisciplinary Negotiations of Sex, Age and Materiality. Diss. Åbo: Åbo Akademi University. Available at http://www.doria.fi/bitstream/handle/10024/61786/irni_sari.pdf, last accessed September 8, 2020.

Khushf, George (2005): The Use of Emergent Technologies for Enhancing Human Performance: Are we Prepared to Address the Ethical and Policy Issues? In: Public Policy and Practice 4, 2, pp. 1–17.

Kunzru, Hari (1997): You Are Cyborg [Interview with Donna Haraway]. In: Wired. Available at http://www.wired.com/1997/02/ffharaway/, last accessed September 8, 2020.

Lee, Edward A. (2015): The Past, Present and Future of Cyber-Physical Systems: A Focus on Models. In: Sensors 15, 3, pp. 4837–4869. Available at https://dx.doi.org/10.3390%2Fs150304837, last accessed September 8, 2020.

Lucky, Robert W. (1999): Connections. In: IEEE Spectrum Magazine. Available at http://www.boblucky.com/reflect/mar99.htm, last accessed September 8, 2020.

Maaß, Susanne/Buchmüller, Sandra (2018): The Crucial Role of Cultural Probes in Participatory Design for and with Older Adults. In: I-com 17, 2, pp. 119–136.

Miah, Andy (2003): Be Very Afraid: Cyborg Athletes, Transhuman Ideals and Posthumanity. In: Journal of Evolution and Technology 13. Available at http://www.jetpress.org/volume13/miah.html, last accessed September 8, 2020.

Moor, James H. (1985): What is Computer Ethics? In: Metaphilosophy 16, 4, pp. 266–275.

N.N. (2010): Caster Semenya's Comeback Statement in Full. In: The Guardian. Available at https://www.theguardian.com/sport/2010/mar/30/caster-semenya-comeback-statement, last accessed September 8, 2020.

N.N. (2020): Sex Verification in Sports. In: Wikipedia. Available at https://en.wikipedia.org/wiki/Sex_verification_in_sports, last accessed September 8, 2020.

Petropoulus, Georgios (2017): Machines That Learn to Do, and Do to Learn: What is Artificial Intelligence? In: Bruegel. Available at http://bruegel.org/2017/04/machines-that-learn-to-do-and-do-to-learn-what-is-artificial-intelligence/, last accessed September 8, 2020.

Savransky, Martin (2016): Modes of Mattering: Barad, Whitehead, and Societies. In: Rhizomes: Cultural Studies in Emerging Knowledge 30. Available at https://doi.org/10.20415/rhiz/030.e08, last accessed September 8, 2020.

Scheman, Naomi (1993): Engenderings: Constructions of Knowledge, Authority, and Privilege. New York: Routledge.

Schinzel, Britta (2018): IT-getriebene Transkriptionen: Zum Gender- und Moral-haltigen Gebrauch von Sprache, Begriffen, Metaphern und Erzählungen in Informatik und Informationstechnik. In: GenderIT '18: Proceedings of the 4th Conference on Gender & IT, pp. 3–9. Available at https://dl.acm.org/doi/proceedings/10.1145/3196839, last accessed September 8, 2020.

Star, Susan Leigh (1991): Invisible Work and Silenced Dialogues in Knowledge Representation. In: Eriksson, Inger V. et al. (eds.): Women, Work and Computerization: Understanding and Overcoming Bias in Work and Education. Proceedings of the IFIP TC9/WG 9.1 Conference on Women, Work and Computerization, Helsinki, Finland, June 30–July 2, 1991. Amsterdam: Elsevier, pp. 81–92.

Star, Susan Leigh/Strauss, Anselm (1999): Layers of Silence, Arenas of Voice: The Ecology of Visible and Invisible Work. In: Computer Supported Cooperative Work 8, 1–2, pp. 9–30.

Suchman, Lucy (1995): Making Work Visible – How People Work is One of the Best Kept Secrets in America. In: Communications of the ACM 38, 9, pp. 56–64. Available at http://citeseerx.ist.psu.edu/viewdoc/summary?doi=10.1.1.174.4331, last accessed September 8, 2020.

Technopolis group (2016): Ethical Aspects of Cyber-Physical Systems: Scientific Foresight Study. European Parliamentary Research Service. Available at https://www.europarl.europa.eu/RegData/etudes/STUD/2016/563501/EPRS_STU%282016%29563501_EN.pdf, last accessed September 8, 2020.

Truman, Sarah E. (2019): Feminist New Materialisms. In: Atkinson, P. A. et al. (eds.): The SAGE Encyclopedia of Research Methods. London: Sage. Available at https://www.researchgate.net/publication/332728422, last accessed September 8, 2020.

Velden, Maja van der (2009): Design for a Common World: On Ethical Agency and Cognitive Justice. In: Ethics and Information Technology 11, 1, pp. 37–47.

Weiser, Mark (1991): The Computer for the 21st Century. In: Scientific American 265, 3, pp. 94–104. Available at https://www.lri.fr/~mbl/Stanford/CS477/papers/Weiser-SciAm.pdf, last accessed September 8, 2020.

Zagorac, Ivana (2008): The Body and Technology: A Contribution to the Bioethical Debate on Sport. In: Synthesis Philosophica 46, 2, pp. 283–295. Available at http://hrcak.srce.hr/file/58346, last accessed September 8, 2020.

Flying into the Future: Potentials and Challenges of Commercial Single-Pilot Operations

Anja K. Faulhaber

1. Introduction

Pilots of commercial aviation aircraft are part of a complex sociotechnical system. In order to complete a flight successfully, they have to interact with each other as well as with the technological environment of the flight deck. Over the past decades, this sociotechnical system has been subject to an evolutionary process marked by a considerable shift regarding the role of the human component (Boy 2014). Due to technological progress, more and more sophisticated technology, such as the autopilot, was implemented in the flight deck, thereby altering the pilots' work environment. Their main tasks shifted from physical flying activities, like stick and rudder control, to cognitive skills, such as decision making, problem solving, supervision, and management of flight operations (Mauro/Barshi 2003). Automated systems took over many tasks originally performed by the cockpit crew. This led to what Harris (2007: 519) called "progressive de-crewing" – a crew reduction from initially five to two cockpit crewmembers. Thus, as the level of automation increased, the involvement of the human in the sociotechnical system changed.

A current trend points towards the next step in this evolutionary process. Research is investigating the feasibility of a further reduction in crew size to commercial single-pilot operations (SPO). Even though it is technically already possible to fly an aircraft with only one pilot in the cockpit, this is only designed as a precautionary measure for cases such as pilot incapacitation. The cockpit is built on the principle of redundancy, so that if one part of the system fails, the another part can take over. Additionally, pilots are highly trained to work together as a team, given that crew resource management is an integral part of their training. A transition from a two-crew context to a single operator in the cockpit would, therefore, require drastic changes to the whole sociotechnical system. In order to find a permanent solution for SPO, we need to redesign the cockpit, redistribute functions between human and machine, and adapt pilot training. All these necessary changes bear potentials and pose challenges at the same time.

This paper aims to shed light on potentials and challenges that need consideration in the development of commercial SPO. The intention is mainly to draw conclusions from research conducted within the scope of my PhD project. My research focused on the human component in the sociotechnical system and I wanted to investigate specifically how a potential transition from two-crew operations (TCO) to SPO in commercial aviation might affect the pilot. I conducted a systematic literature review and an empirical flight simulator study. In the simulator study, 14 pilots flew several approach and landing scenarios either with a second pilot in TCO or alone in SPO. A combination of qualitative and quantitative data were collected to analyze differences in pilot behavior and performance between TCO and SPO (for details see Faulhaber 2019; Faulhaber/Friedrich 2019; Faulhaber et al. 2020). The present paper is far from a comprehensive review of potentials and challenges of commercial SPO, but presents a selective overview with a human-centered perspective, based on my PhD research.

2. Challenges

A key requirement for the transition from TCO to SPO is maintaining safety standards. Operations with only one cockpit crewmember need to be at least at the same level of safety as they are nowadays with two cockpit crewmembers. This is particularly challenging, given that part of the redundancy is lost without a second pilot in the cockpit. With only one pilot in the cockpit, we need to compensate for the missing redundancy by providing alternative fallback options for cases such as pilot incapacitation. There are several potential solutions to this challenge – for example, a cabin crewmember with special training could take over, ground operators could control an aircraft remotely, or automated systems could assume control completely (e.g., Neis et al. 2018; Vu et al. 2018). All of these solutions rely in the first place upon an accurate detection of the incapacitation, which could be achieved via a health monitoring system. It is, however, still questionable whether such systems can reliably detect all possible contexts of incapacitation, while implemented in a nonintrusive and comfortable way (Bilimoria et al. 2014). Moreover, health monitoring comes at the price of continuous observation and implicates serious privacy issues.

The second pilot in current-day TCO is not only a safety net, a second component in a redundant system. Both pilots share the workload throughout the flight and the second pilot is tremendously important for crosschecking and error detection (Dehais et al. 2017). One challenge will be to implement reliable crosschecking and error-detection mechanisms that do not rely upon the presence of a second pilot in the cockpit. With regard to pilot workload, studies have shown that workload may reach critical levels in SPO, particularly during abnormal, unexpected situations, such as system failures (Bailey et al. 2017; Faulhaber 2019). These studies also showed that pilots tended to commit errors when flying alone and that their level of frustration increased significantly. Consequently, future research should consider these workload-related issues when developing support solutions for pilots during normal as well as abnormal operations. Several concepts are already being investigated, particularly in the context of ground-based support during high-workload situations (e.g., Lachter et al. 2017; Koltz et al. 2015) but further research is required.

Several other human factors issues have been studied and discussed in the aviation context for a long time and gain a renewed interest in light of the potential transition to SPO. This concerns primarily the topic of human-automation interaction, given that automation could assume even more control authority in commercial SPO. In the past, human-automation interaction has led to complacency, over- or under-trust in automation, loss of situation awareness, automation surprise, and mode confusion (e.g., Endsley 1996; Sarter/Woods 1995; 1997). The challenge for the introduction of SPO is to learn from the past and design human-automation interaction in a way that avoids these well-studied phenomena. Initial attempts in this direction have been made by designing automation as a team player (e.g., Brandt et al. 2018) but further research is required. Moreover, research should tackle other pressing issues related to automation in SPO, such as boredom, fatigue, and, in the long term, skill degradation.

The last challenge I want to discuss within the scope of this paper concerns the social aspects of the pilots' job. In my study, several pilots reported that they valued the presence of a second person in the cockpit from a social perspective. Flying an aircraft alone might become a tedious task during long-haul flights. Furthermore, pilots reported that they felt more comfortable with a second set of eyes in the cockpit, particularly during abnormal events, and that the mere presence of another human being could have a calming effect. These social aspects of flying open up a new field of research in the context of commercial SPO and it is questionable whether or how the social component can be substituted in SPO. One possible direction is to test whether social bots, meaning software implemented in the cockpit systems to imitate social interaction, may improve the pilot's experience. This is a topic for future work, but one should consider carefully whether technology can really substitute a social human being. Can machines act socially, show empathy, or even perceive social cues the way we do? In the end, it remains to be seen how the loss of the social in SPO would affect the pilot, for example with regard to job satisfaction.

3. Potentials

For the aviation industry, the main drivers in the development towards SPO are of economic nature. Airlines hope to reduce their operating costs and gain more operational flexibility with SPO (Bilimoria et al. 2014). Another aspect is the growing demand for commercial aviation expected to ultimately lead to a pilot shortage (Boeing 2019). Reducing the cockpit crew size would allow the same number of pilots to fly more aircraft. However, human factors seem to be the obstacle impeding the development towards SPO in commercial aviation (Harris 2007). Consequently, most human-centered research focuses on challenges, problems that need solving in order to implement commercial SPO successfully. So, are there even potentials from a human-centered perspective or are there only challenges?

A concept of operation that has gained attention in SPO research is the combination of a single pilot on-board with a remote copilot on the ground (e.g., Schmid et al. 2020). Studies have shown that this concept may offer benefits as compared to current TCO (e.g., Levine/Levine 2007). The remote copilot could support, especially during phases of high workload and during abnormal events, and would not be affected by on-board hazards, such as hypoxia, smoke, or passenger disturbances. In case of emergency, s/he could communicate directly with the relevant personnel and provide optimal information on how to handle a specific situation.

During my empirical study, I could observe that pilots were more alert when they had to fly alone. They had full responsibility and acted accordingly with careful consideration and concentration. Social loafing, the phenomenon of a person devoting less effort when working in a group (e.g., Karau/Williams 1993), would thus not be an issue anymore and neither might be other negative social effects, such as social stress. For concepts without additional ground-based support, the pilot would not need to communicate and coordinate with a second cockpit crewmember, which could reduce the pilot's workload and remove a possible source of error. The question is whether these benefits can balance out the disadvantages of SPO.

There is, however, further potential in transitioning to SPO. Several researchers have suggested that we should abandon the evolutionary de-crewing process and take on a revolutionary approach instead (Boy 2014; Sprengart et al. 2018). This means that we get the opportunity to rethink the whole sociotechnical system and particularly the role of the human operator in this system. A revolutionary de-crewing process gives us the chance to think about how we really want to design human-machine interaction and what role we want to attribute to the human and to the machine.

4. Conclusion

The objective of the present paper was to give an overview of the potentials and challenges of a possible transition from TCO to SPO in commercial aviation. Taking on a human-centered perspective showed that the human factors challenges are a major obstacle in the development of SPO. Transitioning towards SPO would mean partly giving up on redundancy and largely removing the *social* from the sociotechnical system. Thus, the implementation of SPO brings along many issues that require solving and from a human-centered perspective, the challenges seem to outweigh the potentials. This applies particularly if we choose to stay on the road of the evolutionary de-crewing process. However, if we choose to take on a revolutionary approach, we could take the requirements of the human operators into account. We get a chance to reconsider and reconfigure human-machine interaction in aviation, based on the many experiences and scientific findings we were able to collect throughout the past decades. The aviation industry might prefer to stay on the more cost-sensitive evolutionary road, thereby taking the easy way out. Taking the revolutionary approach is, of course, less comfortable and probably more expensive but might reward us with more benefits in the long run.

References

Bailey, Randall E. et al. (2017): An Assessment of Reduced Crew and Single Pilot Operations in Commercial Transport Aircraft Operation. In: 2017 IEEE/AIAA 36th Digital Avionics Systems Conference (DASC), St. Petersburg, FL, pp. 1–15.

Bilimoria, Karl D. et al. (2014): Conceptual Framework for Single Pilot Operations. In: Proceedings of the International Conference on Human-Computer Interaction in Aerospace (HCI-Aero '14). New York, NY: ACM, Article 4.

Boeing (2019): 2019 Pilot & Technician Outlook. Available at https://www.boeing.com/commercial/market/pilot-technician-outlook, last accessed April 14, 2020.

Boy, Guy A. (2014): Requirements for Single Pilot Operations in Commercial Aviation. A First High-Level Cognitive Function Analysis. In: Boulanger, Frédéric et al. (eds.): Proceedings of the Poster Workshop at the 2014 Complex Systems Design & Management International Conference (CSDM 2014 Poster Workshop). Paris, pp. 227–234. Available at http://ceur-ws.org/Vol-1234/paper-19.pdf, last accessed July 20, 2020.

Brandt, Summer L. et al. (2018): A Human-Autonomy Teaming Approach for a Flight-Following Task. In: Baldwin, Carryl (ed.): Advances in Neuroergonomics and Cognitive Engineering. AHFE 2017. Advances in Intelligent Systems and Computing, vol 586. Cham: Springer, pp. 12–22.

Dehais, Frédéric et al. (2017): Pilot Flying and Pilot Monitoring's Aircraft State Awareness During Go-Around Execution in Aviation: A Behavioral and Eye Tracking Study. In: The International Journal of Aerospace Psychology 27, 1-2, pp. 15–28.

Endsley, Mica R. (1996): Automation and Situation Awareness. In: Parasuraman, Raja/Mouloua, Mustapha (eds.): Human Factors in Transportation. Automation and Human Performance. Theory and Applications. Mahwah, NJ: Erlbaum, pp. 163–181.

Faulhaber, Anja K. (2019): From Crewed to Single-Pilot Operations: Pilot Performance and Workload Management. In: Proceeding of the 20th International Symposium on Aviation Psychology, Dayton, OH, pp. 283–288.

Faulhaber, Anja K./Friedrich, Maik (2019): Eye-Tracking Metrics as an Indicator of Workload in Commercial Single-Pilot Operations. In: Longo, Luca/Leva, Chiara M. (eds.): Human Mental Workload: Models and Applications. H-WORKLOAD 2019. Communications in Computer and Information Science, vol 1107. Cham: Springer, pp. 213–225.

Faulhaber, Anja K. et al. (2020): Absence of Pilot Monitoring Affects Scanning Behavior of Pilot Flying: Implications for the Design of Single-Pilot Cockpits. In: Human Factors.

Harris, Don (2007): A Human-Centred Design Agenda for the Development of Single Crew Operated Commercial Aircraft. In: Aircraft Engineering and Aerospace Technology 79, 5, pp. 518–526.

Karau, Steven J./Williams, Kipling D. (1993): Social Loafing: A Meta-Analytic Review and Theoretical Integration. In: Journal of Personality and Social Psychology 65, 4, pp. 681–706.

Koltz, Martin T. et al. (2015): An Investigation of the Harbor Pilot Concept for Single Pilot Operations. In: Procedia Manufacturing 3, pp. 2937–2944.

Lachter, Joel et al. (2017): Enhanced Ground Support: Lessons from Work on Reduced Crew Operations. In: Cognition, Technology & Work 19, 2-3, pp. 279–288.

Levine, Sy/Levine, Leslie Jae Lenell (2007): An Onboard Pilot and Remote Copilot for Aviation Safety, Security & Savings. In: 2007 IEEE/AIAA 26th Digital Avionics Systems Conference, Dallas, TX, pp. 4.E.5-1–4.E.5-13.

Mauro, Robert/Barshi, Immanuel (2003): Cognitive Science and Aviation Training: Foundations for Effective Learning and Operational Application. SAE Technical Paper, 2003-01-3061. Warrendale, PA: SAE.

Neis, Stefan Manuel et al. (2018): Classification and Review of Conceptual Frameworks for Commercial Single Pilot Operations. In: 2018 IEEE/AIAA 37th Digital Avionics Systems Conference (DASC), London, UK, pp. 1–8.

Sarter, Nadine B./Woods, David D. (1995): How in the World Did We Ever Get into That Mode? Mode Error and Awareness in Supervisory Control. In: Human Factors 37, 1, pp. 5–19.

Sarter, Nadine B./Woods, David D. (1997): Team Play with a Powerful and Independent Agent: Operational Experiences and Automation Surprises on the Airbus A-320. In: Human Factors 39, 4, pp. 553–569.

Schmid, Daniela et al. (2020): Evaluating the Reduced Flight Deck Crew Concept Using Cognitive Work Analysis and Social Network Analysis: Comparing Normal and Data-Link Outage Scenarios. In: Cognition, Technology & Work 22, pp. 109–124.

Sprengart, Sebastian Michael et al. (2018): Role of the Human Operator in Future Commercial Reduced Crew Operations. In: 2018 IEEE/AIAA 37th Digital Avionics Systems Conference (DASC), London, UK, pp. 1–10.

Vu, Kim-Phuong L. et al. (2018): Single Pilot Operations in Domestic Commercial Aviation. In: Human Factors 60, 6, pp. 755–762.

Human vs. Machine: Laboratory Automation in the Pharmaceutical Context From a User-Centered Perspective

Rebecca Wiesner

1. Introduction

The aim of the doctoral thesis presented in this chapter is to investigate the potential of automation in pharmaceutical laboratories, especially in quality control (QC). Here, laboratory automation includes the automation of manual processes, such as the use of pipetting robots to dilute and prepare samples for analysis. Data analysis can also be digitized using artificial intelligence (AI) in order to avoid manual errors and achieve uniformity. The main advantages of automation, according to the vendors' specifications, are data integrity, product safety and sterility, employee safety, higher reproducibility caused by fewer errors in sample preparation, reduced workload for the employees, and reliability (Wiesner 2018). Furthermore, the performance of manual and automatic workflows regarding sample preparation and the data evaluation of analytical processes were assessed.

Automation is employed in a variety of fields, such as aviation and the automobile industry. In pharmacy, automation is already used in logistics and the production, as well as assembly of drugs. It is especially useful if large numbers of samples need to be handled. Compared to these sectors, the implementation of automatic solutions in laboratories is highly complex because a variety of glassware, reagents, and sample types need to be considered (Li 2013; Pfannkoch 2013). Typically, samples are prepared for HPLC measurement in a volumetric flask in volumes ranging from 10 to 100 ml. If sample preparation is to be automated, miniaturization is necessary to achieve volumes between 1 µl and 2 ml, the specified working range for most Automated Liquid Handlers (ALHs). Moreover, the change-over from manual to automatic workflows in pharmaceutical quality control is governed by various agencies to ensure the safety of the products. How patients apply them, drugs have to comply with the highest level of regulations in safety, effectiveness, and quality. Correspondingly, method development, which includes the miniaturization and cross-validation of the manual process, is time-consuming and expensive.

2. Exploring Laboratory Automation

Being the first PhD student in the working group of Professor Dr. Hermann Wätzig dealing with laboratory automation, I decided to choose an explorative research design. Experiencing a variety of methodologies in the doctoral program "Gendered Configurations of Humans and Machines," like interviews, participatory observations, or user-centered design methods, opened up different perspectives for me in researching my topic. Combining qualitative and typical pharmaceutical quantitative methods, e.g. measuring and evaluating proteins and drugs on analytical devices, as well as statistical data evaluation, has broadened my horizons and led to a deeper understanding of work processes as well as the misunderstandings that arise in communication between vendors and users. These misunderstandings are due to different fields of expertise: the vendors of lab automation are experts in hardware and software solutions, while laboratory staff are experts in workflows. Below is a brief overview of the methods and results of my research.

In order to examine the existing lab automation solutions concerning sample preparation and data evaluation, I visited the exhibitions "Analytica 2018," "Achema 2018," and "Hannovermesse 2018." Standardized single-expert interviews with 20 questions based on guidelines developed using the GERD model were conducted with approximately 60 vendors of lab automation at these fairs. The *Gender Extended Research and Development* (GERD) model considers the diversity of human circumstances as well as knowledge areas in IT research and development, combining gender and diversity research with informatics (Maaß et al. 2014). Gender and diversity categories, like relevance, benefit, knowledge, values, power relations, ideas about basic characteristics of the human being, language, and working culture were reflected, both during the development process of IT software solutions and throughout the entire project. I have also used these categories and reflected on them in my interview guidelines and my overall research context to link gender and diversity research with pharmacy.

The interviews provided the following preliminary conclusions based on the vendors' opinions. Robots are already available for solid and liquid handling. They can be divided into user-centered, application-related complete solutions, or stand-alone workstations. Two main software solutions are available: flexible open solutions, where the customers must be able to program themselves, and intuitive, easy-to-use solutions, where the customers are limited to changing parameters. I focused on the ALH systems due to the variety of automation solutions (see Figure 1 as an example) on offer in that area.

Figure 1: Automated Liquid Handler by Brand (left) and Axel Semrau (right)

Source: Rebecca Wiesner

They are typically used in food production, biotechnology, diagnostics, the automobile industry, and the pharmaceutical industry. In the latter, applications are focused on High Throughput Screening (HTS), Next Generation Sequencing (NGS), and proteomics, which are parts of research and development (R&D). The drug development process can take 20 years or more and is divided into several parts. The screening of drug libraries is part of the first step, *Discovery and Development*, which examines possible protein target interactions with millions of chemical compounds, which gives it the name HTS. Due to the large number of compounds to be investigated and manual work steps needed, automation is necessary and easy to implement based on easy-to-handle and commonly-used liquids: water and dimethyl sulfoxide (DMSO). The drug substance and protein solutions are pipetted together, followed by a color reaction, which can be evaluated photometrically to determine binding affinity. Other parts of drug development are only partially automated. The workflows in QC, which are intended to confirm the contents and purity of the drug and ensure safety, are not automated yet, because a variety of liquid classes need to be handled. For example, many analysis methods, like *High Pressure Liquid Chromatography* (HPLC) or *Capillary Electrophoresis* (CE), rely on the use of organic solvents, as well as viscous solutions. When automatically preparing samples for these methods, the following issues must be considered: in some cases, organic solvents, such as acetone, cannot be used due to the materials utilized in robot surfaces: acetone, for example, rinses the plasticizers out of plastic tubes, which could contaminate the samples. When using a viscous solution, the speed of dispensing and aspirating the liquid is crucial to avoiding air bubbles and, therefore, pipetting an incorrect volume.

The performance, as well as the possibility, of instrument standardization must be evaluated in order to ensure its establishment in pharmaceutical QC. ALHs from HTS processes were tested for applicability and transferability into QC. A practical study was set up, where manual and automatic workflows were compared. Dilutions series as well as sample preparation using different analysis methods, like HPLC and CE, were investigated. Manual workflows were performed by students and myself. Various ALHs, such as Brand's Liquid Handling Station, and the PAL System of Axel Semrau were tested. They were compared in terms of key analytical elements, like precision, accuracy, and linearity. Comparisons in key usability measures, namely reliability, flexibility, speed, traceability, usability, user-centered design, vendor's support, and sustainability were conducted as well. The provision of a user guide for the implementation of lab automation in a pharmaceutical environment will be the final stage of this process.

Next, the peer group of potential biochemical and pharmaceutical users was studied. The personal attitude of the users is important for a successful cooperation between humans and machines (Parasuraman/Riley 1997). However, this collaboration also involves fear and uncertainty, since human lab technicians are afraid of losing their jobs. The vendors of lab automation and Li assume that there will always be something for humans to do, because "[c]ognitive work such as experimental design and data interpretation cannot be easily automated." (Li 2013) It is only the scope of the duties that changes. Trust, an open-minded approach to new challenges, and system reliability are all prerequisites for good cooperation (Parasuraman/Riley 1997). Nevertheless, the main advantages of automation, according to the users, are nearly identical to the once put forward by the vendors: product and staff protection, reduction of human errors, and less repetitive tasks for staff.

Another crucial point is the financial investment required by automation solutions, which ranges between 20,000 and 250,000 euros. Only the main pharmaceutical companies, like Bayer, Roche, Novartis, Merck, and Boehringer Ingelheim (*The big 5*) are able to make these investments and typically use the pipetting robots in their research and development departments, while in academia, projects rely on obtaining external funding. Unlike mid-sized pharmaceutical companies and academia, big companies have lobbying power and the financial backup to implement innovative devices, like automation solutions. In academia, financial resources are limited and typically used to educate students. New, expensive technologies are, therefore, first tested and implemented in commercial research.

Based on the guidelines described above, a questionnaire, customized to each participant, was designed. Simultaneously, participatory observation, based on the principles of contextual design (Holzblatt 2008), was used to evaluate the possibility of automating their workflows. The participants spoke more freely because they knew that I understood their processes due to my background in pharmacy. The following quote (translated into English) from a user of the Zinsser system *Lissy* is very impressive: "it is difficult for computer scientists and engineers to understand the whole synthesis process and which tasks the robot has to manage" and also demonstrates the main problem of automation: the vendors do not know in detail the workflow the robots are designed for: that's why they need in-depth communication with the users. Furthermore, lab group leaders who would like to implement automation solutions might not normally ask the employees, e.g. technical assistants, about their expertise and expectations. Some new investments, therefore, end up not being used in daily work, since the solution does not fit the problem.

Moreover, 80% of laboratory staff is female, while mainly men develop the robots (Policy Paper 2015; Federal Statistical Office Germany 2019). The I-Methodology of the engineers and informatics specialists involved influences the robots' development process, leading to the exclusion of target groups. The I-Methodology describes the perspective and status of the developers of automation solutions, who take themselves as representatives of the user group (Akrich 1992). Furthermore, based on the disciplinary background, developers tend to focus on their discipline's perspectives, which leads to communication barriers and misinvestments between the users and vendors, as users forget to explain everyday terms they take for granted. At the state of the art, vendors are working in interdisciplinary teams together with collaborators from the natural sciences to minimize the communication barriers with customers and optimize the performance of the automated solutions. In terms of usability and employee acceptance, usability studies, such as user-centered, participatory, and contextual design can be conducted by lab automation vendors to achieve innovative and user-friendly solutions by integrating user perspectives into the development of robots (Muller 2008; Holtzblatt 2008).

3. Conclusion

Reflecting on the entire project, as well as the pharmacy as a discipline, reveals many opportunities to implement Gender Studies and Feminist Science and Technology Studies (STS). Based on the explorative research design, the differences between men and women are only one small part of this project. By using the *GERD* model, my discipline, my research topic, as well as the power relations between industry and academia are reviewed critically and prevailing challenges are highlighted.

This work unites quantitative and qualitative empirical social research methods and usability studies, as well as pharmaceutical analysis methods.

Combining diverse methods from various disciplines has led to a deeper understanding of the communication process between users and vendors and opened possibilities to innovate in products and processes in the pharmaceutical environment. By applying expert interviews, contextual design, as well as participatory observations, developments in the wrong direction or non-use of equipment can be avoided. Tacit knowledge can be used to legitimize the application of new methods. The implementation of automation solutions in pharmacy can be easier if users are part of the development process as workflow experts.

The above-mentioned questionnaires are available to download for free under the following doi: 10.3224/84742494A.

References

Akrich, Madeleine (1992): The De-Scription of Technical Objects. In: Bijker, Wiebe/Law, John (eds.): Shaping Technology/Building Society: Studies in Sociotechnical Change. Cambridge: MIT Press, pp. 205–224.

Bündnis TA: Policy Paper (2015): Technischen Assistenten (TA) - Röntgenbild einer Berufsgruppe. Available at https://idw-online.de/de/attachmentdata48859.pdf, last accessed July 27, 2020.

Federal Statistical Office Germany [Statistisches Bundesamt Deutschland] (2019): Studierende in Mathematik, Informatik, Naturwissenschaft (MINT) und Technik-Fächern [as of October 18, 2019]. Available at https://www.destatis.de/DE/Themen/Gesellschaft-Umwelt/Bildung-Forschung-Kultur/Hochschulen/Tabellen/studierende-mint-faechern.html, last accessed July 27, 2020.

Holtzblatt, Karen (2008): Contextual Design. In: Sears, Andrew/Jacko, Julie A. (eds.): The Human-Computer Interaction Handbook. Fundamentals, Evolving Technologies, and Emerging Applications (Second Edition). New York: Taylor & Francis, pp. 949–964.

Li, Ming (2013): Automation in the Bioanalytical Laboratory: What is the Future? In: Bioanalysis 5, 23, pp. 2859–2861.

Maaß, Susanne et al. (2014): Gender-/Diversity-Aspekte in der Informatikforschung: Das GERD-Model. In: Marsden, Nicola/ Kempf, Ute (eds.): Gender-UseIT – HCI, Web-Usability und User Experience unter Gendergesichtspunkten. Berlin: De Gruyter Oldenbourg, pp. 67–78.

Muller, Michael J. (2008): Participatory Design: The Third Space in HCI. In: Sears, Andrew/Jacko, Julie A. (eds.): The Human-Computer Interaction Handbook. Fundamentals, Evolving Technologies, and Emerging Applications, Second Edition. New York: Taylor & Francis, LLC, pp. 1061–1082.

Parasuraman, Raja/Riley, Victor (1997): Humans and Automation: Use, Misuse, Disuse, Abuse. In: Human Factors 39, 2, pp. 230–253.

Pfannkoch, Edward (2013): Sample Preparation for Chromatography: How Much Can be Automated? In: LC-GC North America, Supplement 31, pp. 34–39.

Wiesner, Rebecca/Wätzig, Hermann (2018): Laborautomatisierung 2018: Eindrücke von der Analytica 2018. In: GIT Labor-Fachzeitschrift 5, pp. 34–35.

Usable Security and Privacy in the Internet of Things – a Pattern-Based Approach

Alexander Gabel

1. Introduction

Internet of Things (IoT) technologies are an emerging trend. Often, however, security and privacy requirements are not adequately considered, leading to flawed products. The lack of transparency and intervenability is especially critical for end users. Therefore, in this dissertation project and in the context of an mHealth (mobile health, i.e. using mobile and wireless technologies for health) use case, several aspects of privacy and security (especially from a user perspective), e.g. pseudonymity, data minimization, confidentiality, etc. are addressed and the usability of the proposed concepts is analyzed. From the experience of this use case, as well as from literature research, security and privacy patterns for the IoT are derived. These patterns ought to facilitate the development of IoT applications, where security and privacy requirements are respected from the design phase, as well as during the operation phase. The use case addresses a diverse range of end users in regard to age, gender, and technological experience, so that they can experience digitalization as an opportunity for them.

2. Use Case: An mHealth Application for Goal Management Training

The main use case considered here is an assistive mobile application for the therapy of patients affected by executive dysfunction. Executive functions include abilities for higher-order planning, such as the ability to select, monitor, and execute plans to reach certain goals (Emmanouel 2017).

An executive dysfunction can be due to acquired brain damage or congenital deficits. Over time our research group, consisting of neuropsychologists and computer scientists, extended the target group, starting from acquired brain damage only, to include congenital deficits as well as hemispatial neglect. Furthermore, therapeutic personnel needed to be considered as well as patients.

In the context of this project, an evidence-based therapy approach (Bertens et al. 2013: 201; Emmanouel et al. 2018; Krasny-Pacini et al. 2014), namely Goal Management Training (GMT), developed by Robertson (1996), was followed. In GMT, a main goal is split into a list of steps, which are executed, while regularly *self-stopping* in order to compare the achieved state with the sub-goals. We further included *errorless learning* (Bertens et al. 2015; Wilson et al. 1994) to avoid the learning of erroneous behavior.

A digitalized version could better integrate into daily activities and assist beyond therapy. However, the possibility of behavioral tracking[1] raised privacy concerns: a privacy-preserving, but usable, application was needed. Instead of creating a list of steps with pen and paper, as in traditional approaches of GMT, therapists and patients are able to model and execute actions as workflows on smart devices (smartphone, tablet, smartwatch, desktop). The risk of behavioral tracking especially in the context of medical studies was addressed by introducing privacy-preserving metrics, which are summarized in chapter 6.

3. Developing an mHealth App for Executive Dysfunction

Our interdisciplinary[2], agile, and iterative development process was based on certain design principles. We applied user-centered design by including ideas and feedback from therapists and patients throughout the process. Furthermore, we chose simplicity over complexity/flexibility in many cases. E.g., in order to formalize the concept *human workflows*, instead of designing a fully-fledged programming language, we searched for a minimal/usable subset of building blocks by analyzing example workflows. To empower people, we tried to build flexible solutions whenever possible, e.g. user-created workflows (made by and for users without technical expertise) or metrics (see chapter 6).

We observed seven project stages, corresponding to a shift in priorities over time, mapping to different work phases. The computer science (CS) team in retrospect recognized the following phases: mock-up, prototyping,

---

1   By tracking I am referring to the possibility of tracking a large part of the (day-to-day) activities of the data subject/participant. In a privacy-insensitive application, this could include movement data e.g. from accelerometers to infer the activity type, or GPS location information, as well as information about what workflow is performed when. From this kind of data, more information may be inferred about the person.
2   Neuropsychologists and computer scientists, with feedback from patients and therapists.

implementation, polishing and refactoring, and study accompaniment. The neuropsychologist (NP) team's phases were theory, exploration, single case and pilot study, evaluation and feedback (of therapists and/or patients), and study and evaluation.

During development we encountered several challenges. For a representation of human workflows, we started with a to-do list and refined this to a more structured approach using visual programming languages. We decided to use a block-based language (Google Blockly) rather than a graph-based one, as it was better understood by therapists. We created a *block language* for human workflows, with elements not present in typical programming languages, but highly relevant to day-to-day tasks (e.g. performing only a selection of possible tasks in any order). Furthermore, the interface needed to be usable across various devices. Accessibility was also taken into consideration by including e.g. text-to-speech, images, and a specialized view for hemispatial neglect patients. Lastly, metrics (chapter 6) required a lot of attention.

The development process was successful, measured by the willingness of organizations, patients, and therapists to use the application, as well as by positive feedback and publications. The integration of participatory design in the context of the project was challenging. Among other things, this was due to the limited availability of patients and therapists (small target group, difficult to access, distributed all across the country, and lack of motivation to participate in such studies in people recovering from brain injury), as well as busy therapists, only willing to cooperate with a promising prototype. Later on, when there was a working prototype, it was still difficult to organize regular meetings for co-design (participants were working and were distributed across the country). This was addressed by the CS team visiting patients as they went through their daily life, along with the NP team, in order to get a feeling of what their challenges and needs are. We also received a lot of feedback from job coaches, i.e. people who are working in occupational rehabilitation, belonging to a partner organization in the same city. The NP and CS cooperation itself improved further after we moved to a shared lab.

4. Privacy By Design in mHealth Applications

To develop the application in a privacy-by-design fashion (as required by the European General Data Protection Regulation (GDPR)), risks, as well as strategies to cope with them, needed to be identified (Gabel et al. 2018). In the mHealth scenario considered here, general risks inherent in smart devices (e.g. tracking by third-party applications) and behavioral tracking in the context of studies were investigated. The model of seven types of privacy, as proposed by Finn et al. (2013) was used and then the privacy requirements were modeled, using the concept of privacy protection goals (Hansen et al. 2015) and privacy design strategies (Hoepman 2014). Different modelling approaches were integrated and appropriate privacy patterns for the use case were determined. Whole catalogues of pre-existing patterns had to be searched through to find appropriate patterns for a specific application and there was high variance in the abstraction level of patterns. In mHealth and IoT in general, pseudonymity is a concept of high importance. However, existing patterns for pseudonymity in literature were either too abstract or too specific. In the next chapter our research results regarding privacy patterns for pseudonymity are summarized.

5. Privacy Patterns for Pseudonymity

While anonymity of the data subject would be preferable, making it non-identifiable and non-trackable, it is also associated with a significant loss in data utility and is often not possible, for example when linking multiple records of the same patient in a medical study is required. The GDPR proposes the use of pseudonyms to limit the risk, while allowing the linking of pseudonymous data. Apart from medical applications, pseudonymity is also gaining importance in vehicular ad-hoc networks, smart grid, billing, and Radio Frequency Identification (RFID) applications. The current state of research already includes some patterns for pseudonymity, but some are rather abstract, such as the Pseudonymous Identity or the Pseudonymous Messaging pattern (Hafiz 2013), while others are quite specific and complex, e.g. Attribute-based Credentials (Colesky et al. 2012) or the Pseudonym Broker Pattern (Hillen 2015). To fill this gap, we first gathered approaches to pseudonymity in literature and analyzed their similarities, trying to cluster them using several of their properties. We then identified common building blocks, which were iteratively improved in order to describe eight new patterns: Minimal Pseudonym Scope, Recoverable Identity, Data hidden from Pseudonymizer, Pseudonym Converter, Data fragments, Encrypted Link, Anonymization Network, and Data owner-based Pseudonymization (Gabel/Schiering 2019). These patterns were constructed from uniting several ways to implement a solution for a certain problem in a given context (abstraction), as well as by breaking down complex approaches into their structural components (separation). An important factor for the identification of such components was also their occurrence in multiple publications, i.e. their use more than once. The resulting patterns were described using the accepted conventions in pattern catalogues. Relations between existing and new patterns, based on the taxonomy proposed by Caiza et al. (2017) were also shown, in order to integrate old and new into a pattern language for pseudonymity.

6. Privacy-Preserving Metrics in Neuropsychological Studies

As part of the planned intervention studies for GMT based on our mHealth application, in addition to neuropsychological tests used as pre- and post-tests, measurements about app usage[3] were integrated. To address the risk of behavioral tracking, a privacy-preserving approach was needed. Often in past studies (e.g. Grünerbl et al. 2015)[4] and frameworks (e.g. Google Fit SDK)[5] privacy was barely considered an integral part of the design and data was collected for future use with no apparent motivation for data minimization. We decided to instead concentrate on a data minimization approach from the beginning and only collect what was really necessary to answer our research questions. This meant that these questions had to be formulated in advance and in greater detail, since we had to know beforehand which kind of (minimal) measurements might be able to give us insight. Of course, this comes with the risk that the collected data might not be expressive enough, which is why we first carried out pilot studies on potentially relevant measurements and built experience based on them. While iterating over the research questions and measurement ideas, we noticed a common structure, which was later on used to design a domain-specific language for the flexible description of such metrics (Gabel et al. 2020). That language also inscribed certain questions regarding data minimization and on-device aggregation (i.e. before the data leaves the device). Because the language is descriptive and common concepts need to be implemented only once, the amount of changes in the source code for adding a new metric are minimal and errors can be largely mitigated. The language may be adapted with reduced effort to other use cases and is therefore kept rather general. The metric architecture was integrated into our application and a set of twenty-eight highly specific and minimal metrics was defined, which at the time of writing are collecting data in the context of the intervention study.

---

3   For example, how often is a workflow started/completed/aborted (per week)? Are reminders answered shortly after they occur or later (i.e. close to working on the next task)? How often is the text-to-speech feature used?
4   Information about phone calls, sound and voice features, physical motion, travel patterns collected to detect mental state.
5   Timestamps are stored in nanosecond precision; data always stored on Google servers instead of an option to store it locally; no or very fine granular aggregation of time series independent of purpose.

7. Conclusion

Digitalization as introduced by Internet of Things technologies has a huge potential in various areas including mHealth (e.g. more efficient usage of resources, faster response to changing conditions, etc.). However, it is important that all participants of these systems can perceive this opportunity. This requires that systems feature a usable design and sufficiently address privacy and security concerns, preventing misuse. The usage of pseudonyms can provide better privacy, without sacrificing much data utility, if used correctly. Privacy patterns are an approach to show ways in which developers can apply best practice techniques. In order to develop usable systems, accepted by the users, our team sees interdisciplinarity as well as continuous collaboration and inclusion of the users as important factors for success.

References

Bertens, Dirk et al. (2013): A Randomized Controlled Trial on Errorless Learning in Goal Management Training: Study Rationale and Protocol. In: BMC Neurology 13, pp. 64–72.

Bertens, Dirk et al. (2015): Do Old Errors Always Lead to New Truths? A Randomized Controlled Trial of Errorless Goal Management Training in Brain-Injured Patients. In: Journal of the International Neuropsychological Society 21, pp. 639–649.

Caiza, Julio C. et al. (2017): Organizing Design Patterns for Privacy: A Taxonomy of Types of Relationships. In: EuroPLoP '17: Proceedings of the 22nd European Conference on Pattern Languages of Programs. New York City: ACM, pp. 32:1–32:11. Available at https://doi.org/10.1145/3147704.3147739, last accessed July 20, 2020.

Colesky, Michael et al. (2012): Privacy Patterns. Available at https://privacypatterns.org/, last accessed at October 20, 2017.

Emmanouel, Anna (2017): Look at the Frontal Side of Life: Anterior Brain Pathology and Everyday Executive Function: Assessment Approaches and Treatment. Radboud University. Available at https://repository.ubn.ru.nl/handle/2066/166754, last accessed at July 22, 2020.

Emmanouel, Anna et al. (2018): Incorporation of a Working Memory Strategy in GMT to Facilitate Serial-Order Behaviour in Brain-Injured Patients. In: Neuropsychological Rehabilitation 30, 5, pp. 1–27.

Finn, Rachel L. et al. (2013): Seven Types of Privacy. In: Gutwirth, Serge et al. (eds.): European Data Protection: Coming of Age, Dordrecht: Springer, pp. 3–32.

Gabel, Alexander et al. (2020): Privacy-Preserving Metrics for an MHealth App in the Context of Neuropsychological Studies. In: Cabitza, Federico et al. (eds.): Proceedings of the 13th International Joint Conference on Biomedical Engineering Systems and Technologies - Volume 5. HEALTHINF, Malta. Valetta: SciTePress, pp. 166–177. Available at https://doi.org/10.5220/0008982801660177, last accessed July 20, 2020.

Gabel, Alexander/Schiering, Ina (2019): Privacy Patterns for Pseudonymity. In: Kosta, Eleni et al. (eds.): Privacy and Identity Management. Fairness, Accountability, and Transparency in the Age of Big Data. Cham: Springer, pp. 155–172. Available at https://doi.org/10.1007/978-3-030-16744-8_11, last accessed July 20, 2020.

Gabel, Alexander et al. (2018): MHealth Applications for Goal Management Training - Privacy Engineering in Neuropsychological Studies. In: Hansen, Marit et al. (eds.): Privacy and Identity Management. The Smart Revolution. Cham: Springer, pp. 330–345. Available at https://doi.org/10.1007/978-3-319-92925-5_22, last accessed July 20, 2020.

Grünerbl, Agnes et al. (2015): Smartphone-Based Recognition of States and State Changes of Bipolar Disorder Patients. In: IEEE Journal of Biomedical and Health Informatics 19, 1: IEEE, pp. 140–148.

Munawar, Hafiz (2013): A Pattern Language for Developing Privacy Enhancing Technologies. In: Software: Practice and Experience 43, 7, pp. 769–787.

Hansen, Marit et al. (2015): Protection Goals for Privacy Engineering. In: 2015 IEEE Security and Privacy Workshops: IEEE, pp. 159–166.

Hillen, Christiaan (2015): The Pseudonym Broker Privacy Pattern in Medical Data Collection. In: 2015 IEEE Trustcom/BigDataSE/ISPA 1: IEEE, pp. 999–1005.

Hoepman, Jaap-Henk (2014): Privacy Design Strategies. In: Cuppens-Boulahia, Nora et al. (eds.): ICT Systems Security and Privacy Protection. Berlin/Heidelberg: Springer, pp. 446–459. Available at https://doi.org/10.1007/978-3-642-55415-5_38, last accessed July 20, 2020.

Krasny-Pacini et al. (2014): Goal Management Training for Rehabilitation of Executive Functions: A Systematic Review of Effectivness in Patients with Acquired Brain Injury. In: Disability and Rehabilitation 36, 2, pp. 105–116.

Robertson, Ian H. (1996): Goal Management Training: A Clinical Manual, Cambridge, UK: PsyConsult.

Wilson, Barbara A. et al. (1994): Errorless Learning in the Rehabilitation of Memory Impaired People. In: Neuropsychological Rehabilitation 4, 3, pp. 307–326.

Solar Delight, Electric Vulnerability and Energy Squandering: Capacities of a More Just Organization of Electricity?

Dagmar Lorenz-Meyer

1. Introduction

The word sexy stirs me when X-Solar describes its photovoltaic installations as *sexy řešení* (sexy solutions) at the 2019 technology fair Amper. The designation calls up the slogan "solar is sexy" on a promotional Rubik's Cube that I had picked up the year before. With prices for photovoltaic panels reduced to less than a quarter of what they were in 2010, the number of Czech solar rooftop installations has been growing – even though the pace of installing capacity remains woefully inadequate for transitioning to a low carbon society by 2030 (Frauenhofer ISE 2020; Government of the Czech Republic 2019). Examining how promissory photovoltaics (dis)articulate, order, and reroute energy practices to enable a more just organization of electricity, I am drawn to the possibility that solar energy is sexy: spurring bodies into new "movements […] and becomings" (Grosz/Probyn 1995: x) and creating conviviality (Illich 1973) or a joyful, creative and responsible becoming-together of "people, tools and a new collectivity" (ibid.: xxiv).[1]

Early Science and Technology Studies scholarship had identified the promises of photovoltaics as realizing "the potential of material abundance" (Etzkowitz 1984: 430) and social equity by "extend[ing] responsibility and control to a greater number of people" (Winner 1986: 57). Leaving affective relations outside the purview of STS at that time, these scholars made clear that the actualization of these potentials would "depend on the specific configurations of both hardware and the social institutions created to bring that energy to us" (ibid.: 47). In the Czech Republic, the institutional configurations that incited the proliferation of photovoltaics over the past decade

1   This research is supported by the Czech Science Foundation (17-14893S). For their help in conducting interviews with solar householders, I thank Alma Benešová and Natalie Drtinová. I'm grateful to Loren Britton, Rebecca Wiesner, and the anonymous reviewer for helpful comments on an earlier draft of the manuscript.

include state support reluctantly introduced in response to an EU Directive to promote energy from renewable sources: between 2009 and 2013, the Green Bonus (Feed-in-Tariff), where the state grid provider guaranteed producers of renewable energy a fixed price over 20 years; and later the New Green Savings (2015–2020), which provides subsidies of up to 40% of the purchase price of solar panels, inverters, and batteries.

Yet the heteronormative fantasy that solar companies propagated as sexy – "a family house" that afforded thermal comfort, low electricity bills, independence from blackouts so "you don't have to care about anything" and the possibility to "transfer surpluses to your parents' weekend house" (X-Solar 2019) – did not tantalize me. The sexy solution was encapsulated in the image of a house whose black roof rendered the array of solar panels nearly imperceptible. This visualization resonates with some of the peculiar pleasures that feminist technoscience scholars have identified among male scientists and engineers: "the erotics of taxonomies, the satisfactions in controlling grids of difference, and the aesthetic pleasures of sameness" (Traweek 1995: 217). For many American high energy physicists, "sexy machines" are those that are "malleable, but a bit fallible and a little mysterious, responsive to the controlling hands of the knowledgeable physicists" (ibid.: 215). Such pleasures of technical prowess are viscerally felt when these men "rearrang[e] the detector" (ibid.: 212) or when "lab hands" (Doing 2009) or mechanics kinesthetically work *with* the material in getting a difficult piece of equipment to work (Mellström 2002).

It is worth underlining the multiplicity and ambiguity of the gendering of technical practices, where masculine-coded control depends on an openness to and the capacity to succumb and learn from materials – that is, "the kinds of characteristics that have been historically attributed to women [and] natives" (Doing 2009: 309; Lorenz-Meyer 2014). Photovoltaic installations, however, are marketed as turnkey technologies, emphasizing the gendered, racialized, and classed sexiness of the comfort of *not* getting involved rather than the possibility of touch, rearrangement, and variation. Lest this render the operator of a photovoltaic power plant insignificant, the evocation of being served by solar power is supplemented by ubiquitous imagery of white young men holding children in meadows suffused in sunlight – a naturalization of both solar technology and the family man as the provider of care, security, and a future that sutures solar power to homo-sex. Women and members of minoritized ethnic groups are notably absent from these harmonious scenes of self-birthing Man that Haraway (1997: 121) aptly describes as the dream of "ultimate control of natural others for the good of the one."

Against the backdrop of these racialized sexual fantasies of solar power this chapter explores what bodies, affects, and environments materialize in and around novel practices of solar microgeneration. What capacities, matters of care and modes of control are expressed or *dis*abled in these practices?

How are they gendered, racialized, and classed? And how might emerging capacities germinate more just energy relations? By examining these questions, the research becomes both critical and constructive: it holds open the possibility that photovoltaic installations are more than neoliberal technological fixes that limit more sustainable electricity provision to affluent households – and that generative capacities which inspire alternative forms of knowing and doing take flight from *within* what is currently emerging.

The argument draws on interviews with 14 solar households, house tours and demonstrations of digital solar apps, as well as photographs taken of solar installations that offer possibilities of sensual engagement. Interviews were conducted in Czech and English with 12 men and two women solar plant owners and where possible with adult cohabitants in single- and multi-generation houses in Czech villages and cities. Half of the photovoltaic power plants (*fotovoltaická elektrárna*) were installed under the Green Bonus/Feed-in-Tariff and the other half under the New Green Savings Program. While holding together the technical, environmental, and affective the following analysis offers three focal points for exploring human-machine-environment configurations. The first section zooms in on micro-producers' *technical practices* to examine how bodies and environments are (trans)formed through contractual subjectification as well as the pleasures of digital immersion and energy squandering that exceed a masculinized logic of economization. Starting from the observation that solar power plants engender attention to the weather, the second section focuses on *environmental entanglements* and the heterogeneous gendering of the capacities of collaboration, subjugation, and refusal in synchronizing energy use with the availability of the sun. The final section examines the potential of *bodily electric vulnerability* in solar microgeneration that underscores that the drive for energy independence is also a realization of inevitable electric entanglement. In conclusion, I discuss how the material capacities identified in the analysis might be harnessed for more solidary and just energy relations.

2. Subjectification and the Pleasures in Solar Micro-Production

2.1 Solar subjectification

Many solar householders started by speaking about the technocratic hindrances they encountered in setting up their solar power plants, which arose from the very schemes that were meant to support them. Commenting on the changing institutional energy landscape, some noted that the government had gradually reduced and ultimately abolished feed-in tariffs in 2013 after political representatives and state-owned electricity utilities had profited from more generous tariffs, sometimes by fraudulent means. Obstacles consisted of difficulties in obtaining the required permits, business licenses, and installation contracts. Solar micro-producer Jitka, a health care provider, and her partner Ivo recalled the state bureaucracies of the energy regulation agency [ERÚ] and the utility provider before tariffs were ended, which required considerable risk-taking and perseverance of prospective solar householders.

Jitka: "You had to get the permit from ERÚ. We had asked three times, it's a lot of paperwork and we always sent it by registered mail and three times they rejected it. And in November the man supposed to install it told us that they were starting to allow it."

Ivo: "It was five to 12 and the installation company said they didn't know whether they could make it in four weeks. We were not the only ones [...]."

Jitka: "They let you build it but only when it was connected would they approve and register it. Then we had it on the roof, but they didn't like the inverter, and it was the last workday before Christmas. I went to [utility] so that they connect me, crying. And the installer, a very decent man, came that afternoon, and modified the invertor and they turned it on [...]. On December 24 I got a terrible fever, I was completely unnerved but because the plant was registered to my name, my husband took me again to [utility] where I personally signed that I renounce the 30-day appeal period that would have ended after the deadline." [multi-generation house, village, feed-in-tariff]

The volume of document folders that micro-producers presented materialized these administrative travails. Licenses legally turned the homeowner into a solar plant owner (colloquially *solarník* or solar man), entrepreneur, and accountant. In a neoliberal modality, utilities transferred the accounting onto individual plant owners who henceforth had to monthly document and sign the documentation of their electricity production, and file taxes and health insurance on their earnings. Retired chemical engineer Martin ironically referred to the frequently changing accounting regime as his "Alzheimer's prevention training."

For householders who set up their photovoltaic installations after 2013, under the New Green Savings subsidies, the possibility to sell solar generated electricity was much reduced and monthly accounting no longer required. Registered solar companies, often subcontracted by the utilities, now took care of the administration, including the application for subsidies. A crucial restriction was the requirement that at least 70% of solar generated electricity must be consumed within the house. For private households with limited electricity consumption during the day, this necessitated the costly acquisition of energy storage or accumulation – either batteries or water boilers, turning solar men into *baterkáře* (battery-men) and *vodaře* (watermen). One research participant astutely observed that in this way the demand for load balance was transferred onto the micro-producer rather than collectively integrated into the grid.

Contractual obligations and electric connections to the utility created vertical relations, responsibilized individual plant owners, and hampered their capacity to considering themselves part of a larger collective. Importantly, people in rented accommodation and homeowners who lacked the investment capital, credit ratings, or linguistic-administrative competencies were excluded from acquiring photovoltaics, while simultaneously contributing to feed-in-tariffs and subsidies that were financed from increased electricity prices and taxes. In this way, solar rooftop installations became a middle-class white initiative that participated in making racial and class distinctions.[2]

2.2   The capacity of tuning into solar activity

In contrast to the sex appeal of not "hav[ing] to care about anything" (X-Solar), it was the active involvement with photovoltaics that frequently generated pleasure amongst solar householders, particularly men with time available for hands-on involvement. Several micro-producers got to know photovoltaics through off-grid panels and enjoyed the tactile interaction that – not unlike the masculinist lineage evoked by the solar industry – businessman and climate activist Josef hoped to impart to his son.

Josef: "I bought a solar panel four years ago, just one, because I like to experience... experiment with the technology. I also wanted my son to have the hands-on because it's really very simple. So we played... when I used to go sailing with the kids, we took just one panel and hooked a small fridge to it [...] When you're at sea, you have to be able to repair it yourself. I always like to have the hands-on!" [single house, city]

Pleasure in *playing with* solar panels extended to grid-connected installations in both single and multigeneration houses. For, despite their standardized configuration, many micro-producers cared to learn about and with their solar power plants. Consider the account of accidental plant owner Martin, who had been prohibited by the utility to register the solar plant in the name of his co-habiting son-in-law, who had been driving the acquisition of photovoltaics.

Martin: "In my old days, we got a toy for me. I'm playing with it. I'm observing in detail how much we are making today, what the processes are. For example, two months ago there was a solar eclipse that was reflected: The curve went up like this, then it had this tooth, then it went up again, so this is interesting! I look at how much we have saved theoretically and how much we spent. I will show you on my mobile! So I can see how it's been in the past few days, you see it does this, it should go smoothly, but there are clouds. I'm comparing it to other power plants around here [...] Every day I do the read-

<hr>

2   On the constitutive exclusion of Roma as laborers and solar power plant owners see Lorenz-Meyer (2017).

ings here, so it's a hobby and I still learn new things!" [multigeneration house, city, feed-in tariff]

Playing with solar rooftop installations does not only involve the tactility of starting the digital application. It consists of the capacity of *tuning into* the panels' activity in setting the flow of electricity that monitoring devices visualize in real time as spikes and numerical values in motion. Underscoring the pleasure in the activity, Martin makes clear that his immersive observations do not directly impact the panels' activity, unless he were to notice an operational error. Like another early adopter, Martin kept a notebook under the electricity meter, where he recorded the kilowatt hours of generated electricity (see Figure 1).

Figure 1: Handwritten Entries of Solar Generated Electricity (Jaroslav's house)

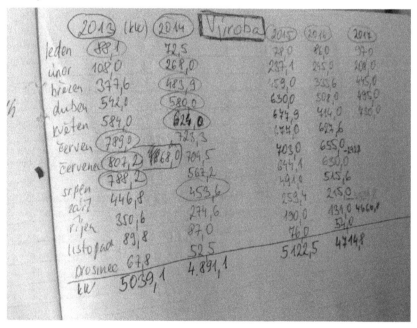

Source: Dagmar Lorenz-Meyer

Such meticulous daily recordings allowed for comparing solar production by day, month, and year. They also marked significant thresholds: "15.2.2014: PRODUCTION 5000 kWh" (Jaroslav). Importantly, handwritten entries were made even though electricity production was registered digitally (Martin: "The meter has a GSM module so every 15 minutes it reports to [the utility] what I'm making here"), and the app could produce comparative charts instantaneously. The notebook of Jaroslav, a younger solar producer, suggests that these entries were not a matter of differential generational digital literacy. Rather, they materialize corporeal immersion by incorporating the electricity production *in their own hand*, changing bodily sensibilities and boundaries in the act of observation and inscription.

In so doing, the gendering of these joyful bodily acts remains heterogeneous. Householders' daily bodily movements and pleasures related, through the app's parameters, to the quantity of solar generated electricity of their own plant (solar apps under the New Green Savings no longer allowed producers to see the electricity production of neighboring power plants). They thereby appear to materialize the calculative energy producer/manager imagined by utilities, who Yolande Strengers (2013) aptly calls "Resource Man." But as with the pleasures of hands-on tinkering, that capacity of attunement seemed to exceed and complicate the logic of calculation and its masculine gendering. Joy was experienced through sensory immersion conventionally coded feminine, and calculation entailed the registering of difference, such as the solar eclipse or a midday cloud, as enticing, not a matter of lost revenue.

Sara Ahmed (2004: 164) has suggested that "pleasures open bodies to worlds through an opening up of the body to others," including to a midday cloud, or the wonderous generativity of solar radiation. It was the abundance of immaterial solar radiation and the ability to tap into it that appeared to create a feeling of joy, wonder, and freedom. Jaroslav who had installed a solar installation in the name of his cohabiting mother, the house owner, started to laugh when thinking of the fullness of solar radiation's nothingness.

> Jaroslav: "It's great that I use free energy! [...] My mother says it's *amazing* that it's possible to have your own electricity from... from nothing! (laughs) It's from *nothing*!!"
> [multi-generational house, city, feed-in-tariff]

This account suggests that women householders take part in the pleasures of solar energy production, specifically the enticing *immateriality* of radiation and electricity – where immaterial denotes the "incorporeal and/or inconsequential" (Pierce/Pauli 2010: 113) and simultaneously draws attention away from the materiality of photovoltaic panels, their production and future waste.

For other solar householders, quotidian encounters with solar companion technologies were limited to a controlling gaze (Krystof: "When I come home, I just have a look at the display, see whether it's really working or not. Just to avoid the possibility that it's broken" [subsidies]). But even Daniel, a rental tenant and environmental activist who could not install solar power and had given his friend a loan so that he could, carried the solar application on his phone as a way of calculating energy savings and participating in the energy transition. Practices of as Daniel put it "just looking what the house is producing" on the app extended micro-producers' bodies and environs, enabling them to be in touch with the electricity production at home – for early adopters, even with the plants of their neighbors. Jitka and Ivo, meanwhile, had installed a light in their living room that brought invisible solar production into their surroundings and sensibility, through flashing when the panels were producing electricity, signaling the availability of what Jaroslav called "free energy." In those ways, solar electricity transformed bodily boundaries, quotidian practices, and environments in ways that were tied to, but exceeded, a masculinized logic of calculation.

2.3 The pleasures of squandering solar generated electricity

This excess of middle-class economization became apparent in another mode of solar delight that concerns the exuberant uses of solar generated electricity: the pleasure of indulgence and squandering or wasting abundant energy rather than giving or selling it to the grid provider. Arnošt laughingly referred to the excessive heating of his swimming pool.

> Arnošt: "The pool is 30 degrees (laughs), I probably went over the top with those panels (laughs). But it's nice at night when it's cold, it's splendid, and the water is fantastic!" [farmhouse, village, feed-in-tariff]

Solar micro-production here affords new practices and tactile enjoyment: a night-time swim, a summer sauna. Such energy intensive practices have also been observed among Australian and British solar micro-producers (Strengers 2013; Turner 2016) – but against the backdrop of normative energy-savings discourses they are rarely considered enjoyable. They caution against equating solar microgeneration with environmental sustainability – and problematize accounts that associate and target energy waste predominantly in lower-class households: the proverbial TV set running in every room (Großmann 2017).

Strengers (2013) notes that solar micro-producers often describe solar generated electricity as "home grown," thereby endowing it with different qualities than other energy. British producers, for example, have justified energy practices, such as using the tumbler dryer when the sun is shining, not as wasteful but as "saving practices": saving homegrown electricity that otherwise would have been "lost" or "just disappears out in the grid and gets wasted" (cited in Turner 2016: 184). Such accounts underscore the heterogeneity of affective valuation referring to a sense of emotional attachment and "care for [homegrown] energy" (Pierce/Pauli 2010: 118) as much as a sense of entitlement to use this electricity at one's pleasure, and a reluctance to gift or sell it to an amorphous grid for the benefit of other users; a joyful capacity nonetheless to waste and squander – like "the sun squanders its light" (Hazard 2019: 3) – copious energy that is at odds with the economizing logic of Resource Man.

3. Synchronizing Electricity Use with the Weather

Even though "enhance[ing] the feeling of harmony with the environment, of closeness to fundamental forces" (Argue et al. 1978: 13) had not been a driving force for the solar micro-producers we spoke to, as it had for some earlier "sun builders" (ibid.) in the 1970s, the capacity to tuning into solar electricity generation brought householders in touch with the environment. For the spikes on the solar application that signal electricity also bring home the weather – and concomitantly its variability and unpredictability.

> Kamil: "I look [at the solar app] quite often, like when the weather is changing, because I work at the other end of Prague, so when it's overcast there and I see that the power plant is running fully, I know that the sun is shining here." [single house, city, subsidies]

Solar apps directly indicate the environmental factor of CO_2 emissions *not* produced calculated by the app's algorithm. When Arnošt showcased his plant's electricity production, this environmental benefit was mentioned as an ethical afterthought: "and in this time you lowered CO_2 emissions by 12.8 tons – so we are doing a good thing!" In comparison to this feel-good indicator, the app's comparison of current electricity production with what was produced a day, month, or year ago was a more tangible reminder of weather anomalies that householders regularly commented on when taking stock of their plant's productivity.

> Martin: "June has always the biggest production. But this June was somewhat weird."

> Arnošt: "March and April were totally catastrophic."

Catastrophic weather was not discussed as a phenomenon of a changing climate, as when large-scale solar plants had those living in proximity notice rising temperatures and drought. Solar householders, it turned out, were often interested in learning to synchronize their electricity use with the weather. In practice, some performed this synchronization work of running household appliances when the sun was shining by using digital timers that were pre-set in the morning; others, performing pervasive gender stereotypes through solar technology, attempted to delegate it "to the women of the house" (Martin).[3]

> Michaela: "So Arnošt might say: "Today you can't iron because the sun is not shining!""

> Arnošt: "We also say: "Today the sun shines, iron, wash, cook!" (laughs) Well, it's good, we learn, and then it works. Somebody might be interested in night-time electricity, we are interested in how the weather is!"

---

3   In the context of utility initiatives that incentivize shifts in domestic energy uses in response to grid load in the UK, Johnson (2020) has suggested the term Flexibility Woman to signal that it is often middleclass women who flex their electricity consumption in what amounts to shouldering an additional under-valued workload.

When it worked, integrating electricity use with the rhythm of the weather – collaborating with the sun – felt satisfying. Ecologically, this practice seems to embody a responsiveness to environmental forces. Synchronization resonates with the idea of *slow energy* in architecture and design that embraces more varied rhythms between periods of intense activity and slow time in times of peak demand or bad weather, rather than an always-on productivity (Strengers 2013). At the same time, responsive synchronization appears to demand the householder's subjugation to a (weather) regime and was guided by the quest to limit energy expenditure – the economizing rationality of Resource Man – which underscores the heterogeneity of actual or potential valuations and their genderings.

In fact, the mobilization of synchronization of gendered household chores became a matter of dispute, "arguments with the family, with the wife about when you do things, and that you need to change your behavior a bit" (Daniel). In light of its multiple valences, the refusal of synchronization by (women) householders was a refusal to be subjected to a new disciplinary regime, Flexibility Woman, as much a rejection of the economizing logic of Resource Man – a refusal also to change and to collaborate with the weather world.

Alice: "I have one washing day..."

Karel: "...whether it rains or the sun shines, it doesn't matter."

Dagmar: "So you'd say life hasn't really changed with all these technologies?"

Karel: "No, because we have an external input of electricity, that is the key. What's special with this [smart] technology – but I don't want to do it – it's able to decide when we have the weather forecasts for the next 2–3 days, it can switch off unnecessary equipment in the house. We have to switch off this functionality. If you want to save money, then you have to plan your electricity consumption, but I don't want to do it. And I think it would be strange for my wife to plan it (laughs)." [single house, village, subsidies]

Karel cast synchronization as an energy-saving strategy mandated by energy scarcity, not environmental concern. He and Alice lived with smart appliances, where blinders responded to sunlight, indoor lights to the movement of bodies. It was in the context of home automation that human autonomy and control of electricity use was asserted the most.

But even where synchronization was pursued, Michaela and Arnošt's practices underline that collaborating with the weather coexisted with practices of energy squandering. Thus, while solar microgeneration brought the environment home it did not necessarily turn it into a matter of care. To be sure, research participants sometimes alluded to social inequities underpinning the support for and questioned the environmental benefits of solar energy applications, including electric vehicles that two solar households owned and many aspired to.

Zuzana: "Always if the state supports something, then something else gets more expensive. It seems to me completely fantastic to use solar energy if there is a possibility. But I don't know if it's distinctly cheaper or if it burdens the environment less." [weekend house, village, off-grid]

Karel: "I think that the future is to build smart grids [...] But it's very odd to say that electric cars are more ecological than standard oil cars. Are you really sure? This production of batteries and the recycling of batteries with unknown sources of energy, is this electricity really green?"

And yet such critical environmental concerns rarely constituted a lens through which solar plant owners interrogated their own practices and responsibilities: Who exactly was paying the price for tariffs and subsidies that helped make their installations viable? Few cared to know where and how minerals, labor and energy were sourced to produce their panels and batteries, or how those will be disposed of and with what effects on bodies and land.

4. Electric Entanglements and the Im/Possibility of Solar Solidarity

4.1 Electric vulnerability

Even though I had been skeptical about the persuasiveness of the threat of a blackout – and the sexiness of eliminating it that solar companies often touted *before* the benefits of financial savings – a sense of bodily vulnerability appeared to have driven some photovoltaic acquisitions. While encompassing the fear of bodily harm through being cut off from electricity denoted by the concept of energy vulnerability (Bouzarovski/Simcock 2017: 640), *electric vulnerability* is decoupled from low income, substandard housing, and diminished health and social participation associated with energy poverty. Grounded in the experience or expectation of corporeal wounding in conditions of relative energy affluence, electric vulnerability is concerned not merely with the quantity but the quality and effects of energy provisioning. Jaroslav, an early-retired pilot, had used the money he received from a work-related disability to finance the solar installation in his mother's house:

Jaroslav: "I had a problem with my ear and backbone, and I said: "You have to do something about the future." [Solar microgeneration means] freedom. Freedom from normal life [...] to not think I have to go to work tomorrow because I need the money to pay the electricity companies."

While the notions of freedom and free energy resonate with the language of capitalist advertising ("Be unlimited" in the words of a prominent Chinese solar panel manufacturer), solar installations here are figured as a means to refuse capitalist productivism, powerful utilities, and the strictures of paid work. For logistics manager Karel, the fear of electricity deprivation was linked to worries about vital food provisioning.

Karel: "Do you have any idea how long you will have food in the stores in Prague when the electricity doesn't work? Retailers have two days' inventory on each level of the supply chain. And I would like to build a place outside civilization to have a chance to be OK for a week or two [...] The question is not *if* but *when* we can expect a blackout. Electric engineers will tell you this is a reality in Europe. I'm not sure that in five years we will have enough energy for our consumption [...] When you have this helicopter view of society, you definitely need to build something like this to prepare your family for a crisis situation."

Dagmar: "And crisis, what could that be?"

Karel: "It could simply be high winds in northern Germany which can break the electricity network here."

These accounts here speak not of the capacity of collaboration with, but a desire for insulation from environmental forces, and corporatist and public infrastructure. Resonating with the gendered advertising of solar companies, they portray solar installations as a tool for assisting family man: not a technology added to the home but one of enabling basic security and nourishment of one's own. Importantly, the perceived need for insulation, "a place outside of civilization", is driven by an awareness of deep material and energetic interconnection. Karel's reference to German wind power damaging the Czech grid (that geographically is a part of German north-south electricity connections) points to a further qualification of electric vulnerability, namely that the electricity that establishes security and well-being is also potentially harmful.

Solar power is not exempt from this double-edged nature of electricity. Josef had encountered the fear of electricity in the opposition of fellow climate activists to participating in a workshop consisting of installing photovoltaic panels on his roof. Another micro-producer had fervently warned that this was *dangerous*, the panels could overheat and start a fire – fears that Josef considered as being fueled by solar companies that prevented hands-on interaction. When I had asked Jaroslav if he would power his home appliances with low-volt solar generated electricity if it were possible, he forcefully ruled out such a direct connection:

Jaroslav: "I don't want that! Because, you know, this frequency of 2.4 gigahertz like your mobile phone, Wi-Fi, is not very healthy and safe. [...] There is an induced current, it's difficult to explain in English. Everything with electricity, you have to be very careful. It is on the same frequency as your glands, and 20 years later you have problems with your hormones, with everything."

Photovoltaics' connectivity here brings home a deep-seated ambivalence about the transformational force of electricity that is impervious to human senses of sight, smell, or hearing (Anusas/Ingold 2015). Electric vulnerability does not only concern the potentially deadly lines of electric conductivity, but more insidiously the low-level interferences between the pulses of electricity outside and inside our neurological synapses that question the boundaries between self and other, inside and outside.

In an anxious and paranoid way, photovoltaic installations are a material reminder of electric kinship and connection, the inhuman electricity around and within humans and other animals. I want to suggest that electric vulnerability thereby entails the potential "to perceive the material world as consisting not of discrete entities with bounded interiors, but rather of knots or nodes in an energetic weave that crisscrosses different states of matter and life, without beginning or end" (Anusas/Ingold 2015: 549). It is this uncanny inhuman kinship and shared electric bodily vulnerability that appears to fuel a desire for insulation, for *cutting* energetic entanglements at home, rather than building energetic lifelines collectively through transversal interconnection and solidarity. Electric vulnerability then is the realization of corporeal openness to life-sustaining electricity that can fuel both attempts at insulation as well as imagination of different electric interconnections that I consider next.

4.2   The impossibility of gifting electricity

As noted, current Czech subsidies for photovoltaic installations are designed to reduce the extent to which solar generated electricity can be fed into the grid. In contrast to the sexy proposition that micro-producers could "transfer surpluses to [their] parents' cottage" (X-Solar 2019), solar householders understood that there was no such grid-based transfer option.

Dagmar: "If you have more electricity than you can save with your battery, could you send it over to [nearby farm]?"

Karel: "Yes, I can send it…"

Dagmar: "…and credit them?"

Karel: "I'm not sure that we can talk about crediting (laughs). So far, it's a penalty rather than a credit […]. Because they [utilities] don't want [you] to send the energy back to the network."

While some utilities had instituted instruments for measuring and penalizing the ostensible overproduction of electricity at the household level, they had not installed a mechanism that would allow micro-producers to transfer excess electricity to other households – a neighbor, a social organization, a school – whose electricity costs would be reduced accordingly. Some participants deemed these prohibitions less a matter of grid stability than the utilities' economic self-interest. The prohibition might inadvertently align with the fears about the density of electric interconnections and sharing "home-grown" electricity I examined above.

Figure 2: Unconnected Photovoltaic Panels (Josef's house)

Source: Dagmar Lorenz-Meyer

And yet, the limitations of lateral electric interconnections under the New Green Savings scheme still incited imaginations of electric solidarity.

Josef: "When I know that there are a couple of neighbors over there who run air conditioning systems, why should I buy expensive batteries to store the energy here if during a sunny day it can be consumed by my neighbors? [...] I could agree with them, if we are ten households, we could buy the panels at a better price and then install it and so on – They don't want people to do this! Why would [utility] want to have a co-op here to produce electricity when it would be competition for them?"

Josef's consideration of forming an energy cooperative raises doubts about the contention that the current absence of community energy in the Czech Republic is simply a result of adverse experiences of collectivization under state communism (solar industry representative, November 7, 2018). Practically, his refusal to purchase energy accumulation devices had meant that more than three months after mounting the panels onto his roof, the photovoltaic panels had remained unconnected to the grid and household appliances (Figure 2).

In closing, I would like to leave the ambiguity in Figure 2 standing – the impossibility of sharing in abundant solar radiation without the acquisition of energy storage – as a provocation for sparking the reader's imagination of more convivial electric interconnections and solar solidarity – for which the capacities of solar delight, electric vulnerability, and energy squandering offer unexpected cues.

5. Concluding Thoughts

Almost four decades after STS scholars had flagged the potentials of photo-voltaics for participation, social equity and material abundance, Winner's (1986: 57) premonition that future photovoltaic systems would be characterized by "institutional and physical centralization [since] our society has [...] delegated decision-making power to those whose plans are narrowly self-interested" appears to be partially vindicated. For although decentralized photovoltaic installations and state support schemes have changed the Czech energy landscape, it is precisely through these regulatory schemes that the configurations of solar power remain controlled by electricity utilities, and the pace of installations slowed down. Centralized control and deceleration are enacted by way of lateral *dis*connections of photovoltaic installations: bureaucratic hurdles, lack of capital or credit ratings cut non-white and lower-class households off from solar microgeneration, while individual licensing, electricity transfer limits and energy accumulation push it towards neoliberal individualization, embodied in so-called solar island systems (panels + batteries). If "break[ing] up the oligopolistic structure of the energy industry" (Etzkowitz 1984: 430) remains a crucial task for more convivial energetic relations, this is achieved by imagining and enabling more exten-sive lateral electric connections at the level of the neighborhood, region, and beyond.

Athwart to the masculinist imaginations of photovoltaics as enabling comfort and economization propagated by the solar industry, *capacities and pleasures of connectivity* come to the fore in interviews with solar micro-producers, house tours, and solar app demonstrations. These include the abil-ity of solar householders to learn tuning into solar machines, synchronizing energy uses with the rhythms of solar radiation, and imagining alternative connections such as energy cooperatives. At the same time, the heterogenous gender valuations and disputes of these practices underline that they do not simply render social equity and environmental justice: the ostensible good of synchronizing energy use with the sun, for example, is often relegated to

Flexibility Woman and is a form of environmental collaboration as much as a subjection to a new disciplinary energy regime. And so, rather than asking whether solar delights and fears of connection are mostly male passions, these heterogeneously valued capacities problematize the prevailing ideology of electricity utilities, the solar industry and the coherence of gender. The troubles of energy synchronization begin to suggest that we hone the capacities of connection and collaboration not as an individual act within a household but as a collective orchestration of networked devices across households and regions, potentially including places where the sun is shining at any one moment (see also Lorenz-Meyer 2017).

The solar app as the material digital interface of quotidian human-environment intra-actions underscores that solar energy is best understood as a human-machine-environment configuration. Designing the solar app for conviviality visualizes lateral networks of interconnected photovoltaic plants and other households or businesses. Drawing on the socio-environmental (un)concerns of solar micro-producers the app might include information on where photovoltaic components are sourced and their "emergy," (Gabrys 2014) or energy that is embodied in panels and batteries and their future disposal, as well as the energy expended in using the solar app to render the environmental impacts of *im/material energy* tangible and accountable.

While such indicators extend concerns of electric vulnerability beyond the household, solar householders' delight in squandering abundant solar generated electricity casts doubt that socio-environmental indicators will lead to a reduction in energy use. And yet, together the capacities of energy squandering, electric vulnerability and tuning into solar activity might enable refiguring electricity and its connections, not as a finite resource that can be owned, but as an abundant flow that can be tapped into, a force that is in and around us – all the while keeping the materials and pathways through which solar generated electricity becomes available in critical visibility. This might include a rethinking of the hatred of wastefulness (Hazard 2019). Reminding us that "'zero-waste' is not a sustainable principle but a death sentence" and that "every ecology on earth springs from the sun's foundational squandering of its rays [where] animals and plants breathe each other's waste" (ibid.: 3–4) Hazard asks, what if we recast waste "as a residual reflex of generosity and networking"? (ibid.: 5) Could the pleasures in squandering help reimagining how electricity breakdown and deprivation are better met by lateral networks than isolation, and turn the waste in solar panel and battery production and recycling into an impulse for responsible connection rather than forgetting or declaring it resolved?

Crucially, building such lateral connections must include and draw on the capacities of those whose labor and taxes have enabled existing photovoltaic installations but who so far have been excluded from solar microgeneration and are all too often considered waste(ful): people who experience energy poverty and energy debt, solar construction, recycling and waste workers, and those who know how to pirate electricity might be well positioned to reroute electric connections and ferment electric kinship and solidarities through overflows and spills, in a more communal squandering of solar energy of a sexiness yet to be known. Such reconfigurations might charge a new "electric sublime" (Nye 1990: 59): not the awe and amazement that electric lighting incited in the early 20th century, but one that holds together the joy in the ability to tap into abundant solar flows, its material pathways and the apprehension of a shared but differential electric vulnerability of entangled participants, human and not. An electric commons where sharing in the energy abundance around us is a matter of material orchestration of solar plants, devices, and grids rather than the promise of innocence, insulation and energy accumulation.

References

Anusas, Mike/Ingold, Tim (2015): The Charge Against Electricity. In: Cultural Anthropology 30, 4, pp. 540–554.

Argue, Robert et al. (1978): The Sun Builders: A People's Guide to Solar, Wind and Wood Energy in Canada. Toronto: Renewable Energy in Canada.

Bouzarovski, Stefan/Simcock, Neil (2017): Spatializing Energy Justice. In: Energy Policy 107, pp. 140–148.

Doing, Park (2009): 'Lab Hands' and the 'Scarlet O.' In: Social Studies of Science 34, 3, pp. 299–323.

Etzkowitz, Henry (1984): Solar Versus Nuclear Energy. In: Social Problems 31, 4, pp. 417–434.

Frauenhofer ISE (2020): Recent Facts About Photovoltaics in Germany. Available at https://www.pv-fakten.de, last accessed May 2, 2020.

Gabrys, Jennifer (2014): Powering the Digital. In: Maxwell, Richard et al. (eds.): Media and the Ecological Crisis. New York: Routledge, pp. 3–18.

Government of the Czech Republic (2019): Vnitrostátní Plán České Republiky v Oblasti Energetiky a Klimatu. Available at https://www.mpo.cz/en/energy/strategic-and-conceptual-documents/the-national-energy-and-climate-plan-of-the-czech-republic--252018, last accessed May 2, 2020.

Großmann, Katrin (2017): Energiearmut als multiple Deprivation vor dem Hintergrund diskriminierender Systeme. In: Großmann, Katrin et al. (eds.): Energie und soziale Ungleichheit. Wiesbaden: Springer, pp. 55–78.

Grosz, Elizabeth/Probyn, Elspeth (1995): Introduction. In: Grosz, Elizabeth/Probyn, Elspeth (eds.): Sexy Bodies. New York: Routledge, pp. ix–xiv.

Haraway, Donna (1997): Modest_Witness@Second_Millenium. New York: Routledge.

Hazard, July (2019): As Lucky and as Trashy as the Sun: Presentation at the 4S Conference. New Orleans (unpubl.).

Illich, Ivan (1973): Tools for Conviviality. New York: Harper & Row.

Johnson, Charlotte (2020): Is Demand Side Response a Woman's Work? In: Energy Research & Social Science 68, pp. 1–9.

Lorenz-Meyer, Dagmar (2014): Reassembling Gender: On the Immanent Politics of Gendering Apparatuses of Bodily Production in Science. In: Women: A Cultural Review 25, 1, pp. 78–98.

Lorenz-Meyer, Dagmar (2017): Becoming Responsible with Solar Power? Extending Feminist Imaginings of Community, Participation and Care. In: Australian Feminist Studies 32, 94, pp. 427–444.

Mellström, Ulf (2002): Patriarchal Machines and Masculine Embodiment. In: Science, Technology & Human Values 27, 4, pp. 460–478.

Nye, David E. (1997): Electrifying America. Cambridge, MA: MIT Press.

Pierce, James/Paulos, Eric (2010): Materializing Energy. In: Halskov, Kim/Petersen, Marianne Graves (eds.): Proceedings of the 8th ACM Conference on Designing Interactive Systems. New York: Association for Computing Machinery, pp. 113–120.

Strengers, Yolande (2013): Smart Energy Technologies in Everyday Life. New York: Palgrave Macmillan.

Traweek, Sharon (1995): Bodies of Evidence: Law and Order, Sexy Machines and the Erotics of Fieldwork Among Physicists. In: Foster, Susan L. (ed.): Choreographing History. Bloomington: Indiana University Press, pp. 211–227.

Turner, Britta (2016): Assemblages of Solar Electricity. Diss. Durham: Durham University/Department of Geography.

Winner, Langdon (1986): The Whale and the Reactor: A Search for Limits in an Age of High Technology. Chicago: University of Chicago Press.

Digitalization and Cultures of Translation

Screens and Ontological Work: Four Projects of Yolŋu Aboriginal Australian Meaning-Making Mobilising ICT Machines

Helen Verran

1. Introduction

In Australia's Northern Territory (NT) over half the land area is owned and governed collectively by members of Indigenous clans, albeit in often tense partnerships with agencies of the Australian state. This article is concerned with the collective life of Yolŋu Aboriginal Australian clans who own the better part of the NT region known as Arnhem Land. Yolŋu collective life is lived through a rich and exhaustive set of non-modern categories which are relational all the way down. There are categorical dichotomies in Yolŋu life, but they differ profoundly from the familiar dualities of modern life. Thus, in the contemporary knowledge and culture work of Arnhem Land, there is a meeting up of two *cosmologies*: a cosmology embedded and expressed in an on-going Indigenous Australian collective life-way, and the cosmology embedded in modernity as enacted in various state institutions.[1] In some situations, this leads to clashes, such as when a Yolŋu member of the NT Legislative Chamber wishes to speak in his clan language in Parliament (Christie 2020), or when Yolŋu community elders struggle to develop a collective caring approach during the Covid-19 disease outbreak, only to find themselves thwarted by public health officials (Spencer 2020). But in most situations, with various degrees of explicitness, work-around practices are contrived to do the necessary work. Very often these work-arounds are invisible, so embedded in culture and knowledge work are their means, and so used are Indigenous Australians to doing this work. The existence, realities, and burdens of this work would surprise almost all non-Indigenous Australi-

---

1   In anthropology a cosmology is an analytical construct and often an object of study. A cosmology guides practitioners in terms of knowledge, beliefs, interpretations of happenings, and cultural practices, offering explanations about the origins and evolution of a cosmos, as well as the role and the meaning of humans, life, and the world. A cosmology involves explanations of the past, present and future forms of existence.

ans, I see its continuing invisibility as an on-going form of epistemic injustice associated with colonising.

This essay brings particular configurations of humans and machines into focus. It first came to life as a talk, and the essay form adopted here seeks to stay true to that occasion, its time and place and its audience. The situated human-machine assemblages attended to here were involved in on-going, long-term, low-intensity, dissensus by members of Yolŋu communities as they work to reproduce Yolŋu institutional norms, and the ontologies in and as which non-modern metaphysical commitments are collectively enacted. I claim that engaging with Indigenous communities in good faith, non-Indigenous Australians must learn to undertake the necessary ontological work to open up and loosen the ontological weave embedded in epistemic aspects of ordinary practices of modern institutions.

I describe four projects of knowledge and culture work that were designed and directed by Yolŋu members of different communities working to strengthen institutions and groupings that were important to them – they all involved promoting the well-being of clan members and clan lands, and sought ways to innovate in how communities might participate in the work of various modern institutions. For the non-Yolŋu participants, of which I was one, in one aspect or another, these projects were disconcerting in their foci. In describing the projects, I interpret these disconcerting aspects as indicating that as a group we were undertaking ontological work. Having described the projects and their disconcertments, I propose three refractive material-semiotic instruments to make the ontological work visible, as such.

Right from the beginning we were aware of information communication technologies (ICTs) as active participants in these projects, and here I offer interpretations that foreground the ontological work involved in messing around with machinic arrays in place. All the four projects I deal with here involved inventing practical routines to sidestep or manage issues to do with the differences between Yolŋu Aboriginal knowledge practices and those in modern institutions. My aim is to show the means by which differences were managed in effecting ontological work-arounds and to worry at the roles played by screens as parts of ICT machinic arrays. The paper proposes that in digital media, expressions of concepts through enscreenments, as image (still and moving), sound, and written words often in combination with each other, in which particular concepts have life in situated collective meaning-making, particular conceptualised entities always *come to* and express their life in forms configured in particular forms. I propose that sometimes in the collective action of such work, conceptual entities that have precisely configured normative forms in collective enactment in modern Australian cultural contexts, can be challenged. When collectively enacted by Yolŋu Aboriginal Australian for *their* purposes, and to express *their* values, these concepts are, to varying extents, ontologically *other* than normative versions. To enact everyday concepts as *other* takes work.

Particular notions of conceptualised entities in action are entailed in the argument of this paper. As participants in collective epistemic practices in a particular situation, conceptualised entities take up differing forms as they participate in the circuits of collective epistemic practices. For example, the conceptualised entity of a diseased human body is invariably a participant in a clinical encounter. But the entity enters the event of that encounter at a particular time and conceptualised in a particular form so that, necessarily, conceptualised entities are always realised in particular, in actual, situated expression.

The analysis I offer here, a form of empirical epistemology, mobilises relational empiricism where all entities involved in epistemic practices are conceptualised as relational (Kenney 2015; Raasch and Lippert 2020; Verran 2007). Working in the broad and varied analytic tradition of material-semiotics in pursuing empirical ethnographic studies of knowledge practices, I push material-semiotics in a different direction than its familiar form as a box of tools useful for characterising networked political agency in society. That sociological focus, which is interested to show how agency is distributed across webs of entities that are simultaneously actors and enacteds, as part of the actor-network analytic repertoire (Law/Mol 2008: 58), is not what I do here. Material-semiotics analysis proposes realised things – conceptualised entities in action, as situated forms that are simultaneously material and semioticised in their manifestation. I work material-semiotics as an analytic framing for familiarising ourselves with the epistemic lives of concepts.

2. Others' Ontological Work

Many of the familiar dichotomies that seem to fit so well in doing modern life are troubled when it comes to participating in contemporary Yolŋu life: the subject/object dichotomy implicitly reinforced every time we speak in an Indo-European language; the nature/society dichotomy routinely enacted in modern sciences; the physical/abstract dichotomy and the real/artificial dichotomies of modern interpretive traditions, all dissolve in participating in collective happenings of contemporary Yolŋu life. In enactments of Yolŋu knowledge and culture work these dualisms are routinely ignored, resisted, actively subverted, and/or explicitly contested. The ontological forms of knowns and of knowers are different in Yolŋu life than in modern life. Work needs to be done if the particular forms of material-semiotic expression that effect the proper enactments of these ontological forms is achieved. This sort of work is not new for Indigenous Australians – in encountering and engaging with written word texts, photographic images, moving images, individually and in groups they have been inventing ways to utilise new media for their own purposes for over two hundred years. Digitised media are just the latest challenge.

Having been the beneficiary of instruction from Yolŋu knowledge authorities since 1987 I respectfully propose the following set of understandings of their cosmology. The singular category of people-place is core to Yolŋu collective and individual going-on, lived in particular explicit, and actively enforced, norms of knowing and meaning-making practices. Existentially each and every Yolŋu person is one with a particular set of places, albeit that the forms of experiencing differing places are divergent. Each and every person has responsibilities for caring for particular other people and places, and also the right to expect to be cared for and welcomed into particular people-places. However, this commitment to Yolŋu ontological forms does not mean that participating in contemporary modernity is proscribed either individually or collectively in contemporary Yolŋu Aboriginal Australian life. A Yolŋu person might also enact the subject/object and nature/culture dichotomies if required by circumstances to do so. Such sophisticated management of existential categories is both highly pragmatic and strongly politicised. It requires constant and attentive work, both individual and collective, even in the most banal of situations, like taking an urban bus ride in the small city of Darwin (Verran 2020a).

In conveying her understanding of the affective consequences of this ontology, anthropologist Frances Tomisari (1998) proposes a statement of the impressionist artist Paul Cézanne: "The landscape thinks itself in me [...] and I am it and I am its consciousness" (Gasquet 1991). I imagine the cosmological difference that is being managed in the stories I tell in this essay as experienced in an intense awareness of rightness/wrongness in situation, a capacity that many Indigenous Australian individuals and groups have honed over many years. I imagine such experience on the basis of my own experiences which I have previously elaborated as epistemic disconcertments that can arise in experiencing experience (Verran 2001; 2013).

The stories below tell of the work several groups of Yolŋu Aboriginal Australians undertook in in collaborating with researchers from Charles Darwin University in struggling to turn various information communication technologies (ICTs) to their own epistemic and meaning-making ends. For these people who *know otherwise* in doing their familiar and routine knowledge practices in their home lands while utilising ICTs, various sorts of material-semiotic work-arounds need to be devised and instituted. The projects that Yolŋu people wanted to undertake with ICT machines variously made use of screened images, both still and moving, recorded talk and song, and enscreened written-word texts. Digital objects which have physical life within ICT machines as various types of electronic files, participate in collective epistemic and meaning making practices through various expressive media – as visual, aural, and linguistic script media. What I am concerned with here is the material-semiotic lives of conceptualised entities as enacted in these expressions, made with the aid of electronic screens and speakers. These expressions participate in, and in varying ways mediate, in on-going collective epistemic and meaning-making practices of contemporary Yolŋu life.

3. Learning to Contribute to Ontological Work in Going-On Together

As I have explained above, in the early years of this century, I was a member of a group of university researchers and research support officers who followed, supported, and encouraged in working with members of land-owning Indigenous Australians, both in groups and individually, as they mobilised these various ICT machines for their own purposes. Four of these Yolŋu projects utilizing ICT machines and their capacities to screen and sound are briefly described as purposeful pursuits. Conceptualised entities came to life in these projects through expression with digital media. The ontological troubles that each project met needed to be managed. The work has previously been elaborated in the form of several websites (Internetworking Communities www.cdu.edu.au/centres/inc/; IKRMNA www.cdu.edu.au/centres/ik/ikhome.html; Teaching from Country learnline.cdu.edu.au/inc/tfc/index.html) and a series of published papers (Christie 2010; Christie/Verran 2013; 2014; Verran 2007; Verran/Christie 2007; 2014; Verran et al. 2007).

I had dual roles in the projects described here. I was a supporter and advisor for the work on the ground, an officially funded member of the team, albeit marginal, *and* I was recognised as an ethnographer, a university researcher, who would contribute as a scholar in the global, modern institution of the academy. In other words, I had a double participation (Pyne Addelson 1994; Pyne Addelson/Verran 1998). Such double participation carries entails accountabilities towards those about whom I tell stories below. Not only must the inquiries on the ground be pursued in good faith and through nurturing an ethos that is generative in the context of the collective life of the communities we work with, but interpretations offered in academic setting must retain this Grounded Inquiry at its core in offering inquiry into that inquiry. Analytic academic inquiry needs to stay with the trouble of the situated inquiry (Haraway 2016; Verran 2020b).

The four episodes I will describe briefly here were carried out in assiduous, collective, situated, on-the-ground inquiry, much of which was institutional translation work, which although epistemic in nature, in the normal course of events remains invisible in the academy (Verran forthcoming). My participation in those inquiries was limited to listening to accounts and watching what those more actively involved in the physical, embodied work were doing. I offered advice and support. In this first iteration of inquiry, members of the groups designed and trialled various socio-material arrays in turning various ICT devices to Yolŋu purposes in projects expressing Yolŋu values. A great deal of attention was paid to developing the appropriate ethos in these working groups, developing an ethos that respected contrasting epistemic values, and differing sets of epistemic concepts. It was towards this end that much of my advice and support was directed.

It seemed that none of the non-Yolŋu researchers and support staff had a clear idea of what exactly would come out of the work. We all hoped that we could make something happen on the ground, make some sort of difference, in something, somewhere for some people. For each of the projects we produced a report. These reports detailed the impact on the ground as economic, societal, environmental or cultural impact on the on-going life in the Northern Territory. These reports were prepared for the specific organisations that had funded the collective action of the inquiry (see for example, ground-up.cdu.edu.au/; learnline.cdu.edu.au/inc/tfc/index.html). Most of these projects were funded with resources channelled through the research arm of Charles Darwin University, so it was not enough to have something happen on the ground, albeit that this was well attested by reports. In a second iterative turn, in inquiry into these inquiries, we offered reflection on our practices and our, usually modest, on-the-ground accomplishments. We identified certain social, cultural, and political issues that were salient and of interest to the professional community of social scientists. Some of us who had been involved in the first iteration of the inquiry albeit in varying roles, turned our attention to crafting these academic papers, offering interpretations and assessments. These reflective/interpretive texts took the form of conference presentations or research papers directed at particular audiences. In all the second iteration research products associated with the projects I have described here, the issue of ontology and ontological work was canvassed. These papers were directed at social science audiences but in focussing on ontology, they were concerned with what can be identified as cosmological issues. The trouble that tarried within these analyses was ontological trouble.

This paper, and the talk it grew out of, can be understood as a third iteration of inquiry that grew in particular, situated, and collective action. Here I have set descriptions of several of the projects side by side in hopes of having them speak to each other, and in doing so reveal some aspects of how the usually invisible ontological work that many Indigenous Australians routinely perform is achieved. In the sections below, this will lead me to the issues that lie at the core of this iteration of inquiry into inquiry around Yolŋu Aboriginal Australians using ICT machines for their purposes and to express their values and metaphysical commitments. I link experiences on the ground to particular sorts of ontological work as revealed by three material-semiotic refractive instruments. In wielding these, I am not attending to the question we associate with Latour about whether machines are to be construed as neutral media working as intermediaries in the doing of knowledge and culture work in contrast to accounting machines as active mediators (Latour 2005: 105). All these projects recognised machines as participants from the start. Nor are they the sorts of track and trace questions that are conventionally asked by ANT researchers who seek to show how the social is (re)assembled (Blok et al. 2020). The questions that concern me are how active/passive interventions made by machines as participants were, and by what material-semiotic means they were made. I confine myself to considering only screens, seeing enscreenment as constituting the interface between the designed machinic arrays and situations of their deployment in knowledge and culture work. The three instruments I have contrived in developing relational empiricism, as a version of material semiotics are designed to focus up epistemic aspects of everyday practices, here they are tuned to reveal ontological aspects of practices. I imagine the devices by analogy to a quartz pyramid used to refract a light beam allowing aspects of a light beam that are in normal circumstances invisible, to become obvious. The first device reveals conceptual multiplicities in opening up possibilities for experiencing experiences in novel ways. The device focusses attention encouraging re-searchers to dwell in what Giddens calls the experience of "ontological insecurity" (Giddens 1991: 53). The second and third devices expand two different aspects of C.S. Peirce's semiology.

4. Describing Four Projects of Yolŋu Meaning Making Mobilising ICT Machines

Before I begin to describe the projects let me briefly describe how in a general sense I understand the tensions we non-Yolŋu participants found ourselves immersed in as we tried to follow and support. Yolŋu group and individual identification with their lands has been described by anthropologists as a corporeal connection in which "Body, spirit, name, shadow, [Ancestral] track and totem, and [...] sacred places are all within the one [...]. They all imply each other" (Stanner 1979). Or alternatively: in "the cosmology of Yolŋu people in Northeast Arnhem Land [enacted] through images of bodily transformations, journeys and traces [...] illustrates how the body is the *hinge* between self and the land" (Tomisari 1998). I have proposed that Yolŋu and other Indigenous Australians have a strong sense of the rightness that goes along with proper collective enactment of the ontology implicit in that cosmology, and are acutely aware of the continual and never-ending interruptions to proper Yolŋu epistemic demeanour and comportment, as they engage with modern institutions. I see this as a powerful stimulus to making other arrangements when they as groups find themselves in a position to arrange situations differently. The sense of ontological rightness/wrongness that our Yolŋu colleagues clearly experienced with varying degrees of intensity was however almost entirely inaccessible for the non-Indigenous participants in this research. This means that for much of the time what we experienced was an anxiety inducing sense of being *all at sea*.

4.1   East of the Arafura Swamp. Struggling with the problem of re-performing Yolŋu clan lands – Wänga (Guyula/Guluya 2005)

The first product of this project I describe is the earliest product generated in our project. The problems it encountered as those who made it tried to turn it to Yolŋu, offered the first sign that care needed to be taken. A DVD, East of the Arafura Swamp, helps to see the serious purposes that Aboriginal curators have for their collections of digital objects. The East of Arafura Swamp DVD displays seventeen short movies about different places around the eastern edge of the UN World Heritage listed Arafura Swamp. Mängay the instigator of this project is a Liya-Dhälinymirr man living at Mirrngatja on the eastern margins of the Arafura swamp in central Arnhem Land. Caring deeply for his country and his people, their pasts, their present, and their futures, Mängay has told some *life stories* of a few important places. With his friend John Greatorex, Mängay travelled from place to place. In each place, while John filmed and recorded sound, Mängay spoke of history, the Ancestral Journeys it features in, its location in the complex patterns of Yolŋu land ownership, and the varied responsibilities that different groups of Yolŋu people have for the place.

These short biographies of significant places are delivered in Mängay's Liya-Dhälinymirr language. Mängay's Yolŋu compatriots are a primary audience for these recitals or (re)performances of place. However, Mängay and his family are determined that other Australians should also understand that these lands are owned and also learn who owns them and by what means that ownership is evidenced. In subsequent filming, Mängay's younger brother Yingiya, while listening to and watching the recording of his brother speaking in-place, translated the talks into English. This second recording is inserted on the screen as a *talking head*. The Yolŋu sound track is set to emerge from the right speaker, the English from the left (www.cdu.edu.au/centres/ik/db_mangay.html).

Mängay was concerned that many Yolŋu growing up in communities like Galiwin'ku and Gapuwiyak had never seen parts of the country which

212

were important to them and for which they have significant care responsibilities. They didn't know the histories of places and the stories, and the patterns of its ownership and responsibility. And in addition, for some time he had been concerned that many non-Yolŋu people, especially those working for mining companies and people working on a proposed gas pipeline, were doing things without involving all those who should be included in making decisions. So in 2003 Mängay and his friend John Greatorex visited Mirrngatja with a video camera. Subsequently they travelled from place to place. In each place, while John filmed, Mängay told some stories of the place. And when he pointed out particular features of a place we focussed the camera on them so people could clearly see what he was talking about. What he told and showed were only *outside* or *beginners* stories. In addition to these collections of video clips and texts about each place, for many of the places Mängay spoke of there are other images that have been returned to him from the Donald Thompson collection at the Melbourne Museum. In some of the original videos he is holding up one of these images. The museum has now given him digital versions to be associated with the videos in storage.

The problem: Once assembled, using proprietary software like DVD Media Pro, or iView Media Pro the collection is stuck in a particular array. Its capacity to be tailored specifically for each type of audience and each time-place of performance is very limited – yet *this* capacity is crucial for the digital objects to be useful in Yolŋu life. There is a very real danger that the movies on the DVD will come to seem like a scientific report, because the display is set and stabilised. It plays without explicit recognition that like the stories Mängay tells, any particular viewing should be understood as also a particular performance of place – they are the clan land coming to life and *consciousness* through Mängay as he stands in place speaking. The tendency for the digital objects to present as immutable representations of the land rather than particular situated re-performances will prevail.

4.2   TAMI File Management Device – Storage of digital objects in translating ontology (Verran et al. 2007: 132)

TAMI (standing for Texts, Audio, Movies, Images) is the acronym of a digital platform with several unique features. It is difficult to define the device; is it best thought of as a file-management system, a small database, software for community informatics, or local archiving software? Any or all of those general descriptors are applicable. TAMI was designed with and for Aboriginal Australian teachers, parents and grandparents so that they might work with the children of their communities inducting them into the collective life of the various places to which they belong and from which they derive their identity. TAMI imagines parents, children, teachers, grandpas and grandmas generating and collecting digital objects of various types. It sees users as presenting their places and collective life by designing and presenting/performing collections of these items for many sorts of purposes (cdu.edu.au/centres/ik/db_TAMI.html). The project out of which the TAMI device emerged was concerned with designing a device to allow all control of use of the digital objects in the hands of the user.

Functionally TAMI is software that allows users to collect and store digital objects, and to use them in various arrays and forms to *do* their places and their collective lives in ways that make sense to them. Its use in both generating collections and performing (showing) them, is interaction, involving conversation, performance, selection, display, reactions, reconfigurations, assessments and so on. In TAMI digital objects are stored solely on the basis of their file type, and the interface of this software privileges and prioritises visual searching mechanisms. It is possible for users to identify a file on the basis of the thumbnail and pick it up drag it and drop it into an emerging collection that expresses something of their understanding of place or an episode, event or person. There is also a fuzzy text search mechanism for those who do use written words to search, but whose grasp of literacy is minimal. There is a capacity to arrange folders of objects that have been collected and put together, in this way or that onto the figure of a map. So, folders can be dragged and dropped into places on a map.

TAMI has been designed:

- with and for people with few or no literacy skills.
- people who want to manage their own digital resources for perpetuating local knowledge traditions.
- assuming that by and large, each TAMI database will be very small and users will generally have a good idea of what they are looking for in the database.
- to make smaller amounts of valued resources easily enrichable for the purposes of on-going collective memory making, not to store large amounts of anonymous information.
- to be ontologically flat: as far as possible it encodes no assumptions about the nature of the world or the nature of knowledge, it is the user who encodes structure into the arrangements of resources and metadata.
- for the users to become the designers of their archives as they bring together resources, then group and order them, and create products (like DVDs and printouts). The ways in which truth claims are assembled and validated collectively within the knowledge traditions of particular knowledge traditions, can be left fluid.

- so that one single screen enables search, upload and view. A workspace enables different objects to be viewed simultaneously, and arranged into folders.
- to enable users to upload resources into the database by a simple drag-and-drop.
- so that the only a priori ontological distinction at work in the database is the distinction between texts, audios, movies, and images. Apart from that there are no pre-existing categories, as there are in other database where metadata are sequestered into fields. This provides ontological flatness so local knowledge traditions are not pre-empted by scientific assumptions.
- objects can be uploaded and searched without metadata. Metadata can be added at any time. Its sole purpose is to help text-based searching.
- the usual way to find objects in the database is without a text-string search, that is, without a text driven FIND function. Texts, audio files, movies, and images can be searched by flicking through the full set of thumbnail resources.
- users can make assemblages, *folders* of associated and linked resources. They can give these folders metadata. So the database can hold collections of resources based on a theme and these folders can be labelled and found through text search.

TAMI is designed as a clunky piece of software. All its *mechanical* processes lie on the surface. It is a learning/teaching surface designed to recognise and manage ontic incoherence, interference, and interruption, and to make that managing obvious and explicit. Consequently, TAMI will never be a very comfortable experience either for teachers or learners. Users would be constantly aware that representations stored in TAMI, and the various configurations in which they might be arrayed are mutable. Any particular collection that *does* people-place is provisional.

4.3 Teaching from Country – Experimenting to find ways to enable teaching of a university course in Yolŋu language and culture from Ancestral people-places (Christie 2010)

How can digital technologies be mobilised so that Indigenous knowledges are actively and effectively incorporated into the Yolŋu Studies higher education teaching programs while remaining faithful to the ancestral practices and protocols which govern them? With the roll-out of broadband throughout remote Australia, we are increasingly in a position to investigate carefully, ways in which knowledge owners and authorities can become actively and appropriately involved in e-teaching from very remote locations. In 2008, the time was ripe for the expertise which Aboriginal elders and interpreters have developed in teaching, consulting and the use of information technologies, to be brought to benefit our University teaching programs. The program was designed to invigorate the University's engagement with Aboriginal knowledge authorities, as well as to address carefully and publicly the valuing of Aboriginal knowledge in academic contexts, and its protection in the digital and academic worlds.

A further impetus for the program was the desire to shift at least some of the locus of the teaching of Yolŋu knowledge from Darwin (the traditional land of the Larrakiya people) to the lands to which the Yolŋu languages and cultures belong, in eastern Arnhem Land. The program only succeeded because of the difficult and complex philosophical work which preceded and underpinned the collaborative work. The work was fundamentally epistemological. It found the Yolŋu talking about knowledge as distributed in the Yolŋu environment. About trees, for example, having agency in growing knowledge, about the breezes, the sounds of waves breaking, the roar of floodwater, contributing to one's learning about one's self. (Many of these references were implicitly to totemic elements in ancestral song – those parts of Yolŋu ceremonial practice which specifically define particular clan identities.) These discussions, particularly in the context of the seminar, found the International visitors talking about the always local nature of knowledge, the processes of silencing and marginalisation of knowledge, the work of the screen, and how we break down the assumed boundaries between the social and the technical, the person and the technology.

From the beginning we contrived to not separate the social from the technical. That division, pervasive in western metaphysics, has little validity in Yolŋu philosophy, as we came to see. The Yolŋu teachers on country were already experimenting with technical arrangements which suited their purposes (in teaching but in other ICT work as well, such as internet banking), which responded to the particular sorts of connectivity they had available, the sorts of hardware that came to hand, the sorts of software that became available, and the sorts of everyday goals of living and teaching that they find themselves addressing. As the teaching program developed, we all moved slowly from the static webpage and PowerPoint development work towards real-time on-line teaching.

By June 2009, we had passed a semester of feeling our way forward with many teaching trials from remote places, and different people explaining and performing their ancestral knowledge in confusing and frustrating contexts. Yet as they all point out, these contexts are no more confusing or frustrating than a classroom. In the same way that each place is unique – with its particular ancestral story, its different connections with other people and places, different owners and managers of its stories and ceremonies – so from each site emerged a unique socio-technical configuration of hardware, software, connectivity, spaces, images, elders, kin networks, children and passers-by. Some trial sites failed despite a huge amount of effort, others emerged successfully almost spontaneously. Success was more a function of ongoing shared experience, seized opportunity, good faith, nurturing and serendipity than of detailed planning.

Yoḻŋu began to participate in the work of the university in complex different ways. Senior elders took to sitting silently in the background supervising the use of knowledge by younger bilingual kin folk, knowledge for which they were the ultimate custodians. Young children were to be found keeping the technologies connected, or acting as go-betweens for elders who – for kinship reasons – must not meet or speak to each other. We as university teachers were learning without being taught. Knowledge and how to *do* it appropriately in a university setting was unfolding through the screen, and as advisors we had the rare privilege of rethinking so many of the settled categories through which we have for so long understood our work.

4.4 The TouchPad Body – Explicitly managing the body-multiple through screens to effect a singular body emergent in the here and now of a clinical encounter (Christie/Verran 2014)

The TouchPad Body is a design for an application that can be screened on an iPad ICT machine: a digital device for use in those times and places where health professionals and Aboriginal patients and their families are struggling to go on together in generating plans and collective proceedings to achieve healthier Aboriginal individuals, families, and communities. The design came together as a product of a project commissioned to attend to *health literacy*. Of course, the received opinion health services authorities assumed it is the Yoḻŋu clients who are deficient when it came to being literate about health practices.

However, when we, a mixed group of linguists, designers, programmers, and ethnographers went to talk to Yoḻŋu people and groups about how they worked with medical personnel and translators, we were given a different story. Many medical people were seen as ignorant and deficient in their understandings of much of what mattered when it came to ensuring the on-going well-being of Yoḻŋu individuals and groups. The Yoḻŋu people we spoke with were tired of researchers coming to troubleshoot the system, tired of the overwhelming and increasingly differentiated health workforce, and tired of the top-down disciplinary health literacy messages. Yet, we also heard many stories of unusual, highly productive collaborations across boundaries of professional responsibility and across the boundaries of culture which were invisible from above, unsupported, but carried out through long conversations with commitment and good faith and good results.

Good health literacy, we concluded, especially in remote Aboriginal context of extended family and community living, is better understood not so much as what the individual client knows about biomedicine, and what individual medical people understand about Yolŋu life-ways and values, but rather the productive working together of the people and resources which could generate shared understandings and agreement in the moment of the clinical encounter. It involves easy access to clear information, and honest respectful discussion and agreement making across the divides between providers and consumers. Often, we found this already happening, that health professionals, clients and families were often using ingenuity and discretion to create good open collaborative ways of working together. How could we support this work? Adopting a collective approach to dealing with the problems of the moment allows us to remain respectful of both services providers and Aboriginal community members, and the various non-human participants in their worlds – even though they may be quite different. A collective approach allows us to avoid assuming the biomedical model of the human body as the sole salient entity in the clinical encounter. It offers also a robust way around the excessive individualism of western ethics and political philosophies.

We proposed a radically different sort of resource, that disconcerted many medical personnel and challenged many Yolŋu clients. Exploiting inter-active possibilities of touch screens, we devised a user-friendly touch pad animation of a minimal diagrammed human body which has no overt message. It is manipulable, zoomable, transparent, and three dimensional, and detailed in particular areas (heart, lungs, kidneys, liver, pancreas, ears). Such bodily structures are familiar to patients and their families and to health professionals, albeit in different ways. The diagramming of the *TouchPad Body* de-emphasises biomedical details and assumptions. It stimulates conversation – in any language or mixture of languages. Designed collaboratively, in any situation development and its use of a diagram will be coterminous. Which parts it shows and which it conceals, its genders and its pathologies will all be designed and developed collaboratively, in the situation of the clinical encounter, so it emerges as itself *a body* albeit not flesh and blood, but nevertheless one which is both Aboriginal and biomedical; a body which is emergent in exchange in particular times and places.

As itself an emerging body in the here and now of the clinical encounter – albeit of a very different corporeality than a flesh and blood knowingful human body, the diagram will interrupt the presumptions of all contributing parties presuming – neither biomedical certainties about physical human bodies, nor Aboriginal certainties about bodies as always knowingful placed bodies will prevail. By using the device as a diagram to pilot a conversation around the individual problems of the moment, accepting the constraints of that particular here and now, and not obliged to import and to promote particular concepts of what human bodies *are*, the device evades *a priori* assumptions at work in the stories of all these different participants (the bio-

218

medics, the Aboriginal patients, the social workers, family members, *etc.*), each of which entrench received assumptions, and prevent the group from thinking and acting together in new ways (Christie/Verran 2014).

Figure 1 below offers a vision of the *TouchPad Body* in action in a clinical encounter involving many human participants along with many non-human participants, including four enscreened *TouchPad Bodies*. The trees in the background help the reader of the image understand that this is a family living in a remote Yolŋu homeland and their ill family member is being visited by a medical team. The research which led to the design of the prototype grew out of working with doctors and nurses and translators and ill people transferred from their homelands into hospitals, and their family members. One important capacity of the enscreened interactive iPad diagrammatic body is that it can be used in a clinical consultation to negotiate a robust form of medical consent in a group situation, where family members, nurses, doctors, translators are all present and where an on-the-spot translation of what doctors are planning is available.

Figure 1: The *TouchPad Body*

The image visualises the digital object of the diagrammatic *TouchPad Body* enscreened, in being deployed in a clinical encounter involving medical personnel, translators, Yolŋu patient and family members in the process of negotiating biomedical treatment. The interactivity of the screen enables both Yolŋu and biomedical *theories of the body functions* to be talked about and, if necessary, illustrated. Artist: Trevor van Weeran

What is important in this story is that the screen of the touch pad enables multiple conceptualisations of the human body to be screened simultaneously without clashing which would get in the way of agreement making. Expressed diagrammatically the concept of the human body bears on its screened surface a capacity for material-semiotic multiplicity. This achieves a necessary keeping vague in the complex but also very ordinary situation of clinical encounter where it is more usual for there to be a precise specification of the conceptualised entity of the human body.

5. Introducing the Material-Semiotic Refractive Instruments and Describing the Ontological Work They Do in the Four Projects

The first contrast I draw in this inquiry into inquiry concerns multiplicities of concepts-in-action. I am understanding work that Indigenous Australians routinely undertake in mobilising ICT machines to maintain and nurture their traditional practices in collective and individual knowledge and culture work, as involving conceptualised entities whose involvement in the confluence of cosmologies necessarily engenders conceptual multiplicity. This conceptual multiplicity needs to be explicitly and actively managed in action if a sense of Yolŋu rightness in meaning making is to eventuate in the collective action. Sometimes the multiplicity may need to be made explicit and managed as such, and in other situations both a singularity and the multiplicity may need to be maintained in explicit tension.

In the STS literature Mol (2002) and Verran (2001) are two studies we might turn to for interpretive inspiration. Mol (2002) focuses up the multiplicity of the medical concept of atherosclerosis in a Dutch hospital. But in a hospital treating ill patients with a quite wide variety of practices in which many atherosclerosis concepts are to be found in action, the requirement is to foreground the singularity of this scientific concept (albeit that is necessarily vague), and background the multiplicity which is maintained as implicit, but best not talked about. There the ontological trouble needs to be explained away, and Mol interferes with that in focussing up the awkward actualities. In the postcolonial Yoruba classrooms that Verran participates in however, making the multiplicity of numbers explicit serves useful political purposes of everyday decolonising – the incommensurability of the two number concepts yet it usually is not made visible, is generally acceptable to practitioners. Nevertheless, the singularity of number in a made measurement, still needs to be allowed for. Nurturing ways to stay with the ontological trouble generatively and recognise the actuality of multiplicity and the achieved singularity, is desirable (Verran 2001: 117–119; 2020b).

In the first two stories I tell here, the concept around which tensions circulate is named in English as clan-lands. This is routinely translated by the Yolŋu term *wänga*. But there are profound differences between what *clan-lands* and *wänga* mean, and how they are *done*. In the first project I described, a multiplicity discernible as contesting material semiotic referential expressions inevitably emerges, in generating a meaningful cultural product. The expression of the multiple known clan-lands/*wänga* needs to simultaneously point to the modern concept of land area as ownable property, *and* to subvert and refuse to index that concept, while affording possibilities for proper Yolŋu re-enactment in enscreenment by offering an acceptable form of presence of Mängay along with the situation of his performance. If a good enough *cosmological confluence* is to be achieved in use of this product, transition between the concepts as knowns must be both technically feasible and explicit. A very evident duplicity is required, so that the bad-will in meaning making and the resulting assertion of incommensurability in multiplicity emerges with some clarity. Achieving this actually proved to be very difficult and only partially achievable (Verran/Christie 2007).

The second project circumvented this problem by radically reconceiving what a digital resource storage device *is*. TAMI allows landowners total control of a very small data set in which resources are stored and retrievable by reference solely to the concrete form of the digital object. Material-semiotic properties of concepts actioned in cultural and epistemic expressions using this data storage device are controllable by Yolŋu knowledge authorities. The need for material-semiotic management of multiplicity is worked around, by rather extreme technical means.

The second two projects involve *the person side* of the core singular concept of Yolŋu life which here I am glossing as *people-place*. Using ICT machines Yolŋu set about managing expressions of the concept *knowing persons*. In one case this involved Yolŋu persons as authoritative knowers, and in the second as patients in clinical settings. As Yolŋu explain the issue, the conceptual trouble to be managed here concerns the ontological configuration of persons. As knowing persons Yolŋu are configured as radically distributed in the form of people-place, they are *not* configured as the dualistic mind/body figure of modernity who has existence in any and in all places (and in no particular place).

Recognising the reality of the difference and attempting to foreground people-place as a distributed knower (Verran 2015a) was the motivation behind the *Teaching from Country* project. Gratifyingly, it was revealed in the project that taking the trouble institutionally, and aligning the technology to enable teaching from *wänga*, enabled Yolŋu clans to devise ways and means for this reality to be enacted in the university classroom. The differences in conceptualising the knowing person was managed through the screen in the university classroom and this difference could be made explicit in the lesson content being conveyed – form and content of Yolŋu knowledge became aligned for the first time in this life of this university subject. In the case of the *TouchPad Body* this explicitness around multiplicity of the conceptual figure of the knowing person emerged in a quite different way. But here too a differently conceptualised entity in action could be glimpsed and managed in doing the conceptual multiplicity that inevitably arises in cosmological confluence is explicitly set against the singularity of the patient as emergent in a particular explicitly negotiated clinical encounter.

This first resource for *seeing* ontological work concerns the need to recognise differing ontological configurations of knowns and knowers as relational concepts in action, it is just one of the analytic resources that relational empiricism hones in designing a "tool-box" of means for empirically studying conceptualised entities in action as an element of an empirical epistemology that works through ethnography of knowledge practices (Raasch/Lippert 2020). This analytic tool develops accounts of a working relation between knower and known within experience which first emerged within the epistemology of empiricism around the beginning of the twentieth century. The work of American pragmatist John Dewey (1896) offers a beginning here. Relational empiricism makes a virtue of the claimed relation between knowers and knowns in knowledge generation, whereas most empiricist social scientists aspire to explain it away (Holmes 1986). The epistemology of relational empiricism is neither naturalistic, nor *a priori*, but rather experiential.

Further contrasts by which I propose ontological work might be made visible in pursuing an empirical epistemology, looks to a Peircean semiotics for inspiration. Two typological elements of the Peircean model of semiotics are mobilised in relational empiricism to inform its working imaginary. This use of Peircean semiotic instruments is in contrast to the Greimasian model of material semiotics as mobilised in ANT and feminist material semiotics. Two aspects of the Peircean approach make the typologies useful. First is the processual aspect that the Peircean instruments emphasise, is significant, revealing that materialising, in potently signifying meaningfully, always leads onwards, in unending processes of sociability, struggle, and contingency. Second, the Peircean formulation helps us see the wide range of possible means of materialised happenings, richly varied expressions of material semiotic being, become visible.

The first Peircean typology of I mobilise here picks up on indexicality and iconicity as material-semiotic properties of conceptualised entities in action. Thus, I am concerned with just part of the range that Peircean typology makes possible, omitting symbolism as involved in theorising (see Keane's (2003) use of Peirce). I use the terms indexical and iconic as relational, describing ways of materialising meaningfully in the course of the happening of collective action, imagining them as ends of a continuum of contingent possibilities in materialising. I am not proposing them as a dichotomous state of affairs but rather as modal continuum. In happening indexically, a conceptualised entity points to, or indicates a known as *out-there*, materialised in an on-going set and stable state of being. This form

222

enacts a metaphysical commitment to what Latour has called "the modern constitution" (Latour 1993), or in conventional anthropological terms, a modern cosmology. This is the aggressively normative world of meaning making of modern science. There indexicality can be escaped only by recourse to the abstract, and the symbols of theory, or more colourfully by resorting to social technologies of metaphor and allegory. But neither indexicality nor symbolisation will enact a Yolŋu cosmology. Thrust on to *others*, as these modes of expression often are in the doing modernity, has us perpetrating the epistemic injustice of a colonising modernity.

Indexes represent a world *out-there* that has already happened, and happened for always. In stark contrast the actualities enacted in iconic expressions, are worlds that are happening in the here-and-now, in the *as we speak* so to say. Iconicity in meaning making is forever dragging pasts into presents in continuing re-presentations, as re-enactments. For Yolŋu Aboriginal Australians, iconicity has a certain past made in Ancestral journeys, (re)enacted in the present. In each and every (re)performance the metaphysical commitments entailed in the particular forms of being of this or that people-place are expressed in certain particular and explicitly articulated re-performance. Note however that it is not only Yolŋu who in this paper are shown as enacting iconicity in their analyses. This is also the mode of expression that I am mobilising in my analysis (Verran 2019).

Utilizing the contrast of indexicality-iconicity to reveal ontological politics, we see how in the second project described above which involved design of a small data storage device with resort solely to machinic meta categories, the device allows Yolŋu knowers to work comfortably with digital objects as iconic in their re-enactments of clan-lands in enscreenment. In contrast the three other projects described above all struggle to allow possibilities for simultaneous iconic and indexical enscreenment. Enscreenment opens up possibilities but must always be accompanied by attempts to have viewers differentiate. So Mängay attempted a design of a DVD presentation that has clan-lands as *out-there* while also insisting on them as *re-enacted here and now*, attempting to make viewers/listeners do the work. And similarly, Yolŋu knowledge authorities *Teaching from Country* try in their dialogue to head-off interpretations of their role as mere *experts*. While the diagrammatic *TouchPad Body* presents unproblematically on the screen as index for some, and icon for others. Screens here are participating in the collective action in allowing for possibilities for the necessary multiplicities associated with concepts in action. But their interventions remain open. They are not intervening in a determining way, differentiations depend on further social, linguistic, and political work.

The two analytic resources that I have so far wielded, emphasise multiplicity in showing up a cosmopolitics that necessarily accompanies cosmological confluence. But emphasising a cosmopolitics that depends on the good will that involves trusting viewers to do the necessary ontological work, has its drawbacks. Resort to multiplicity is fraught here, for *doing difference* is construed as a form of concession granted by the others to Indigenous knowledge communities. Epistemologically this cosmopolitics depends on doing multiplicity in enacting relativism. And as Indigenous Australians have found out again and again, good will often goes along with bad faith, it is easy to shift to a position that denies difference and refuse to recognise distinctions which allow for the continuation of efforts to nurture the Yolŋu cosmology. Such a shift is not always politically motivated however, it might express a more mundane ignorance or ontological laziness.

There is however a third contrast that allows us to glimpse the possibility of screens participating more determinatively in a more robust cosmopolitics of dissensus, one that decisively stays with the ontological troubles involved in cosmological confluence. This analytic instrument mobilises the Peircean typology that articulates what I tell as a continuum between ontics and ontology possessed of varying degrees of reflexivity, but which Peirce names as the continuum of *firstness, secondness* and *thirdness* (see Kockleman's (2017: 150) use of Peirce).

This is a contrast of vagueness/precision associated with concepts in action which values the processual relation between experience of experience at one end and reflexive ontological specification at the other. Vagueness has a bad name in social science research, where it is assumed that concepts need to define "the features of the thing to which the concept refers" (Blumer 1940: 707). In analysis pursued within iconicity however, which I read Yolŋu knowledge practices as doing, and which my version of material semiotics does, vagueness is a crucial resource that enables cultivation of generative tensions in analysis, which can be brought into the present, into the here-and-now of the analysis. This vagueness however is not the vagueness that social science deplores. That is a form of linguistic vagueness, the vagueness that is conceptually advantageous is vagueness as Ludwig Wittgenstein develops it in his final work *On Certainty* (1969). While acknowledging that there is a form of vagueness associated with uncertainty that is debilitating in meaning making, this analytic instrument asserts that there is also a form of vagueness that enables "certainties-in-action" (Pihlström 2012: 3). This is the sort of vagueness associated with ontics, or what Peirce names as "firstness."

Contriving to cultivate a tension that sets ontic vagueness within which an in-the-here-and-now certainty holds, against the uncertainty of an explicit multiplicity, can be achieved. This renders ontological troubles as a politics of dissensus, and this is what skilful Yolŋu knowledge authorities have learned to strategically cultivate in some situations of confluence of cosmologies. Screens of ICT machines can enable a vague singularity set against multiple conceptualisations of entities in action, to held in tension in the here and now of a particular collective action. This is for example what we see in a clinical encounter negotiated through the *TouchPad Body*. (I have also witnessed it in land management firing workshops, see Verran 2015b). A technological framing solidifies. The *TouchPad Body*, a material technology – a screen, has a vague singularity kept in the foreground, and the uncertainty of the dual Yolŋu and biomedical bodies is backgrounded (but not absented). The singular vagueness enables generative going-on doing difference together. It is here that the screen itself becomes an active participant in framing the collective going-on. The screened diagrammatic body is tension filled yet vague, and most importantly for the process of informed consent, it is singular. The screen is the participant in the collective action of the clinical encounter that *is* that singular body enscreened. Screens here are actively opening up possibilities and participating in enacting a particular dissensual cosmopolitics.

6. Concluding

Mobilising instruments I have devised in developing relational empiricism, an analytic platform proposing a version of material semiotics designed to bring epistemic practices into focus, I have described three types of ontological work that is involved in a situation of cosmological confluence. First I sketched the managing of multiplicities in action; second the contriving of shiftings in referential expression between iconicity and indexicality; and third the workings of degrees of ontological explicitness between vague experiential certainty in action and situated precision. The four projects of meaning making I briefly described in this inquiry into inquiry have been shown as, variably, allowing for all these sorts of ontological work to be carried out *in situ* by virtue of the possibilities that participation by ICT machinic screens open up.

One of the possibilities can be seen in the project of TAMI – a small data storage device of extremely limited local capacity. This device enables control of digital resources for Indigenous knowledge and culture work to remain with traditional knowledge authorities. Screens displaying results of using TAMI participate in enacting Yolŋu people-places in proper Yolŋu forms in the right expressive mode and with the appropriate degree of situated precision. The *TouchPad Body* offers a glimpse of quite different ontological work associated with cosmopolitics. In this case enscreenment intervenes in a form of decisive ontological work to enact a form of cosmological confluence that makes a difference to those participating in what are often fraught clinical encounters. The enscreened *TouchPad Body* allows all participants to stay with the ontological politics of the confluence. In other projects we saw screens opening up possibilities for on-going ontological negotiation. Albeit that this inevitably requires social work which may be resented, and epistemic skills that may be absent, we have glimpsed screens embedded in ICT machinic arrays as worthy and worthwhile participants in the collective action of knowledge and culture work.

References

Blok, Anders et al. (2020): The Routledge Companion to Actor-Network Theory. London/New York: Routledge.

Christie, Michael (2010): Report: Teaching from Country, pp. 1–18. Available at http://learnline.cdu.edu.au/inc/tfc/report.pdf, last accessed August 26, 2020.

Christie, Michael (2020): Sociotechnologies, Sovereignty, and Transdisciplinary Research. In: Learning Communities: International Journal of Learning in Social Contexts 26, pp. 3–8.

Christie, Michael/Verran, Helen (2013): Digital Lives in Postcolonial Aboriginal Australia. In: Journal of Material Culture 18, pp. 299–317.

Christie, Michael/Verran, Helen (2014): The Touchpad Body: A Generative Transcultural Digital Device Interrupting Received Ideas and Practices in Aboriginal Health. In: Societies 4, pp. 256–264.

Dewey, John (1896): The Reflex Arc Concept in Psychology. In: Psychological Review 3, 4, pp. 357–370. Available at https://doi.org/10.1037/h0070405, last accessed August 26, 2020.

Gasquet, Joachim (1991): Cézanne: A Memoir with Conversations. London: Thames and Hudson.

Giddens, Anthony (1991): Modernity and Self-Identity: Self and Society in the Late Modern Age. Stanford: Stanford University Press.

Guyula, Mängay/Guluya, Yingiya (2005): East of the Arafura Swamp [DVD]. Darwin, Australia: Charles Darwin University.

Haraway, Donna (2016): Staying with the Trouble. Making Kin in the Chthulucene. Durham: Duke University Press.

Holmes (1986): The Knower and the Known. In: Sociological Forum 1, 4, pp. 610–631.

Keane, Webb (2003): Semiotics and the Social Analysis of Material Things. Language and Communication 23, pp. 409–425.

Kenney, Martha (2015): Counting, Accounting, and Accountability: Helen Verran's Relational Empiricism. In: Social Studies of Science 45, 5, pp. 749–771.

Kockelman, Paul (2017): The Art of Interpretation in the Age of Computation. Oxford: Oxford University Press.

Latour, Bruno (1993): We Have Never Been Modern. Cambridge: Harvard University Press.

Latour, Bruno (2005): Reassembling the Social: An Introduction to Actor-Network-Theory. Oxford: Oxford University Press.

Law, John/Mol, Annemarie (2008): The Actor-Enacted: Cumbrian Sheep in 2001. In: Knappett, Carl/Malafouris, Lambros (eds.): Material Agency. Boston: Springer, pp. 57–77.

Mol, Annemarie (2002): The Body Multiple: Ontology in Medical Practice. Durham: Duke University Press.

Pihlström, Sami (2012): A New Look at Wittgenstein and Pragmatism. In: European Journal of Pragmatism and American Philosophy IV, 2. Available at http://journals.openedition.org/ejpap/715, last accessed August 26, 2020.

Pyne Addelson, Kathryn (1994): Moral Passages: Towards a Collectivist Moral Theory. New York: Routledge.

Pyne Addelson, Kathryn (2002): The Emergence of the Fetus. In: Mui, C.L./Murphy, J.S. (eds.): Gender Struggles: Practical Approaches to Contemporary Feminism. Lanham, Maryland: Rowman & Littlefield, pp. 118–136.

Pyne Addelson, Kathryn/Verran, Helen (1998): Inquiry into a Feminist Way of Life. In: Bar On, Bat-Ami/Ferguson, Anne (eds.): Daring to Be Good: Essays in Feminist Ethico-Politics. London/New York: Routledge, pp. 168–182.

Raasch, Josefine/Lippert, Ingmar (2020): Helen Verran. In: SAGE Research Methods Foundations. Available at https://methods.sagepub.com/BrowseFoundations?type =Pioneers, last accessed August 26, 2020.

Spencer, Michaela (2020): Micro-Credentialing as Making and Doing STS. In: Learning Communities: International Journal of Learning in Social Contexts 26.

Stanner, W.E.H. (1979): Religion, Totemism and Symbolism. In: White Man Got No Dreaming: Essays 1938–1973. Canberra: The Australian National University Press, pp. 106–143.

Tamisari, Franca (1998): Body, Vision and Movement: In the Footprints of the Ancestors. In: Oceania 68, 4, pp. 249–270.

Verran, Helen (2001): Science and an African Logic. Chicago: University of Chicago Press.

Verran, Helen (2007): Knowledge Traditions of Aboriginal Australians: Questions and Answers Arising in a Databasing Project. In: Selin, Helaine (ed.): Encyclopaedia of the History of Non-Western Science: Natural Sciences, Technology and Medicine. Berlin/Heidelberg/New York: Springer.

Verran, Helen (2013): Engagements Between Disparate Knowledge Traditions: Toward Doing Difference Good Faith. In: Green, Lesley (ed.): Contested Ecologies: Dialogues in the South on Nature and Knowledge. Cape Town, South Africa: HSRC Press, pp. 141–161.

Verran, Helen (2015a): Afterword: On the Distributedness of Leigh. In: Bowker, Geoffrey et al. (eds.): Boundary Objects and Beyond: Working with Leigh Star. Cambridge, MA: MIT Press, pp. 499–500.

Verran, Helen (2015b): Governance and Land Management Fires Understanding Objects of Governance as Expressing an Ethics of Dissensus. In: Learning Communities: International Journal of Learning in Social Contexts 15, Special Issue: Governance, pp. 52–59. Available at www.cdu.edu.au/sites/default/files/ the-northern-institute/cdu_ni_learning_communities_journal_2015.pdf, last accessed August 26, 2020.

Verran, Helen (2020a): Writing an Ethnographic Story in Working Towards Responsibly Unearthing Ontological Troubles. In: Ballestero, Andrea/Winthereik, Brit Ross (eds.): Experimenting with Ethnography. Durham: Duke University Press.

Verran, Helen (2020b): Narrating a Number and Staying with the Trouble of Value. In: Gray, Jonathan/Bounegru, Liliana (eds.): Data Journalism Handbook. Amsterdam: Amsterdam University Press.

Verran, Helen (forthcoming): Practices in Ordinary Institutional Life: Making Epistemic Work Visible. In: Bangham, Jenny et al. (eds.): (In)visible Labour: Knowledge Production in Twentieth Century Science. Rowman and Littlefield.

Verran, Helen/Christie, Michael (2007): Using/Designing Digital Technologies of Representation in Aboriginal Australian Knowledge Practices. In: Human Technology 3, 2, pp. 214–227.

Verran, Helen/Christie, Michael (2014): Postcolonial Databasing? Subverting Old Appropriations Developing New Associations. In: Leach, James/Wilson, Lee (eds.): Subversion, Conversion, Development: Diversity and the Adoption and Use of Information and Communication Technologies. Massachusetts: MIT Press, pp. 57–78.

Verran, Helen et al. (2007): Designing Digital Knowledge Management Tools with Aboriginal Australians. In: Digital Creativity 18, 3, pp. 129–142.

Wittgenstein, Ludwig (1969): On Certainty. Oxford: Basil Blackwell.

Acknowledgements

The many Yolŋu groups and individuals who have invited me to participate in their knowledge and culture work projects since 1987. My life and thinking have been transformed by these experiences. The groups of designers and skilled technicians without whose work none of this would have been possible, especially Trevor van Weeren, Juli Cathcart, and Bryce Anbins-King. My fellow CDU Ground-Up academic researchers Michael Christie and Michaela Spencer, and my academic colleagues in Berlin, Josefine Raasch and Ingmar Lippert. An engaged audience of members of the KoMMa.G collective was a great help in supporting this paper's coming to life, and I am grateful for the careful reading and helpful suggestions from Thomas Nyckel.

"A Kingdom of Bullshit." A Few Thoughts on Working on Surveillance in 21st Century Academia

Nadine Dannenberg

Jeri Hogarth: Pull yourself together. You are coming across distinctly paranoid.

Jessica Jones: Everyone keeps saying that. It's like a conspiracy.[1]

1. Prologue Pt. 1: Working on Bullshit

The initial title of my PhD project was "The cluster's mother in a kingdom of bullshit," an agglomeration quote from the tv shows I planned on analyzing with a focus on their depictions of surveillance.[2] Truth be told, I just wanted to see the phrase *kingdom of bullshit* in my title. The phrase seemed as fitting for the show it was taken from ("Mr. Robot"), as it was for the Anglocentric cultures it was applied to and the androcentric academic landscape the project would take place in: an all-encompassing, inescapable kingdom of bullshit. I got a lot of feedback on that title: "Love that bullshit in there, gives great vibes!" "How do you even analyze bullshit?" "This bullshit is quite frivolous, maybe reconsider the title." Ironically, I never cared much for the bullshit. To me that was always just a word to describe a myriad of symptoms that structure everyday life under neoliberal capitalism. The root of this whole bullshit however is the kingdom – and that is what we need to talk about.

There were two things I knew about surveillance before I started working on this project:

Whoever thinks that the surveillance state is an invention of the digital age has never lived in the countryside. (Weber 2016)

---

1   Excerpt from "Jessica Jones" (Netflix, 2015–2019), Season 01, Episode 04 "99 Friends" (2015), 00:14:02–00:14:07.

2   The cluster = a diegetical concept in "Sense8" (Netflix, 2015–2018), the mother = guiding archetypal figure in "Sense8" and "Mr. Robot" (USA Network, 2015–2019), a kingdom of bullshit = an in-show reference and marketing tool for "Mr. Robot".

Surveillance is the historical tool of patriarchy, used to control and restrict women's bodies, speech and activism.[3] (Feminist Principles of the Internet)

The first quote points to the fact that surveillance is not a distinctive problem of the data societies of the 21st century, but as old as humanity,[4] and the second one indicates that surveillance is a tool used to structure life in social ecosystems, to control and regulate social relations.[5] My first draft posed the following question as a guideline: "How are (different kinds of) surveillance techniques gendered in contemporary US-American TV shows?" The question was born out of frustration over the existing literature on surveillance in fictional films and TV shows – and on surveillance in general – which tended to maintain a blind spot when it came to the constitutive sexual component of all surveillance (and its consequent distinctive gendered dynamics). Over time, the range of TV shows included widened, and so did my focus and techniques: I jumped from Tech Noir Paranoia[6] over Romantic(izing) Comedy Stalking[7] to queer (TV) closets,[8] from original contents over transmedia extensions to fanfics, from queer reading over discourse analysis[9] to autoethnography (see Ellis 2004).

It became clear that my project – like every queer and feminist project – needed a methodological, theoretical and practical framework that considered specific materials just as much as the modes of their production, and the modes of knowledge-making in general. The TV shows became a vehicle to illustrate the complex surveillance relationship between culture, academia, power, and my Self. Over the past three years I formulated (and repeatedly reformulated) the following three propositions about surveillance, which reflect the work on my materials as much as the act of working in Western academia in the late 2010s.

---

3   From a queer standpoint I take issue with the term *women* but leave it here as a synonym for femininity (in all shapes and forms). This goes for all bodies, speeches and activisms that challenge patriarchal institutions in one way or another of course.
4   See Reichardt (2016) for a compact overview.
5   This is a basic principle for surveillance scholars, in the tradition of Michel Foucault (see Hier/Greenberg 2007).
6   The literature on Film Noir's obsession with paranoia is quite extensive, as are feminist and queer takes on the genres. See for example Kaplan (1978), or Dyer (1977).
7   Nicol (2006) traces this trend that is currently taken under deconstruction in TV shows like "Crazy Ex-Girlfriend" (The CW, 2015–2019) or "Jane the Virgin" (The CW, 2014–2019).
8   See Sedgwick (1990) for the concept of the "closet" in queer (literary) theory, and Joyrich (2001) for its adaptation onto TV.
9   In the tradition of British Cultural Studies, following Stuart Hall and the CCCS.

2. Proposition 1: It's About (Damn) Time (We Start Talking About the Kingdom)

> When you expose a problem you pose a problem. It might then be assumed that the problem would go away if you would just stop talking about it or if you went away. (Ahmed 2017: 38)

Like most issues analyzed in academia (and elsewhere) surveillance is often contextualized as a technique of governance in generalized terms.[10] But it has also been a longstanding issue for feminist and queer scholars, although in different terms. Three of the main foci of feminist thinking have always been the gendered dichotomy of the public and the private, control and care, and power and resistance.[11] Queer Theory builds on this tradition and widens the scope onto processes of (hetero)normativization, subjectivization, and the pleasure(s) of power.[12] Surveillance – in whatever form – relies on these dichotomies and processes and shapes them.

The fight about the right to, and the protection of, privacy for example, becomes much more complex when you take into consideration that *the private* has been an inherently sexualized, and rather violent realm for many subjects since at least the 18th century – precisely because it was (and is) deemed a *private space*, and thereby already under a questionable *protection*.[13] In order to critically analyze privacy (the heart of current debates about surveillance) it needs to be historicized in terms of patriarchal power, in order to get a more nuanced picture of the effects and implications of an androcentric, heteronormative culture without repeating patronizing patterns that uphold inequal social structures.[14] With this demand to politicize scientific research, feminist and queer perspectives complicate research processes, but the complication is inevitable because the world is complicated. This realization was one of the main reasons for the turn to *interdisciplinarity* in academic spaces since the 1970s, and it was also the mantra for our program.[15] But complication (and complexity) demands time and resources –

---

10   See David Lyon's model of "social sorting" (2003), or Haggerty/Ericson (2000).
11   Karin Hausen outlined the historical dimension of these dichotomies in her definitive essay "Die Polarisierung der Geschlechtscharaktere" (1976). Kortendiek et al. (2018) provide an overview of feminist theorizing.
12   A quick and easy introductory read would be Jagose (1996).
13   To get an idea of the complex relationship of surveillance and the sexualized right to privacy see Berlant/Warner (1998). Also: watch "Jessica Jones" (Netflix, 2015–2019) and "Orange is the New Black" (Netflix, 2013–2019) for feminist takes on the (barely- to nonexistent) right to privacy for women in patriarchal Western societies of the 21st century.
14   Some of these blind spots in Surveillance Studies were recently assembled (e.g. in Dubrofsky/Magnet 2015).
15   "The need for this kind of interdisciplinary reflection results from the complexity of human-machine-configurations." (See Gendered Configurations of Humans and Machines)

two things contemporary fast academia (and western societies in general) struggle with.[16]

Doing feminist and queer research doesn't mean to look at *men* and *women* in an essentialist definition and look for the differences. It means to ask what the terms *men* and *women*, *masculine* and *feminine* even mean, what (and whom) they include and exclude, what consequences they carry, and why they exist in such a dualistic manner in the first place. It means looking at, and questioning, existing power structures – in your project but also in your environment at large. It's not a framework you can apply, nor a method. It's a mind-set, a way of being in the world.[17] It means taking up a decidedly political position that is conscious of one's own social responsibility and at unease with the existing status quo of an inherently unequal society. It is a position that is rarely and barely taught in schools, and that is eyed very suspiciously, precisely because it challenges the status quo. It is, as Sara Ahmed has pointedly noted, an inherently dangerous position because it means to be "*perceived* as dangerous" (Ahmed 2017: 130). It's huge. And it takes time to grasp that dimension. And yet, it's necessary because the status quo won't change freely.

3. Proposition 2: It's About Discipline(s)

[I]t is [not] easy to cross disciplinary boundaries or [to expect] that eventually they would disappear and disciplines merge. As in "real life" one needs visas and the right passport in order to cross borders. (Hark 2007: 17)

At one of our first lectures, the guest professor told us that interdisciplinary work demands first a core knowledge of one's own discipline; a specific expertise that one brings to the table. This notion lingered, even as we discussed how hindering this notion actually is; and not just within our program. The pressure to discipline ourselves is omnipresent, because surveillance is omnipresent: watch your steps, behave yourself, always carry your passport with you.[18]

According to poststructuralist and surveillance studies pioneer Michel Foucault, disciplinarity is a technique of power in the modern nation-state that relies upon normativization, tradition, convention, and routine to produce experts and institutions that surveil and guarantee the existent structures of

---

16   Gill (2013) outlined the term "fast academia."
17   This notion has been outlined by feminist and queer thinkers for a very long time, see Firestone (1970), hooks (1984), or more recently Ahmed (2017).
18   Here and now, in Germany in April 2020, this holds true in a metaphorical sense (passport = academic certificate) but of also in a very literal sense, considering the rights and benefits that a German passport offers (to access any form of health care to name just one).

society.[19] In academia, disciplines define themselves through a very rigid framework of normative curricula and methodological lines; exclusionary strategies to secure a feeling of homogeneity among their members. The problem is that these notions of homogeneity, this question of what belongs to the frame of a certain discipline and what does not, is always already biased through the discursive framework of the hegemonic culture. Meaning: The disciplines themselves are infused with patriarchal, heteronormative, colonial bullshit because for centuries the people who created theories, methods, and analytical frameworks were mostly straight, white, able-bodied cismen from the middle- to upper-classes.[20]

Taking up a feminist perspective means by definition to question and cross the borders of disciplines and to go against your own home, so to speak, because it means to admit that the academy, in its existent form, is in and of itself heavily involved in the execution of power. Those of us who work in the fully normalized precarious conditions of fast academia physically feel that execution every day while we wander through an environment where the main leitmotif has always been the war on resources, funding, and societal recognition.[21] The pressure to be disciplined, to not act up but keep up (with the ever-increasing pace of knowledge production) is high, the wine barely enough to numb the existential dread. There's never enough time, and always too much at stake to risk going wild. Fear is the motor of paranoia.

4. Proposition 3: It's About (Who To) Trust.

We're all living in each other's paranoia.[22]

As I'm writing this, Germany is on partial lockdown due to the Sars-CoV2 pandemic. The government has instructed people to stay home and social distance, police and security control and regulate access to public space. Neighbors watch each other to make sure everybody follows the rules. Vendors make sure nobody buys more than one pack of toilet paper. German free TV airs video conferences with celebrities at home as entertainment. The German phone company Telekom handed a pack of anonymized user data to the Robert Koch Institute for research purposes. In the ad-hoc conversion to digital work from home, cybersecurity has been a secondary issue. Collective work from home undermines every notion of a work-life balance. We wash

---

19   The best outline of this can be found in Foucault (1977).
20   See the extensive feminist research on this history in Scott (1986), over Keller (1985), to Halberstam's outline of "Low Theory" (2011).
21   Hark (2007) pointedly explained this setting.
22   Reference from "Mr. Robot", 2015, Season 01, Episode 08, 00:25:35.

our hands every hour and make sure not to touch our faces. As the fear, boredom, and misinformation grow, surveillance (of ourselves and others) intensifies and becomes even more normalized; top-down as well as bottom-up, in acts of care as well as of control.

I started writing this essay in January 2020 and now I'm trying to figure out a way to finish it. My mind is a blur, oversaturated by information on the current situation and the ways people are dealing with it. We're waiting for (and manically discuss) the day when *things go back to normal* (Hoben 2020). All I can think about is how *normal* wasn't so great to begin with.[23] *Normal* was people coming into work sick because they feared for their jobs. *Normal* was hugely underpaid and overworked people in the (vastly feminized) health and care sectors. *Normal* was a broad lack of hygiene. *Normal* was restricted access to public places at different times of the day for a huge part of society (women, PoC, teenagers and children, disabled people, Trans* people, to name just a few). *Normal* was (and still is) the synonym for a kingdom of bullshit. So let's finish this piece off with an inspirational quote:

Proposition 1: It's About (Damn) Time (We Start Talking About the Kingdom).

---

23   Shoutout to Adorno who had the same issue in an interview with "Der Spiegel" in 1969.

References

Ahmed, Sara (2017): Living a Feminist Life. Durham/London: Duke.

Berlant, Lauren/Warner, Michael (1998): Sex in Public. In: Critical Inquiry 24, 2, pp. 547–566.

Der Spiegel (1969): Keine Angst vor dem Elfenbeinturm. Spiegel-Gespräch mit dem Frankfurter Sozialphilosophen Professor Theodor W. Adorno. In: Der Spiegel 19, pp. 205–209.

Dubrofsky, Rachel E./Magnet, Shoshana Amielle M. (eds.) (2015): Feminist Surveillance Studies. Durham/London: Duke.

Dyer, Richard (1977): Homosexuality and Film Noir. In: Jump Cut 16, pp. 18–21.

Ellis, Carolyn (2004): The Ethnographic I: A Methodological Novel About Autoethnography. Walnut Creek: AltaMira Press.

Feminist Principles of the Internet: Privacy and Data. Available at https://feministinternet.org/en/principle/privacy-data, last accessed August 14, 2020.

Firestone, Shulamith (1983) [1970]: The Dialectic of Sex: The Case of Feminist Revolution. New York: Farrar, Straus and Giroux.

Foucault, Michel (1977) [1975]: Discipline and Punish: The Birth of the Prison. New York: Vintage Books.

Fox Keller, Evelyn (1985): Reflections on Gender and Science. New Haven: Yale University Press.

Gendered Configurations of Humans and Machines (KoMMa.G): Interdisciplinary Analyses of Technology: Program: Research Focus and Transdisciplinary Perspectives. Available at https://www.tu-braunschweig.de/en/kommag/programm, last accessed August 14, 2020.

Gill, Rosalind (2015): Breaking the Silence: The Hidden Injuries of Neo-Liberal Academia. In: Gill, Rosalind/Ryan-Flood, Róisín (eds.): Secrecy and Silence in the Research Process: Feminist Reflections. New York: Routledge, pp. 228–244.

Haggerty, David/Ericson, Richard V. (2000): The Surveillant Assemblage. In: British Journal of Sociology 51, 4, pp. 605–622.

Halberstam, J. Jack (2011): The Queer Art of Failure. Durham/London: Duke.

Hark, Sabine (2007): Magical Sign: On the Politics of Inter- and Transdisciplinarity. In: Graduate Journal of Social Science 4, Special Issue 2, pp. 11–23.

Hier, Sean P./Greenberg, Josh (2013): The Surveillance Studies Reader. Berkshire: McGraw-Hill.

Hoben, Anna (2020): Die Sehnsucht nach Normalität in der Schuhschachtel. SZOnline. Available at https://www.sueddeutsche.de/muenchen/coronavirus-muenchen-sehnsucht-normalitaet-1.4859358, last accessed August 14, 2020.

hooks, bell (1984): Feminist Theory: From Margin to Center. Boston: South End Press.

Jagose, Annamarie (1996): Queer Theory. New York: New York University Press.

Joyrich, Lynne (2001): Epistemology of the Console. In: Davis, Glynn/Needham, Gary (eds.): Queer TV: Theories, Histories, Politics. London: Routledge, pp. 15–47.

Kaplan, E. Ann (1978): Women in Film Noir. London: bfi Publishing.

Kortendiek, Beate et al. (eds.) (2018): Handbuch Interdisziplinäre Geschlechterforschung. Wiesbaden: Springer VS.

Lyon, David (ed.) (2003): Surveillance as Social Sorting. London/New York: Routledge.

Nicol, Bran (2006): Stalking. London: Reaktion Books.

Reichardt, Sven (2016): Introduction: Histor(ies) of Surveillance. In: Geschichte und Gesellschaft 42, 1: Surveillance Studies, pp. 5–33.

Scott, Joan W. (1986): Gender – A Useful Category of Historical Analysis. In: The American Historical Review 91, 5, pp. 1053–1075.

Sedgwick, Eve K. (1990): Epistemology of the Closet. Berkeley/Los Angeles: University of California Press.

Weber, Ute (2016): Tweet, March 28, 2016. Available at https://twitter.com/Ute Weber/status/714409765028433920, last accessed August 14, 2020.

New Transcultural Perspectives on Gender Analysis in STEM[1]: Chinese and Indian Female Doctoral Researchers in Computer Science in Germany

Katharina Losch

1. Introduction

A traditional focus on culture that treats culture as limited to a certain (geographical) area is still widespread in research on gender relations in STEM fields, e.g. computer science.[2] Many studies with such a traditional concept of culture have arrived at the conclusion that the masculine image of computer science remains stable (Mellström 2009: 888). The masculine image of computer science derives from a strong association of that discipline with technology that is personified in the *nerd* stereotype (Schinzel 2014: 141). Following such a traditional approach to culture in research makes discovering challenges to traditional views of a masculine computer science difficult. In contrast to that, in this article I present the potential of a transcultural perspective on gender analysis in STEM, taking the example of my doctoral project about Chinese and Indian doctoral researchers in computer science in Germany. In order to do so, first of all, I am going to clarify the meanings of the *traditional concept of culture* and the *transcultural concept* of culture. After highlighting a transcultural perspective based on the example of my doctoral project, I will mention some methodological issues that such a research approach leads to. At the end of this article, a short conclusion summarizes the most important arguments for a new transcultural perspective on gender analysis in computer science that can be extended to other STEM fields with similar gender problematics.

---

1   STEM refers to Science, Technology, Engineering and Mathematics.
2   I especially want to thank Prof. Dr. Helene Götschel and Jan Büssers who reviewed my article and gave valuable comments.

2. Traditional Concept of Culture

According to the traditional concept of culture, certain cultural beliefs and practices are ascribed to particular, e.g. geographical, national, or ethnic, areas. The "meaning of culture *with regards to content*"[3] (Welsch 2010: 39) and the "*extensional* meaning of culture" (ibid.) are interlinked. This thinking is quite prevalent in modern society (speaking generally about the living together of people beyond (geographical) borders). Additionally, the extensional meaning of culture is considered the most important one. Cultures are also seen as internally homogeneous and exclusive towards influences from the *outside* (ibid.: 39–40). Culture is considered to be something static that cannot be changed (Saal 2014: 22). Charles Tilly points out that clear-cut categorizations can stabilize power relations, e.g. between different genders (Tilly 1998). Deeply rooted beliefs in many *Western* countries of a masculine computer science (Mellström 2009) can be explained by such underlying power relations. By keeping these beliefs alive, the prestigious working sector of computer science continues to be dominated by men, while women usually don't feel attracted to this field (Etzkowitz et al. 2008: 404). It's striking that knowledge of a women-friendly image of computer science in other non-Western countries, e.g. in India (Varma 2009), doesn't open a global discourse that would have been able to question those gendered beliefs. Instead, this knowledge is somehow ignored in Western societies. Acknowledging that other non-Western countries have possibly more gender equality than one's own country might affect one's global power status (Rommelspacher 2008: 198). Holding on to the belief of a masculine image of computer science in our society does not, therefore, only reproduce *male dominance* (Bourdieu 2013) but also the performance of *cultural dominance* towards non-Western knowledge. Especially nowadays, power relations are mostly symbolic and covert, embedded in daily routine and, hence, not directly visible to us (Kron/Reddig 2011: 463). Additionally, traditional categories serve as protection from unknown risks that might cause fear (Bauman 1991: 252). This way, cultural categories that imply power relations are constantly reproduced.

3. Transcultural Concept

In the center of the transcultural concept is the content-based meaning of culture. This meaning is characterized by a mixing of cultural influences that

---

3   This quotation and the following one are translations of the original German text.

transcend (geographical) boundaries. Culture is understood as heterogeneous and inclusive towards different cultural influences from *outside* and this understanding is of growing importance in present (global) societies (Welsch 2010: 42). Transculturality does not only influence society on a macro level but also the individual. Nowadays, most people have several cultural origins or connections. This way, they can combine elements of different cultural origin (ibid.: 45–46). The traditional concept of culture reflects an artificial, rather than a real, description of *living* societies. Therefore, taking a transcultural perspective instead of the traditional understanding of culture offers new creative and empowering possibilities, questioning traditional power relations in society (Welsch 2010: 48). By considering culture fluid (Saal 2014: 22) moments of resistance to gender hierarchies (and cultural dominance) can be identified. At the same time, the researcher conducting research in a specific cultural setting has to be sensitive to existing forms of domination that are still widespread in society (see above).

4. New Transcultural Perspectives – The Example of My Doctoral Project

Now I come to the potential of a transcultural perspective on gender analysis in STEM, using the example of my doctoral research on Chinese and Indian female doctoral researchers in computer science in Germany. In India especially, there is a women-friendly image of computer science (Varma 2009) that supports women in pursuing a career in such a booming working sector (ibid.: 206). The percentage of women in computer science in India is more than 40% (Government of India 2018). In contrast, the percentage of women in computer science in Germany is about 23% (Bitkom 2018). In China as well, computer science promises good job opportunities for women (Zhang/Lo 2010: 396), even though traditionally it's seen as a profession for men (Li/Kirkup 2007). The ratio of women in computer science in China is 32%, according to China's university and college admission system, which is slightly higher than the German one (CUCAS 2020).

The rising internationalization of higher education (Bauschke-Urban 2011) lead me to investigate the mobility of Chinese and Indian women into computer science in Germany, and through this to the cultural transmission of more woman-friendly understandings of computer science from China/India to Germany. The focus of my research is on the doctorate as a door towards academia, where knowledge about science is negotiated (Engler 2004). This leads to my research question of *how can female doctoral researchers from China and India contribute to questioning a masculine image of computer science in Germany*? An important connected question is, how do these women find their way into a doctorate in computer science in Germany? Both experiences in their country of origin and experiences in the German context are taken into account. Since research is still scarce in that field, a qualitative study is at the center of the analysis. However, there are several methodological issues that I have to consider while following a transcultural research approach. In the following section, I mention a few and how I address them.

5. Methodological Issues

Firstly, besides the analytical focus on the cultural image of women in computer science, the cultural understanding around women following an academic career beyond the classical study path at all has to be considered as well. While in India computer science is considered suitable for women, climbing the academic ladder in higher education might cause problems due to a *patrifocal order*[4] that ascribes household tasks to the woman (Gupta 2012: 154–155). In China as well, doing a PhD conflicts with traditional gender roles (Brokate/Günther 2019: 13). However, when culture is understood as static it cannot really grasp *movements* in society, in this case, the decision of Chinese and Indian women to do a PhD in computer science in Germany. Therefore, methodologically, attention has to be paid to the influences of different life-worlds (Pfaff-Czarnecka 2013), e.g. family, school, university, or earlier experiences abroad, that impact in different ways on those women's unique pathways. Another aspect that has to be considered is that gender might be influenced by other social categories, such as social class or ethnicity. Despite a focus on gender, my analysis is sensitive to intersectionality (Winker 2012).

Against the background of a new and culturally complex field, I decided on qualitative interviews as the primary method of data collection, giving access to necessary insights through the principle of openness (Hopf 2012: 350). Bourdieu's theory, and particularly his concepts of *habitus* and *social field* (Bourdieu/Wacquant 2012) play a crucial role in the theoretical foundation of the research. These analytical tools allow me to analyze the attitudes of the researched group that reflect their (potentially more open) image of computer science.

---

4   Indian *patrifocal order* refers to a male privilege that is expressed in family in kindship ties (Gupta 2012: 154).

6. Conclusion

This article aimed to show the potential of a transcultural perspective on gender analysis in STEM. For this purpose, I first defined the meaning of a transcultural understanding in contrast to the traditional concept of cultural and then related it to my doctoral project about Chinese and Indian female doctoral researchers in computer science in Germany. Since the transcultural approach treats culture as something vivid and fluid that finds itself in constant transformation, a masculine image of STEM, here specifically computer science, no longer appears to be stable. Instead, this broader view of culture sensitizes the analytical eye to detect settings where transformation is taking place. Mobility that transcends geographical boundaries, and thus brings different understandings to the country of immigration, is maybe the most evident example. In this context, the researched group in my doctoral project, female doctoral researchers from China and India, potentially bring more women-friendly images on women in computer science to Germany. However, there are many more research settings to be explored – also within one country – since the *movements* of culture aren't restricted to (geographical) boundaries that are nothing but socially constructed.

References

Bauman, Zygmunt (1991): Modernity and Ambivalence. Cambridge: Polity Press.

Bauschke-Urban, Carola (2011): Mobile Wissenschaftlerinnen: Transnationale Verortungen und biographische Perspektiven. In: Gender – Zeitschrift für Geschlecht, Kultur und Gesellschaft 3, 1, pp. 81–98.

Bitkom (2018): Informatik-Hörsäle werden langsam weiblicher. Available at https://www.bitkom.org/Presse/Presseinformation/Informatik-Hoersaele-werden-langsam-weiblicher.html, last accessed April 13, 2020.

Bourdieu, Pierre/Waquant, Loïc J.D. (2012): Reflexive Anthropologie. Frankfurt am Main: Suhrkamp.

Bourdieu, Pierre (2013): Die männliche Herrschaft. Frankfurt am Main: Suhrkamp.

Brokate, Jana/Günther, Susanne (2017): China: Daten & Analysen zum Hochschul- und Wissenschaftsstandort. Bonn: DAAD, pp. 1–47.

CUCAS (2020): Study Software Engineering in China. Available at https://www.cucas.cn/studyinchina/programs/professional/Software_Engineering_73.html, last accessed April 13, 2020.

Engler, Steffanie (2004): Von klugen Köpfen und Genies: Zum Selbstverständnis von Professoren. In: Ebrecht, Jörg/Hillebrand, Frank (eds.): Bourdieus Theorie der Praxis: Erklärungskraft, Anwendung, Perspektiven. Wiesbaden: VS Verlag für Sozialwissenschaften, pp. 153–169.

Etzkowitz, Henry et al. (2008): The Coming Gender Revolution in Science. In: Hackett, Edward J. et al. (eds.): The Handbook of Science and Technology Studies. Cambridge, Massachusetts/London, England: The MIT Press, pp. 403–428.

Government of India (2018): All India Survey on Higher Education 2017-18. Available at https://epsiindia.org/wp-content/uploads/2019/02/AISHE-2017-18.pdf, last accessed September 4, 2020.

Gupta, Namrata (2012): Women Undergraduates in Engineering Education in India: A Study of Growing Participation. In: Gender, Technology and Development 16, 2, pp. 153–176.

Hopf, Christel (2012): Qualitative Interviews – ein Überblick. In: Flick, Uwe et al. (eds.): Qualitative Forschung: Ein Handbuch. Reinbek bei Heimburg: Rowohlt, pp. 349–359.

Kron, Thomas/Reddig, Melanie (2011): Zygmunt Bauman: Die ambivalente Verfassung moderner und postmoderner Kultur. In: Moebius, Stephan/Quadflieg, Dirk (eds.): Kultur: Theorien der Gegenwart. Wiesbaden: VS Verlag für Sozialwissenschaften, pp. 452–466.

Li, Nai/Kirkup, Gill (2007): Gender and Cultural Differences in Internet Use: A Case Study of China and the UK. In: Computer & Education 48, 2, pp. 301–317.

Mellström, Ulf (2009): The Intersection of Gender, Race and Cultural Boundaries, or Why is Computer Science in Malaysia Dominated by Women? In: Social Studies of Science 39, 6, pp. 885–907.

Pfaff-Czarnecka, Joanna (2013): Multiple Belonging and the Challenges to Biographic Navigation. In: MMG Working Papers 13, 5, pp. 1–32.

Rommelspacher, Birgit (2008): Hegemonial Femininity. In: Grzinic, Marina/Reitsamer, Rosa (eds.): New Feminism: Worlds of Feminism, Queer and Networking Conditions. Wien: Löcker, pp. 192–199.

Saal, Britta (2014): Kultur in Bewegung: Zur Begrifflichkeit von Transkulturalität. In: Mae, Michiko/Saal, Britta (eds.): Transkulturelle Genderforschung: Ein Studienbuch zum Verhältnis von Kultur und Geschlecht. Wiesbaden: VS Verlag für Sozialwissenschaften, pp. 21–47.

Schinzel, Britta (2014): Studierende der Informatik sprechen über ihre Weltbilder: Verantwortung, Vielfalt und Geschlecht. In: Bittner, Peter et al. (eds.): Gesellschaftliche Verantwortung in der digital vernetzten Welt. Berlin: Lit, pp. 141–153.

Tilly, Charles (1998): Durable Inequality. Berkeley: University of California Press.

Varma, Roli (2009): Exposure, Training, and Environment: Women's Participation in Computing Education in the United States and India. In: Journal of Women and Minorities in Science and Engineering 15, 3, pp. 205–222.

Welsch, Wolfgang (2010): Was ist eigentlich Transkultur? In: Darowska, Lucyna et al. (eds.): Hochschule als transkultureller Raum? Kultur, Bildung und Differenz in der Universität. Bielefeld: Transcript, pp. 39–66.

Winker, Gabriele (2012): Intersektionalität als Gesellschaftskritik. In: Widersprüche 32, 126, pp. 13–26.

Zhang, Ming/Lo, Virginia M. (2010): Undergraduate Computer Science Education in China. In: SIGCSE '10: Proceedings of the 41st ACM Technical Symposium on Computer Science Education, pp. 396–400. Available at https://doi.org/10.1145/1734263.1734401, last accessed April 14, 2020.

On the Role of the Script in Posthuman Educational Theatre

Hannes Leuschner and Imme Petersen

1. Introduction

When different disciplines conduct performance studies, staging is usually differentiated from performance, with the latter being valued as the unique moment of physical co-presence of actors and audience (comp. Fischer-Lichte/Roselt 2001: 239). Less visible, there is a third level of the play that precedes its staging and performance: the text or the script. In the tradition of European theatre, great importance has been attached to the script and during the formation of theatres studies in the beginning of the 20th century, the dominant role of the script was extensively discussed in terms of its primacy in relation to the performance (see Fischer-Lichte/Roselt 2001; for the performance of musical compositions Eikels 2016). Meanwhile, the performativity of the text itself tends to be overlooked in contemporary performance studies. In this paper, we therefore want to discuss the agency of script itself. Elaborating on two examples from the realm of education, we will explore the performativity of scripts, transported and transformed by different media of translation (paper, power point, internet, audio, audiovisual) and their relation to the human actor on the social stage. We thereby follow Goffman's (1959) approach of understanding everyday life as a kind of social play. Furthermore, we want to extend William Shakespeare's famous lines "All the world's a stage / And all the men and women merely players"[1] to non-human actors. Both empirical examples refer to teaching and learning processes, but they are embedded in two very different contexts: The first example given is part of an ethnographic study conducted in a lecture on automotive engineering during winter semester 2018/2019 at a department of mechanical engineering at a technical university in northern Germany. The second example refers to the participation in a 10-day-class of Vipassana meditation in the tradition of the Buddhist teacher S.N. Goenka, held in a rented facility in southwestern Germany over the turn of the year 2018/2019. Even though the

---

1   Jaques in "As you like it", act II, scene VII.

ethnographic settings seem extremely different, we will argue that both examples are class performances that are oriented and directed by the faithfulness to the original script. In a brief discussion we want to reflect on these observations and discuss them in the light of both an affirmative technological and a critical posthumanist approach (Ferrando 2018).

2. First Example: University Lecture on the Fundamentals of Automotive Engineering

Mechanical engineering is a popular study program at German universities with tens of thousands of students starting every year. I carried out an ethnographic study on higher education at a large technical university in the northwest of Germany, in the bachelor program of mechanical engineering in the winter semester 2018/2019. During that semester, 1.494 students were enrolled, of which 276 were in their first year[2]. I used participatory observation in different lectures and classes and conducted interviews with the lecturer before and after my observation period. One of the chosen lectures was the introductory lecture "The fundamentals of automotive engineering."

As it is a compulsory lecture for bachelor students, it is regularly attended by about 160 students, once a week for 1,5 hours during the semester. Taking place in an auditorium building at the main campus, the students enter a classical lecture hall with eight ascending sequences of seats and 24 seats per row. The seats and tables are fold-up, narrow, and wooden. They are permanently mounted, often leading to creaky noises. In the middle of the rows of seats, a stepped aisle leads down to an open space at the ground level, which is furnished by a table in front of a blackboard and a screen for the digital beamer to the right of the blackboard. The configuration of the space enables a good view of the area at ground level, which is reserved for the lecturer, from all seats. At the ground level, the lecturer performs and the seated students, united as an audience, follow the performance taking place downstairs. I will, therefore, refer to those sections of the room as performance space and audience space.

It is Monday morning at 9:45 a.m. Mr. Schmidt, the professor's assistant, enters the room and sets up a laptop on the table in the performance space. He looks like a young man in his early thirties with dark hair and designer stubble, wearing a casual sweatshirt and jeans. The lecture starts when the lecturer, Professor Garbo, shows up. He is usually a few minutes behind the official schedule. The waiting time is filled by Mr. Schmidt, who shows

---

2   The information is given on the university homepage, data source not shown due to data
     anonymization.

videos. They are either US commercials full of zippy sports cars and race drivers, or video clips created by the German magazine "Automotor und Sport" (automotive engines and sport) explaining engineering-related topics in an easy and understandable way. While a video is running, Prof. Garbo enters the performance space like a theatre stage, by using one of the two doors next to the blackboard. Prof. Garbo is physically small, white-haired, and well-groomed. Every Monday he wears black or grey suits, white shirts with cufflinks or a turtleneck pullover, ties or stylish braces, and horn-rimmed glasses. Prof. Garbo is just a step away from retirement, while Mr. Schmidt is pursuing his career at the institute of automotive engineering. One of his tasks at the institute is assisting with Prof. Garbo's introductory lecture; he also conducts the associated tutorial.

Before Prof. Garbo begins, Mr. Schmidt hands him the portable micro-phone which Prof. Garbo places behind his ear. The video has already ended, and the first slide of the power point presentation is on the screen. The presentation runs steadily and Prof. Garbo starts straightforwardly presenting the slides, which consist of notes, formulas, graphs, and figures. To perform the prepared slides, Prof. Garbo stays on the right-hand side of the screen. His body is laterally rotated towards the screen and he holds a pointer in his right hand. While he is reading and talking, he focuses the red pointer light on the notes or figures he is talking about.

The content of the presented slides, in particular the formulas, graphs, and figures, is taken from a script that is handed out to the students in the first week of the semester. Prof. Garbo has given the lecture for 20 years, and he has re-used his script over and over again. However, this semester he has distributed a new edition of the previous script, because he is currently pre-paring a book on the foundations of automotive engineering and he built up the new edition of the script from the book manuscript. He told me in our interview after the period of participatory observation that the general ap-proach for his manuscript and his script is to include all the relevant basic knowledge that students and engineers would need to work in practice. That is why it aims at combining existing knowledge on mechanics, thermody-namics, or vibration theory with current examples of application. According to Prof. Garbo, the applications are the part of the script that permanently develops and changes, whereas the foundations are sound knowledge that the students usually should have gained at an earlier point in their studies. "When something new, something interesting in automotive engineering is brought into the world, these new ideas are always based on the foundations, every time," explained Prof. Garbo his deep conviction behind his thinking, and continued: "Having a new idea accidentally would be quite an accident. Any such idea must always be explainable through the fundamentals."

Prof. Garbo is convinced that improvement and progress in application must always be explainable by the fundamentals. That is why the script is organized to be of benefit later on in practice. Prof. Garbo: "Knowledge should not disappear in the drawer, but should rather be still in use after 20 years of their [the students'] professional life. That is how I do it in the subject of thermodynamics today, I open my scripts from those days and look something up."

But this does not mean that the content of the script is fixed or unchangeable. Prof. Garbo revises the script, if necessary due to new developments in the applications he wants to depict. Together with his assistant, they usually evaluate the script before the lecture starts and decide if they want to improve it. Three to four days before each lecture, Prof. Garbo and Mr. Schmidt meet again to go through the slides. "I update my slides in terms of two criteria: topicality and clarity," Prof. Garbo said. As most of the students coming into his lecture would be more or less unfamiliar with automotive engineering (some would not even have a driver license), Prof. Garbo wants to catch their attention during the lecture through clear and high-quality slides including attractive design and animations. Even during the lecture, Prof. Garbo has an eye out for possible slide improvements; at times he directly addresses his assistant during his presentation and gives him hints of how to revise terms or figures, or even little details regarding layout.

These instructions for improvements give the impression that Prof. Garbo is ultimately responsible for the slides and the script, but it is Mr. Schmidt who explains to the students how to use the script and how the script and the slides fit together. Due to his initiative, the slides are provided to the students as an online version, in addition to the longer and more extensive printed version of the script. The online version contains the exact content of the slides, but the slides' notes are formulated into more explanatory sentences. During the lecture, I could observe that a few students had a laptop in front of them with the online version running; nearly all others had the print version opened up before them on the desks. When Prof. Garbo had started with a new chapter, the rustling of pages filled the lecture hall. Nearly no one took individual notes, neither in the script, nor on a notebook. Hence, it seems as if Prof. Garbo was right and the script would answer all open questions and include all the required knowledge. In particular, the students request the knowledge that is necessary to pass the exam at the end of the semester. Mr. Schmidt explained to me in our interview that he usually provides both script versions to support the students in their exam preparation: "I make both script versions available to them, so that they are able to pick a little bit which parts of the script are really relevant for the exam." By comparing both script versions, they can see what was presented in the lecture and what is probably additional information.

The printed script, once written and continuously adapted and optimized, represents the body of knowledge that seems necessary to succeed in automotive engineering, as a student passing the exam or as a professional engineer working in the field. The online script is a condensed version of the printed one, highlighting and accentuating the most important knowledge regarding exams (and as well as regarding application). Therefore, the script could be orally presented by a different person than the one who wrote it. And in fact, this is common in the department of mechanical engineering at the researched university: Once an introductory lecture is handed over to the next person, the script and/or slides are usually handed over, too. The newly appointed lecturers have to become acquainted with the existing script and slides that were not of their own composition. Normally, professors have the power to change or discard the inherited script, but I got to know cases in which post-docs were not allowed to revise the existing script, or only in consultation with the head of the department.

3. Second Example: Vipassana Course in the Tradition of S.N. Goenka

Satya Naravan Goenka was born in 1924 in Burma (today Myanmar) and died recently in 2013. Raised in a Hindu family, he initially was introduced to the Buddhist Vipassana tradition while seeking help for strong migraine attacks, from which he suffered while leading a life as a successful business-man. He learned the Vipassana meditation technique by the influential Burmese teacher Sayagyi U Ba Khin by whom he was authorized to teach in 1969. Goenka left his business to his family and started giving courses in India. One of the first assistant teachers appointed by him was William Hart, who describes the meditation in the lines of Buddha's meditation tradition, in accordance with other followers: "Certainly, the technique agrees with the instructions of the Buddha on meditation, with the simplest, most literal meaning of his words" (Hart 2019 [1982]: 19). This claim on original purity brings to mind the protestant principle of *sola scriptura*, which means that the holy message is sufficiently transmitted by the Bible and does not need any addition. The difference is that in Christianity there is a scripture canon-ized as a fundament, while the script behind Goenka's script refers to words spoken hundreds of years before having been written down for the first time. Due to these circumstances, Vipassana still receives criticism for referring to a consensual and referenceable fundament that does not exist as such[3].

From India, Vipassana Meditation as taught by S.N. Goenka spread all over the world. Today, there are around 350 locations in nearly 100 countries where you can participate in a standardized course. All of these courses are

---

3   Comp. the extended discussion in http://www.buddha-heute.de/blog/die-tradition-des-vipa ssana-von-s-n-goenka-und-ihre-reine-technik-des-buddha/.

ten days long, they are free of charge, and do not require any prior meditation experience. Vipassana, following the glossary in "The Art of Living" (Hart 2019: 215), means "Introspection, insight that totally purifies the mind. Specifically, insight into the impermanent nature of mind and body" (ibid.). Under the same entry, "Vipassana-bhavana" is described as "the systematic development of insight through the meditation technique of observing the reality of oneself by observing sensations within the body" (ibid). Practically, that means: "Move your attention systematically from head to feet and from feet to head, observing in order each and every part of the body by feeling all the sensations that you come across. Observe objectively; that is, remain equanimous with all the sensations that you experience, whether pleasant, unpleasant or neutral, by appreciating their impermanent nature. Keep your attention moving [...]." This information about the technique is taken from the international organization's website[4]. The idea behind this practice is explained on the website as well as in the above-cited book: Living unawakened in the Buddhist sense means that you're permanently entangling yourself to the world by emotional reactions. Thereby you condition yourself to react to certain experiences in certain ways, binding yourself to illusional patterns. These patterns are understood by Goenka as a mind/matter combination: What you have in your mind, you can experience as a sensation in your body. By observing these sensations with equanimity, you can eradicate these old conditions, called *sankhara*. The idea seems as simple as it is technical. Visualizing the principle, I had to think of Pacman: Like Pacman is eating all the dots, you have to *sweep away* all the old *sankhara* by scanning your body.

I have known of these Vipassana courses, which are something of a must do in the German alternative milieu, long before I eventually registered for a course over the turn of the year in 2018/2019. I did some, but not too much, research before by studying the webpage, reading the standard introduction by Wilhelm Hart (already cited above) and Andreas Altmann's (2013) autobiographic descriptions of his Vipassana experiences. Nevertheless, I arrived at the southwestern German community where the course was being held in a facility rented from a Rosicrucian church, knowing – at least for the beginner that I was – all there was to know about how the course would function: A leaflet given to the arriving participants gave the same information you find on the website, and a spoken introduction repeated it again before *noble silence* began. *Noble silence* is one of the basic rules during the course and means not talking at all (with minor exceptions mentioned below). It includes avoiding any non-verbal communication as well, as far as possible. Other important rules are the *acceptance of the teacher and the technique* without questioning it; abstaining from any intoxicants (including tobacco, but ex-

---

4   Comp. https://www.dhamma.org/en/osguide.

cluding coffee), any distraction by listening to music, reading, or writing (books and multimedia devices were kept by the staff) and segregation of women and men in order to avoid (nota bene: hetero-)sexual temptation[5]. Following these and more rules[6] was facilitated by the closed environment and its algorithmic[7] preparation. Warning tape in red and white closed off the ways leading from the small park behind the facility to the surrounding area. The men had to cross this park to access the eating hall in another building, while the women's meals were served elsewhere. Between altogether more than ten hours of seated meditation, men were allowed to walk in circles there. Women had their own area for walking. With partitions and closed doors, the main building was prepared in such a way, that men and women did not meet on their way to the only place where they were in the same room, i.e. the meditation hall.

There, women formed one block of bodies and men another. Individual places in these blocks were allotted to the participants as numbers. The older students who had already participated in other courses were allocated places closer to the teacher[8] than the new ones. The teacher meditated on a small podium in front of the students. The few distances that participants had to handle during the course – from the sleeping room to the meditation hall to the eating hall – were unequivocally indicated by information signs on paper fixed on the walls and doors. The electronically broadcasted sound of a gong structured the day, from wake-up bell at 4:00 a.m. until lights-out at 9:30 p.m., i.e. the times to meditate, eat, and rest as they are presented on the website, in the leaflet, and pinned near the access to the meditation hall again. There was hardly any reason to ask anyone for anything. The only distraction from the routine was the so-called *teacher's discourse* in the meditation hall from 7:00 till 8:15 p.m. This meant listening to a recording of Goenka's lectures (one for every day of the course)[9]. After this *discourse*, half an hour was planned for questions to the present (assistant) teacher, but during my course there never were any public questions. Another possibility for talking to the teacher – in case of individual problems with the technique and the like – was to book a five-minute timeslot between noon and 1 p.m. by putting your name on a list. A third moment to legitimately break noble silence was when

---

5   The concept of the courses stipulates as much privacy as possible so as to enable a most concentrated meditation practice, but the spatial arrangement of the centres does not always provide private rooms. So, in my Vipassana experience, I had to share a room with two male roommates, and we sincerely distracted each other by snoring.

6   Comp. https://www.dhamma.org/en/about/code.

7   In the sense of Marvin Minsky's characterisation of an algorithm as "a set of rules which tell us, from moment to moment, precisely how to behave" (1967: 106).

8   The teachers of the courses are sometimes referred to as *teachers*, sometimes as *assistant teachers* in relation to Goenka.

9   They are available on YouTube: https://www.youtube.com/watch?v=cz7QHNvNFfA. Many of the aspects and stories given by Goenka are part of Harding's above-cited book.

the teacher called a number of students to sit nearer to his person on special places in front of him and asked them a number of standardized questions concerning the understanding of the practice as it was instructed by recordings of Goenka. The most appropriate answer to the question, if one understood the instructions, was obviously a *yes*, because longer conversations – as some tried to start – were gently stopped. The present teacher's role was not a very active one. He rather figured as an assistant of the materially absent, but virtually present Goenka. Only once the teacher intervened during meditation time by raising his voice. Songs in the Pali language, sung by Goenka, were played on tape. Some of the students started to laugh about them, as if they did not want, but were not able to suppress a long-held-in desire to act out any longer. I had the feeling that this laughter could spark much more laughter, and probably the teacher, who normally performed a very soft and friendly attitude, felt the same. He ordered sharply: "Please stop laughing immediately!" It stopped.

I do not know if I *swept away* a lot of *sankhara* during the ten days, but, whatever, I managed to conclude the course without smoking, crying, or some other misbehavior. Consequently, in the electronic system where I registered to apply, my status automatically changed from a new student's to an older student's. Now, I can fill in my username and password on the initial webpage and move by just one click to the page for older students. Some new features, information and instructions appear, amongst others a section about *meditation in day-to-day life*. There, I am strongly advised to maintain a meditation practice and participate in regional groups and further ten-day courses at least once a year. And the sole claim of the tradition is underlined once more in the following paragraph, titled "One Path only": "Do not mix this technique with others. If you have been practicing something else, you may attend two or three Vipassana courses to help you decide which technique you prefer. Then choose the one you find most suitable and beneficial, and devote yourself to it." To my knowledge, they are strict on this – having practiced other techniques can lead to exclusion from further Goenka courses. As in the idea behind the meditation practice, a strong concept of purity is at work.

Other features, opened for older students only, include the possibility to give *dana*, financial support to the organization or *dhamma* service, which means, e.g., to be a helper in the kitchen during a course. After a certain number of further courses and special instructions, you can give *dhamma* service as an assistant teacher as well. Furthermore, you get some extended features in the *dhamma.org mobile app*, which you can download from Apple's app store or Google Play. This app, in general, offers one more variation of Goenka's script. It includes a one-hour meditation session introduced by Goenka's chanting in Pali, which means you have some *personal Goenka* in your pocket whenever you need him.

4. Comparison / Commonalities

In both examples – the university lecture and the meditation exercise – we ask about the performativity of scripts used for educational purposes and the relation of the scripts to the human actors on the social stage. We will call them the Garbo script and the Goenka script.

Both scripts have in common that they are adaptable to, and manifesting themselves in, various media. The Garbo script exists as a) book, b) reader, c) slideshow, d) internet version, and e) the spoken word performances of Prof. Garbo assisted by Mr. Schmidt. The Goenka script, as far as it is introduced here, manifests as a) various writings and lectures by Goenka, b) audio and video material by Goenka, c) the book written by William Hart referencing this material, c) webpage, d) printed booklet handed over to participants, e) the spoken word performance of the assistant teacher, and f) even an app. Looking at both scripts through Karen Barad's concept of apparatuses, they have "no intrinsic boundaries but are open ended practices" (Barad 2007: 146)[10]. By being adapted to various media, the extension of the scripts expands and diminishes. Of course, it should be noticed that in this research article (yet another script out of another apparatus) we are the ones who set the limits and finally define the given lists of the script's transformations. We do not, for example, list further manifestations of the scripts, such as working with the Garbo script in student working groups. Nevertheless, as far as we observed, the scripts' use (with the acknowledgement that it is something that may change in student work groups or small Vipassana meditation groups) their basic informative and /or instructive structure, their *fundamentals* remained the same.

Prof. Garbo himself makes a hierarchical distinction between unchangeable foundations and their applications as specific examples: "When something new, something interesting in automotive engineering is brought into the world, these new ideas are always based on the foundations, every time." These foundations are not created by Prof. Garbo, but they are understood and canonized by him. The same contribution of authority happens when William Hart writes about the technique instructed by Goenka, that it "agrees with the instructions of the Buddha on meditation, with the simplest, most literal meaning of his words." Goenka did not invent Buddhism, but he and his script are believed to represent and present the fundamentals of it.

Interestingly, both scripts' prime mediums – Goenka and Garbo – are elderly men: In the case of Prof. Garbo, who is situated in the, still very mas-

---

10 Karen Barad is a US-American philosopher and physicist. In her concept of *agential realism* (2007), referring to Niels Bohr, Donna Haraway, Judith Butler and others, she brings together quantum physics, feminist and queer studies in the framework of science and technology studies.

culine, culture of mechanical engineering, his possible successor, Mr. Schmidt, and most of the students are male as well. So, masculine authority is negotiated in a predominantly male environment. Concerning the students, gender ratio (conceptualized as binary) seems overall balanced in the world of Goenka's Vipassana; the corresponding ratio in the Vipassana organization or among the assistant teachers is unknown to us. It may have been purely by chance that Hannes Leuschner attended a course led by a male teacher. The often-masculine authorship of powerful scripts, which can only be touched upon here, is of high concern, both for classical feminist literature studies (e.g. Ruthven 1984) and for more recent discussions on bias in algorithms built upon Artificial Intelligence (e.g. Wachter-Boettcher 2017; Eubanks 2018; Loh/Coeckelbergh 2019).

Both scripts not only manifest in various mediums, but some of these mediums are bound to certain physical locations, which we are understanding as social stages: These stages determine a certain use of the mediums. In the case of the Vipassana course, the environment is dictated by and, if necessary, manipulated following the script's logic. In its algorithmized structure it repeats and enables the algorithms of the script by enabling as much separation and lack of distraction as possible. Compared to the theatrical form in a narrower sense, it calls to mind approaches that include the theatre visitor as an actor of the play (like blurring, exceeding, or dissolving the line between actors and audience in various forms of contemporary arts and theatre; for many examples see Fischer-Lichte 2017). Only the spatial arrangement in the meditation hall is interpretable as a setting of a more bourgeois theatre, with the assistant teacher performing his meditation in front of the students, although they are instructed to hold their eyes closed. The university lecture takes place in a classical academic architecture, which reminds us more of a classical stage of the bourgeois theatre: there is a clear separation between audience and the two human actors, Prof. Garbo and Mr. Schmidt.

So, what about these and the other human actors? It appears as if there is more interaction between Prof. Garbo and Mr. Schmidt than between either of them and the audience. Performing at the stage in front of the audience, they appear as a show master with his assistant. This impression might be strengthened by the installation of the headset in the introduction, or the fact that advertising clips are shown before the spoken part of the lecture begins. On the stage of the Vipassana course, all actors – the assistant teacher, the helpers, the students – are expected to do their best to follow the very clear script that is not meant to be questioned in any way. In Garbo's lecture the situation is differentiated by the fact that the script is improved upon during the lecture: Such a process wouldn't fit into Vipassana courses at all. When we analogize Garbo to Goenka and Schmidt to the assistant teacher, another interesting difference appears: Goenka is not bodily present, but Garbo is, albeit near to retirement. Goenka's script, in some way, transformed into a

Goenka algorithm – is Garbo's script on the same trajectory? While the inter-action between performers and the audience is nearly zero during the lecture, the underlying algorithm is interactively unveiled in the tutorials conducted by Mr. Schmidt. There, he becomes an ally of the students by indicating the algorithmic logic of the script, which is blurred in Garbo's lecture, but of high importance for the students: Mr. Schmidt indicates how to use the different medium of the script to better understand what is important for the exam, and what is not. In the Vipassana course there is neither a final test, nor a comparable lack of clarity. Their setting belongs (to say it with Deleuze 1992) more to the control societies, where you never finish, than to the disci-plinary societies, where you always have to begin again (as in university culture from course to course, from semester to semester, from bachelor to master, etc.).

5. Discussion

Notwithstanding the discussed differences, in both cases it seems as if the script does not support the lecturer's performance during class. It rather ap-pears as if the personally-present lecturer or teacher assists in presenting the script. Now we want to raise the question: Wouldn't it be possible to change the medium of Prof. Garbo's lecture from personal performance to digital performance, for instance, as a podcast or video performance that can be consumed at home? The digital performance would separate and individual-ize the students as is attempted in Vipassana courses, to which the same kind of question might be asked: When you have Goenka on your smartphone, what do you need the presence of the other students (who are a potential source of distraction) and the assistant teacher for? And if this were true: Could just anybody be empowered to speak in the required language and act as a medium for the Garbo and Goenka script, as in the Catholic church where even a non-baptized unbeliever can perform a baptism in case of life-threatening emergency? These are pressing questions in the context of current political initiatives on digitalizing teaching in educational institutions, such as the "Digital Gipfel" (digital summit) of the German Federal Ministry of Education and Research. The politically driven discussion focuses on the opportunities and challenges, to refer to the contemporary neoliberal new speak, of such processes. We want to contrast different viewpoints, based on the two cases given here, from the perspective of trans- and posthumanist ideas.

The philosopher and critical posthumanist Janina Loh (2018: 31) provides a basic scheme for understanding the differences between prominent schools of trans- and posthumanism in comparison to classical humanism in the 18th century's sense. To start with the basic idea of transhumanism, it follows the dream of creating a human imagined as *better* by enhancing the contemporary human technologically. In its vision, the human being stays the crown of creation. In contrast, the core idea of technological posthumanists is concentrated on creating an artificial intelligence that is more intelligent than the human: After having played the God role, physical humanity as we know it would cease to exist and at best survive outside the body in a digitally or quantumlogically transformed way. Both traditions are strongly dominated by male and partly masculinist writers and scientists, as is the classical European humanism. A newer tradition of thinking beyond the human, rooted in French deconstructivism and poststructuralism, continued in feminist, gender and queer studies, is widely called *critical posthumanism* to differentiate it from the prior mentioned visions (see Ferrando 2018). It differs from classical humanism and post-humanism by highlighting a post-anthropocentrism without denying (wo*)mankind as one kind of being entangled with other kinds and modes of living (see e.g. the considerations in Barad 2014). Where transhumanism shows tendencies of valuing the mental over the physical and where technological posthumanism shows a strong tendency to value (artificial) mind over (natural) matter, critical posthumanism aims to overcome such dichotomies in a more holistic and egalitarian approach: "Posthuman critical thought can thus be understood as a multi-directional philosophy of relational ethics" (Braidotti 2018: 342).

At a first glance, both examples seem to fit into a technological understanding of posthumanism: An abstract script, once created by humans, is gaining independent (even posthuman) authority and agency, which is able to manifest in different mediums, like software running on different hardware, and is therefore materialized in different matters. Prof. Garbo refers to their different qualities when he describes the intention of his script as presenting foundations, because they are primary and fixed, while applications are flexible and concrete, and therefore less important. Hence, in Garbo's script matter and meaning seem somehow separated. In Goenka's Buddhist line of thought, matter and meaning are entangled in the *sankhara,* but the aim of his technique is to disentangle them in order to release the mind from the matter[11].

In a technological posthumanist line of thinking you can isolate mind from body, matter from meaning, and – here it meets with transhumanism – transfer a mind from one body to another as the script from one medium to another. So, reading our examples from there: Why still meet in the lecture hall with Garbo and Schmidt; why still meet in the meditation hall with the

---

11 Concerning private matters, Goenka himself was a family father and does not advice against sexual intercourse in general (but from sexual misconduct, whatever he and his followers may imagine as such). But he states that sexual desire would automatically pass away by ongoing training in his technique.

assistant teacher? Regarding Vipassana meditation, a pragmatic reason to perform it in a protected, heterotopic environment is the aim to release the participants from as many worries of daily life and therein potential distractions as possible. The script, as a care- and therein rather motherly connotated algorithm written by a father, becomes responsible for the participants' basic wellbeing as far as possible by giving them shelter, food, and water. But only during some of the meditation hours participants can choose to meditate in their rooms instead of the meditation hall. Other hours have to be spent obligatorily in the hall. Obviously, a certain level of physical co-presence is considered important. In contrast to the facility where the meditation course was held, the university's lecture hall does not provide any relief from daily duties. On the contrary, it means collateral work for the students to get there at certain hours, to find a place to sit, and maybe even to sit there hungry, because they did not find time to eat before and are not allowed to eat during lecture. So, why not let them study more comfortably and much more cheaply (for everyone) at their private computer at home (e.g., very euphoric: Mendenhall 2012)?

From a critical posthumanist point of view, the medium is not only the message (McLuhan 1964), but the message is the medium as well. That is why they are, to use another baradian term, entangled. To ask with a classical Zen Buddhist question: What is the sound of one hand clapping? Like nothing, because there is nothing observed without an observer, nothing thought without a teacher, no script without performance, on the one hand, and on the other: There is no observer without the observed, no teacher without something to teach and no performance without a script to be performed. Concerning the performance (distinguished from the previous staging as a rehearsal) the physical co-presence of the actors' and the audience's bodies and consequently the synchronicity of production and reception is highlighted (Fischer-Lichte/Roselt 2001: 239). Hence, the co-experience of these bodies at the same space was crucial for any theatrical performance in the understanding of Max Hermann (quoted in ibid.: 340), the founding figure of the German *Theaterwissenschaft* (theatre studies). This happens in the lecture hall and in the meditation hall, but not when you are alone in your study room with your smartphone or computer. Regarding the ongoing digitalization and thereby algorithmizing of learning situations, there are two main concerns. First, algorithms used in teaching software tend to be fixed and not negotiable; their basis still is a binary one: One and zero, yes and no, right and wrong. This binary order is a scheme at the center of posthumanist criticism. A second doubt concerns the power structure of authorship. The French poet Charles Baudelaire wrote about the visions of the hashish eaters that they want to dream to be governed by the dream – but that such dream will always remain "its fathers sun" (comp. Kupfer 1996: 19). With this in mind, a critical posthumanism would question any script and program on whether it is indeed posthuman, or if it merely functions as a channel for a still anthropocentric world order. The question of how to escape such a persistent order then opens the adventure of a serious critical posthumanism: the attempt to theorize as a human in a non-human(ist) way.

So, what might a critical posthumanist educational theatre look like in contrast to the still anthropocentric practices presented in this paper? An important step towards such a theatre would be to de-binarize any algorithmic structure. That finally means to destroy the algorithm that in Minsky's Definition (already cited above) is "a set of rules which tell us, from moment to moment, precisely how to behave" (1967: 106). For this reason, it is constituted as essentially binary in showing us how not to behave at the same time as well. For instance, if two persons meet each other, gender attribution will basically be a question of negotiation between the self and the external perception, however biased and power-determined it may be. For a digital algorithm or for an architectural algorithm, like the existence of two toilet doors signed respectively as *Ladies* and *Gentlemen*, it is a question of definition; an *either ... or* instead of an *as well as* or something completely different that could be negotiated. Maybe with quantum technology, one day it might be otherwise – but for now, everything a human-made computer can do is reduceable to zero and one. Another step towards a posthumanist education would be to overcome the centrality of the human teacher as the educand's educator. This transgression is highlighted in Johann Friedrich Herbart's didactic triangle (see Benner 1997) and is comparable to the emphasis on the physical co-presence of the actor's and the audience's bodies in Max Hermann's understanding of theatre. However, this point is even more tricky than the binary problem. Finally, it would be about deconstructing humanity, which means to question the attribution *human* in the same way that the attributions *female* and *male* have been questioned by Goffman (1977), Butler (1990) and many others. Regarding the gender stereotyping, women can help men, men can help women and transwo*men can help women and men (and so on) to deconstruct binary gender orders. But, looking from an educational point of view, is there a non-human teacher that can help humanity to deconstruct itself as such? A possible answer can be given quite simply: Any sky you look at, any dog looking at you, any mosquito biting you, and any water touching your body can be such a teacher, and learning is about perceiving this. From this perspective, human educational theatre is just a subset and finally part of all-surrounding non-human educational theatre[12]. In this context, Hölderlin's call to Landauer can be read as an educational invitation: "Komm! ins Offene, Freund" [Come! Into the open, my friend!] (Hölderlin 1958: 87–89). You can even read it as an imperative, but

---

12   Like the play in the play in Shakespeares Hamlet, act III, scene 2.

as a strictly non-algorithmic one, because the *open* cannot be reduced to binary schemes that are by definition closed.

References

Altmann, Andreas (2013): Triffst du den Buddha, töte ihn! Ein Selbstversuch. Köln: Dumont.

Barad, Karen (2007): Meeting the Universe Halfway. Durham/London: Duke University Press.

Barad, Karen (2014): On Touching – The Inhuman That Therefore I Am (v1.1). In: Witzgall, Susanne/Stakemeier, Kerstin (eds.): Power of Material/Politics of Materiality. Zürich/Berlin: Diaphenes, pp. 153–164.

Benner, Dietrich (1997): Johann Friedrich Herbart: Systematische Pädagogik. Weinheim: Deutscher Studienverlag.

Braidotti, Rosi (2018): Posthuman Critical Theory. In: Braidotti, Rosi/Hlavajova, Maria (eds.): Posthuman Glossary. London/New York: Bloomsbury Academic, pp. 339–342.

Butler, Judith (1990): Gender Trouble. Feminism and the Subversion of Identity. New York: Routledge.

Deleuze, Gilles (1992): Postscript on the Societies of Control. In: October 59, pp. 3–7.

Eikels, Kai van (2016): Virtuosen-Herrschaft: Überlegungen zu Ausnahme-Performances und Macht – vom Bühnenstar des 19. Jahrhunderts bis zu den Souveränitätsversprechen des Postfordismus. In: Brandstetter, Gabriele et al. (eds.): Szenen des Virtuosen. Bielefeld: Transcript, pp. 77–102.

Eubanks, Virginia (2018): Automating Inequality: How High-Tech Tools Profile, Police, and Punish the Poor. New York: St. Martin's Press.

Ferrando, Francesca (2018): Transhumanism/Posthumanism. In: Braidotti, Rosi/Hlavajova, Maria (eds.): Posthuman Glossary. London and New York: Bloomsbury Academic, pp. 438–439.

Fischer-Lichte, Erika (2017): Ästhetik des Performativen. Frankfurt am Main: Suhrkamp.

Fischer-Lichte, Erika/Roselt, Jens (2001): Attraktion des Augenblicks – Aufführung, Performance, performativ und Performativität als theaterwissenschaftliche Begriffe. In: Paragana, Theorien des Performativen 10, 1, pp. 237–253.

Goffman, Erving (1959): The Presentation of Self in Everyday Life. New York: Doubleday & Company.

Goffman, Erving (1977): The Arrangement Between the Sexes. In: Theory and Society 4, pp. 301–331.

Hart, William (2019): The Art of Living: Vipassana Meditation as Taught by Shri S.N. Goenka. Mumbai: Ambassy Book Distributors.

Hölderlin, Friedrich (1958): Der Gang aufs Land. In: Hölderlin, Friedrich: Sämtliche Werke. 6 Bände, Band 2. Stuttgart: Cottasche Buchhandlung, pp. 87–89.

Kupfer, Alexander (1996): Göttliche Gifte: Kleine Kulturgeschichte des Rausches seit dem Garten Eden. Stuttgart und Weimar: Metzler.

Loh, Janina (2018): Trans- und Posthumanismus: Eine Einführung. Hamburg: Junius Verlag.

Loh, Janina/Coeckelbergh, Mark (eds.) (2019): Feminist Philosophy of Technology. Book Series Techno: Phil – Aktuelle Herausforderungen der Technikphilosophie, Volume 2. Stuttgart: J.B. Metzler.

McLuhan, Marshall (1964): Understanding Media. New York: McGraw-Hill.

Mendenhall, Robert (2012): What is Competency-Based Education? In: HuffPost. Available at https://www.huffpost.com/entry/competency-based-learning-_b_1855374?^, last accessed July 30, 2020.

Minsky, Marvin (1967): Computation: Finite and Infinite Machines. Englewood Cliffs, NJ: Prentice-Hall.

Ruthven, K. K. (1984): Feminist Literary Studies: An Introduction. Cambridge: Cambridge University Press.

Wachter-Boettcher, Sara (2017): Technically Wrong: Sexist Apps, Biased Algorithms, and Other Threats of Toxic Tech. New York: W. W. Norton & Company.

Getting a Handle on Critical Pedagogies: Notes on Interdependencies and Care in Interdisciplinary Technoscience

Loren Britton, Goda Klumbytė, Claude Draude and Isabel Paehr

1. Introduction

A suggestion for a different manner of experiencing this text would be to provide a brief hand massage to yourself or a companion. We invite you to use your fingers to massage fingertips, joints, and palms, thereby paying attention to the various parts of the hand and other non/humans around you throughout this text. If you wish, you can start by focusing on the index finger, loosening and massaging it.

Forms of theoretical production and exchange are often strict and limited in academia. Lectures are provided with a single person lecturing in front of an audience, classrooms are structured in a largely similar architectural and pedagogical manner, publications are issued with the hierarchy and rank of authors in mind, and forms of research subject engagement are premised on metaphors of mastery. While pedagogical and research formats are addressed within teaching and methodological concerns, an active understanding of form co-producing content is seldom explicitly addressed. This encourages us to ask: which kinds of exclusions are imbued in academic artifacts such as *the lecture, the classroom, the research project,* and *the technological object* that continue to assume who is welcome to learn or be in those spaces and who is not?

Questions multiply once we enter the domain of interdisciplinary research and knowledge. In which ways might theories impact the modes in which various disciplinary knowledges are taught in class? For example, if you are researching Karen Barad's concept of intra-action, which pertains to the relational co-constitution of entities, could there be an embodied dance practice taught alongside the theoretical points to model how solidity and movement can be thought together? Could theories of care be addressed by exercising care towards the readers of those theories? Even if the theoretical underpinnings of the work that is being engaged in critical feminist technoscience suggest a re-making, re-configuring, re-addressing, the bodies in the learning and research environment often remain unaffected.

The focus of this paper is to outline an experimental, explorative, and care-based interdisciplinary critical pedagogy framework and to address how the latter could be used in interdisciplinary feminist technoscience research. Critical pedagogy provides suggestions for thinking with negotiation, openness, and indeterminacy as practices towards re-formatting interdisciplinary collective work towards more accessible and liveable presents. In this paper, we will claim that integrating critical pedagogy into technofeminist research is crucial for doing research with more care, attention to interdependence, and accountability.

Particularly, we argue that a critical pedagogical framework for interdisciplinary feminist technoscience research enables a sharp focus on accountability, a drive towards less oppressive research and design outcomes and processes. This framework enables the construction of what bell hooks calls "learning communities" (hooks 1994: 8) by reframing research as a matter of learning and teaching between the researcher and the researched. This paper centers on the pursuit of "education as the practice of freedom" (hooks 1994) that considers pedagogy a major system that participates in upholding systems of oppression and suggests that critical pedagogy is a mode that works towards that system's undoing.

We will start by outlining some of critical pedagogy's main ideas and will document how these ideas could be enriched using technoscientific approaches centering on care and interdependence. Apart from critical pedagogues, such as Freire and hooks, we rely strongly on the work of Puig de la Bellacasa on care and crip (techno)science scholars on interdependence. This article is a work-in-progress that documents our current state of thinking and research on these matters and should be read as a proposition towards conducting interdisciplinary technoscientific research otherwise. By presenting a work-in-progress, we also hope to nudge the uncomfortably rigid academic standard of providing a finished, polished, and somewhat stabilized end product for publication and point out that research is an ongoing process that retains space for the unexpected.

2. Critical Pedagogy: Challenging Hierarchies in Teaching and Learning

Continuing your hand massage; we suggest that you close one hand around the other hand's middle finger. Does it feel warm? If you like, walk your fingertips up and down to create and release some light pressure. Repeat with the ring finger if you are enjoying this movement. Alternatively, you can try using your toes or, instead of touching physically, you could touch fingers or toes with your gaze.

The emergence of critical pedagogy is often traced back to the works of Paulo Friere (1968), Henry Giroux (1998), bell hooks (1994; 2003) and other radical educators from the second half of the 20th century. Critical pedagogy's basis is the understanding of teaching and learning as political acts and the linking of critical theoretical perspectives to pedagogical implications. As a theory and practice, it focuses on shifting more conventional pedagogies towards theories of social change that reimagine the teaching space as less oppressive and the study of culture as critical. Drawing on various philosophical and activist traditions, such as anarchist, feminist, and Marxist theories, critical pedagogy contributes to a decolonial paradigm that challenges domination and the underlying beliefs of dominant practices.

As a philosophy of education and a social movement, critical pedagogy was first conceptualized in Brazilian educator Paulo Freire's work "Pedagogy of the Oppressed" (1968), in which he bases the relationships between teacher, student, and society on co-creation. Freire critiques the so-called banking model of education[1] and instead proposes a dialogue-based approach in which the learner is positioned as an active co-creator. Freire and other critical pedagogues highlight praxis as indispensable to teaching and learning and define it as a situation or an action during which theory, lesson, or skill are enacted, embodied, or realized through practice. The role of praxis is crucial to the political project of critical pedagogy, which rests on the three main assumptions: That praxis can enable social transformation, that teaching and learning are laden with power relations, and that society can be transformed by those who are critically conscious (Gruenewald 2003: 3).

Critical consciousness for Freire is an in-depth understanding of the world, allowing clashes between social and political contradictions to emerge, creating the conditions for the opportunity to take action against oppressive elements in life. Taking action is key to the process of self-determination, which for Freire is fundamental for ending a culture of silence wherein oppressed students (and oppressed people more generally) do not speak their truth back to oppressive power. In notable contrast to pedagogy, critical pedagogy is about engendering a critical mindset in students that enables a transformation of the power relations. This is a praxis that creates thinking, reading, writing, and speaking habits that question surface meanings and ideological myths or traditional forms (Shor 1992). These habits are set up to generate deeper understandings of meanings, causes, contexts, and ideological repercussions of any object of knowledge – be it an academic text, a political event, or a performance.

---

1 The banking model of education is characterised by a teacher providing and students receiving knowledge in a disciplined, passive manner. A "good student" is the one who can "empty" themselves to receive information from the teacher. Information is not to be questioned, but accepted, deposited and rendered available upon request (Freire 1970).

Such habits of thought and praxis require different subjects and modes of engagement. Freire suggests that if the teacher understands their students to be objects or empty *banks* to be filled with state-sanctioned knowledge, then the latter will never leave the classroom as critically thinking subjects. Freire proposes rethinking the subject as student-teacher/teacher-student and positioning dialogue at the heart of pedagogical praxis. He writes:

> Through dialogue, the teachers-of-the-students and the students-of-the-teachers cease to exist and a new term emerges; teacher-student with student-teacher, the teacher is no longer merely the one who teaches, but the one who is himself [sic[2]] taught in dialogue with the students, who in turn while being taught also teach. They become jointly responsible for the process in which all grow (Freire 1970: 16).

For Freire, this dialogical mode of engagement and the resulting transformation of the teaching and learning subject is that which enables critical pedagogy to become a "practice of freedom" (ibid.) that helps bring forth change in a collective manner.

The banking model of education and the racial and other hierarchies that come with it were also actively criticized by bell hooks, particularly in her work "Teaching to Transgress: Education as Practice of Freedom" (1994). Analyzing educational experiences in desegregated US schools, hooks exposes how norms of whiteness are reinforced and exemplified by limiting learning to the memorization of information and modeling the dialectic teacher/student relationship on that of dominance/obedience, authority/subservience, and provider/recipient – models that resonate with racialized hierarchies of white supremacy. Such dynamics are reproduced not only in classrooms but in many other institutional contexts as well.[3] One of hooks' and Freire's joint concerns with these white supremacist institutional practices is that they dehumanize both those that engage in them, i.e., those that reenforce whiteness, as well as those who become excluded or are disengaged because of these modes of operation.

An alternative proposed by hooks is to develop learning communities – learning situations in which everyone, including the teacher-student, has the opportunity to behave, enact, and understand themselves to be creative experts. To be a creative expert is to be entangled in body, space, and time whilst learning. Such a practice counters the traditional authoritarian space and opens up the "magic that is always present when individuals are active learners" (hooks 2003: 43). It allows people to be engaged in not just striving

---

2   This quote is an indicator one of the reasons that bell hooks was dissatisfied with Freire's work because he was understood to be a misogynist.
3   For instance, US activist group "Standing up for Racial Justice" presents a list of "characteristics of white supremacy culture" that appear within institutions and educational settings (SURJ 2001) and help reproduce and reinforce racial hierarchies, including: individualism, fear of open conflict, perfectionism, either/or thinking, a "sense of urgency," quantity over quality, worship of the written word and defensiveness.

for theoretical knowledge (or only applicable knowledge for that matter), but in learning how to live together in the world, to actively participate in the unfolding of being. When "critical awareness and engagement is practiced" (hooks 1994: 14) so that the student-teacher/teacher-student is an active participant and not a passive consumer, it ensures that learning and teaching is not an act of cultural transmission, but of co-production. This opens up opportunities for student-teachers to engage with their own situated experiences concerning whatever material they are dealing with.

These definitions position critical pedagogy as a process that theoretically and practically addresses power dynamics. Critical pedagogy highlights a multiplicity of knowledges by taking each person as an agent of teaching-learning and advocates collective knowledge building using dialogical forms of engagement, situated learning, and various methods of subject formation. For these reasons, exploring critical pedagogy's role in interdisciplinary and collaborative research spaces is an approach that focuses on co-creation, that challenges hierarchies, and that can help create an open space to work towards the goals that interdisciplinary collaborations often seek.

3. Critical Pedagogy and Interdisciplinary Technoscience

Have your little finger and thumb touched today? If you feel like it, slowly bring them closer to each other. When do each finger's nerves register the other finger's presence? When they touch, and if you are into trying this, rotate them gently around one another. Perhaps use both hands, so that your left little finger can play with your right thumb.

Critical pedagogy has been adopted by several interdisciplinary fields adjacent to feminist science and technology studies or FSTS. Anna Hickey-Moody's and Tara Page's work (2016) as well as Jessica Ringrose, Kate Warfield, and Shiva Zarabadi's edited volume (2018) have provided critical pedagogical insights into the field of feminist new materialism. Fred Moten and Stefano Harney's work "the Undercommons" (2013) is prominent in black studies. Anti-racist and decolonial studies have also received several single-author and edited volumes, by Zeus Leonardo (2009) and Michalinos Zembylas (2019) among others. Bernardo Pohl has published "The Pedagogy of the Disabled" (2014) and several volumes have appeared on queer pedagogy, e.g., by Cris Mayo and Nelson Rodriguez (2019) or Elizabeth McNeil et al. (2017). Within feminist technoscience, critical pedagogical approaches are often addressed in the framework of science education or education for science and technology studies (e.g. Hudson 2020; Lasker/Simcox 2020;

McNeil 2013). FSTS[4] itself has recently been positioned as a critical pedagogy within this framework. Another route to pedagogy in feminist technoscience is through technology design and design methods and research, including participatory research and design (Bardzell 2018; Gabrys/Pritchard 2015; Rommes 2014; among others), co-creation methods (e.g. Liu et al. 2019; Paxling 2019) and hybrid pedagogies, particularly in computing and engineering (Britton et al. 2019; Ratto et al. 2019).[5] All have strong resonances with critical pedagogy due to their focus on collaborative making and knowledge generation.

We would like to argue that pedagogy is addressed somewhat less as a significant source for conducting research in interdisciplinary feminist technoscience. This is perhaps due to pedagogy's relegation to studies of education or, alternatively, being understood as a tool for conveying rather than producing knowledge. This is noticeable even in technoscience that employs theories developed to focus on entanglements, interdependency, and relational ethics – such as feminist new materialism or feminist post-humanist approaches. While the methodological implications of such theories are addressed (e.g. Åsberg/Braidotti 2018; Fox/Aldred 2016; Hinton/Treusch 2015; Ringrose et al. 2018), the pedagogical implications are often not explicitly drawn or only addressed marginally, even if the theory itself suggests pedagogical shifts. Even if a theory is about instantiating ethical, political, social change, the way we teach, communicate, and work with it, is often not subject to change.

This is interesting, given that some FSTS theories resonate especially well with critical pedagogical work. For example, the distinction between the positions of student subjects and objects within Freire's work aligns with Karen Barad's conceptualization of agency as something that is distributed along the non/human continuum (Barad 2007). Critical pedagogy's focus on challenging the teacher-student dualism and the clear separation between knowledge and that person who acquires or provides knowledge relates closely to the undoing of a Cartesian perspective. This is taken up by our co-author, Claude Draude, who considers how Barad distinguishes between description and reality. Draude (2019: 20) writes that a description is regarded as independent of the description/representation and, importantly, of how the description was attained, even though from a critical pedagogy perspective, it may be less so.

---

4   See, for instance, the panel on "STS as critical pedagogy" organised by Emily York, Shannon Conley and Marisa R. Brandt during the 2019 Society for Social Studies of Science annual meeting in New Orleans, https://www.4s2019.org/. See also York/Conley 2019.

5   In more mainstream science education and technological education, a constructivist approach to learning has been proposed as an innovative and more student-oriented and problem-based approach (see the work of Seymour Papert, for example Papert/Harel 1991).

Critical pedagogy continues to be challenging to bring into academic spaces because it disrupts the clear-cut lines of sexual, racial, and other forms of domination that most institutions are not free from. Taking on critical pedagogies requires a radical redistribution of hierarchy and the creation of conditions of agency for each participant. The maintenance of acknowledging presence, working at the pace of trust, and sharing knowledge with an anti-racist direction requires a lot of letting go and making a collective open to not knowing what forms something might take.[6] We argue that critical pedagogy not only contributes to liberatory agendas by developing learning communities but also creates context for interdisciplinary cultural production rather than disciplinary (or otherwise) cultural domination. Holding the tension of the interdependencies of knowledge production, critical pedagogical modes is a place to practice an otherwise space where violent co-option of knowledges and practices is undone.

Critical pedagogy is grounded in decolonial and anti-racist work, thereby providing space for and tools to address racial and power hegemonies that emerge, are reproduced, and configured anew by the interdisciplinary field of technoscience today. Interdisciplinary projects can find an exciting partner in critical pedagogy using naturecultures, sociotechnical systems, and experimental modes of academic/scientific/artistic work. Thinking with interdependence, anti-racist co-creation, and sociotechnical worldings of care, we offer theoretical pillows to rest on as well as some materials to work with, in support of those who wish their work to affect and be affected by this critical opportunity and the generous space of unknowing.

4. Care, Interdependence and Crip (Techno)science

Activating the potential of critical pedagogy creates space within interdisciplinary technoscientific research that allows for learning communities that are conducive to creating more liveable techno-nature-cultural worlds. We argue that critical pedagogy needs to be figured together with care and interdependence practices. Such a critical pedagogy can perform several important moves. One, it does not presume which kind of care is needed; two, it takes the non/human actant in question as the expert on their circumstances; three, it focuses on liberatory practices towards enacting these worlds; and four, it positions care as an ethico-political framework for these worlds. To engage

---

6   To be clear, this is not merely a practice of institutional critique, but an acknowledgment that we reproduce the same structures that perpetuate oppression through our conforming to their structures. To quote Athena Athanasiou (2016: 683): "institutions sustain us and wipe us out at the same time."

with such a framework, we turn to Maria Puig de la Bellacasa's definition of care as context-specific, perspective-dependent, and ethico-political, as well as to an understanding of interdependence informed by crip (techno)scientific and disability justice perspectives.

In feminist scholarship and activism, care is historically linked to considerations of the material concerns regarding reproductive and domestic labor (Duffy 2007; Federici 1975; Hochschild 1989). Figuring care as a material concern points to questions such as where do care relations start and who are they performed and sustained by. Within technoscience, this extends to include questions surrounding interdependence and agency: Who is assumed to be the user and creator, beneficiary and provider? How is the distribution of agency figured within and between these categories? It also addresses the dismissal[7] of certain forms of labor and infrastructures: Care and production workers are underpaid, the existence of data centers and submarine cables is overwritten by metaphors like immateriality (Mattern 2016) or "the cloud" (Halpern 2015). This enacts a split along the lines of what is publicly valued and taken into account – which materials, labor, concerns, activities[8]? This split is reproduced in technoscientific institutions, but also historically and geographically harks back to racialized and sexualized forms of the division of labor. Consider, for instance, the childcare forced upon black enslaved women (Collins 1986) or contemporary (often feminized) migrant care and tech workers in the globalized "chain of care" (Precarias a la Deriva 2004). This is part of the human and non-human infrastructures and networks of care that support technoscientific activities "proper."

Some plants absorb light and photosynthesize better when their leaves are clean. This is an invitation to gently wipe the leaves of any plants around you with water and a soft cloth to support their growth. Make sure to support the underside of the leaves with your hand when wiping to prevent any scratches or rips to the leaf surface.

Care creates the opportunity to understand that we are all in mutually dependent relationships. Care also creates the context for challenging what is conventionally understood as technology.

Proposing woven bag technology as a care tool, Ursula K. Le Guin (1986) considers the labor of gathering and carrying this bag a starting point for human technologies. As something essential to survival, care has always had multiple tools at its fingertips. Textiles are the kind of tool or quotidian

---

7   Invisibilized labour, even though the binary of in/visibility is often used in the feminist canon, we align with Schaffer's critique that more visibility doesn't necessarily result in more power (Schaffer 2008) and attempt to be more precise in our naming of modes of domination.

8   For example, consider how during the Covid-19 pandemic a discourse regarding "closing" the economy emerged. However, large parts of the economy were in fact re-distributed towards forms that are not deemed part of the economy including cooking, housekeeping, teaching, food delivery, etc.

everyday material that is not usually configured as a technology today. Textiles, soft, woven, mendable, flexible, and fibrous have different kinds of material histories than technological artifacts associated with stability, metal, plastic, and breakability. Textiles hold, wrap, and create semi-permeabilities that soften homes or bodies and are technologies of carrying life and carrying on living.[9]

Le Guin suggests that the idea of technology evokes a distinctly Western dominant perspective through its universality (technosolutionism) and mastery over nature (furthering the natureculture divide) that has come to flourish in contemporary late capitalism. This definition of technology is weaponized within Western, colonial concepts of non/humans and in post-colonial contexts of advanced or developing nation states. To uphold Western supremacy, this concept of technology ignores the scientific hallmarks and discoveries of non-Western cultures, and devalues the manifold, highly complex technologies of the home: midwifery, weaving, gardening, and cooking, to name a few (Le Guin 1986). Quotidian knowledges sustain life everywhere in the margins of public life: maintenance, sustenance, and repetition provide infrastructures needed to sustain our emotional economies, while also providing the foundations for the high-tech superstructures that continue to generate and unfairly distribute wealth within capitalism.

Care challenges Western concepts of what counts as a technology through mutual relations of interdependency and repositions sociotechnical systems as processes of care. Specifically, care and interdependence frameworks challenge the white, western tradition of the subject-object dichotomy and the power relations that accompany it. Lucy Suchman (2007: 219–220) has shown how some "assistant technologies" make everyday care labor irrelevant and position normative values of autonomy as a privileged site of agency, while dependency is rendered as something that forecloses agency. This is an example of how technological artifacts impose a value judgment onto relations of inter/dependence by assuming the wants and needs of users. It also situates users as having agency based on their autonomy and technology as lacking agency, as it is understood as a passive object for use. Furthermore, Puig de la Bellacasa (2017: 9) connects this particular distribution of agency to "particular forms of design [that] recall the image of slavery: a skillful (self) erasure, it must do the mediations but not let us know how vital that work is, how much we depend on it." Technology here reproduces the denial of the slave, the woman, the black body; the design of technology and technological lifeworlds, therefore, often rests on models of objectification.

As an alternative, Puig de la Bellacasa suggests that paying attention to care allows for a perspective that takes technosciences and naturecultures as

---

9 This thinking with Ursula Le Guin was inspired by ALT_CPH 2020, "Patterns in Resistance," the Copenhagen Biennale that was unfortunately cancelled due to the Covid-19 virus. For more info about their amazing work please see here: https://altcph.dk.

inseparably entangled. Responding to Latour's (2004) "matters of concern," de la Bellacasa (2017) offers "matters of care" as a lens for scrutinizing those entanglements and uses care as an affirmative, ethical connective framework that surpasses that of being concerned. She proposes that human existence has to be inseparably intertwined with the non/human and de-centered, if less exploitative forms of co-existence are to be invented. In this framework, speculative ethics is a crucial element that helps steer such an invention towards less violent forms of living together. Speculative ethics is presented as an open ended, non-predetermined mode of thinking/doing that is care oriented and re-molds contexts and situations against neglect in the face of constant change. It renders both ethics and care as situated, proposing an ethics involving a hands-on, ongoing process of making relations "as well as possible" (Tronto 1990: 36) and, therefore, one that requires the speculative work of inventing what "the possible" involves. The imperative is to understand care as both context/perspective-specific and implying interdependence.

In addition to care, we conceive of interdependence as driving sociotechnical change towards less oppressive world makings. While care frameworks propose interdependence as a given, crip (techno)science focuses more closely on the implications of inter/dependence. A term coined by Leah Lakshmi Piepzna-Samarasinha (2018), crip (techno)science highlights the skills, wisdom, resources, and hacks disabled people utilize for navigating and altering inaccessible worlds. It weaves together concepts of crip – the non-compliant, anti-assimilationist position that disability is a desirable part of the world and technoscience – the co-production of science, technology, and political life. In crip (techno)sciences' mapping of interdependence, disabled people are knowers, innovators, collaborators, and makers (Hamraie/Fitsch 2019). The idea of "access as friction" is defined by the double meaning of access: "as an opportunity enabling contact, as well as a kind of attack" (Hamraie/Fitsch 2019: 23). A crip (techno)scientific sensibility enables what Mingus (2011) calls "access intimacy," a crip relational practice produced when interdependence informs the creation of access. Accessible futures thus require interdependence.

5. Technoscientific Research: Building a Learning Community

This is an invitation to observe: which kinds of technologies do you have around you? Which materials are they composed of and how were these materials brought together? If you wish, spend some time listing the materials in the technologies around you. Linen, cotton, gallium, plastic, aluminum, glass...

The above delved into the traditions of critical pedagogy and technoscientific thought unfolding around care and speculative ethics and interdependence (crip (techno)science). The following reveals how critical pedagogy, enriched by care and interdependence perspectives, helps create a framework for feminist technoscience conducive to creating more liveable and ethical sociotechnical worldings.

Let us consider some questions that emerged within the interdisciplinary technoscientific practices of the authors, which will hopefully resonate with many readers too. How much time is dedicated to establishing common methodological and conceptual ground at the beginning of interdisciplinary projects? Similarly, whose disciplinary standards count towards *acceptable* and *reasonable* research goals and outcomes? As we noted elsewhere (Britton et al. 2019), knowledge making in disciplinary-diverse research teams is also laden with power differentials and silences, which, even if reflected in the theories used, often remain ignored in forms of approach to research and design.

Entangled theories of care, interdependence, and critical pedagogy, which radically unsettle the assumptions of any research because they require the situated positionality of the object of research and the researchers themselves, function as the bedrock at the beginning of any interdisciplinary research. Some questions worth asking to situate care as the core to a set of concerns include: Who is being centered on as a knower and maker of interdependent worlds? How is care defined within a project? Which kinds of caring questions are the researchers asked and are addressed to the topic and the proposed outcome? Which forms of care are imagined and enacted in the project? Using critical pedagogy with technoscience in interdisciplinary research already signifies a significant step outside normative conceptions of what technology development does and who it is intended for. To Puig de la Bellacasa, this might entail requirements such as moving at the speed of trust, considering which models of thought are present and what they do, as well as establishing common languages. Crafting and designing a research process and technological artifacts for others who are not present within interdisciplinary settings, poses significant challenges to technoscience. A variety of knowledge creation methods, people, and considerations meet to unthink oppressions, instead of re-encoding them (Benjamin 2019).

Critical pedagogy, when rethought with interdependency and care, enables a move away from a strictly humanist perspective and its masculinist undertones (especially in Freire's early work). The concept of care entails sorting out caring for non-humans, more-than-humans, and humans alike (Puig de la Bellacasa 2017), a zoe-egalitarianism (Braidotti 2006) that traverses the living world. Crip (techno)scientific perspectives point out that interdependence goes beyond specific abilities and is, in fact, an ontological condition. This condition is both productive and non-innocent: interdependence spells vulnerability, permeability of boundaries, just as much as it entails empowering affirmation and collective liberation. Critical pedagogy adds radical attentiveness to forms of racial embodiment and processes of racialization and oppression as well as anti-racist liberation opportunities to frameworks of care and interdependence. Specifically, it questions who is interdependent with whom and in which ways this interdependence is potentially mutually exploitative. It also draws attention to forms of care that are used for subjugation and infantilization instead of support.

Linking all the three strands together – care, critical pedagogy, interdependence – allows for greater radical liberatory potential. Critical pedagogy casts technoscience research as a form of learning community building. In other words, it casts research as necessarily pertaining to learning with, from, and about the world. It refigures the researcher-researched relation to that of a teacherlearner dynamic that has the capacity to challenge the extractivist approach that so often becomes embedded in research methodologies (Tuhiwai Smith 1999). Teacherlearner dynamics require working with material in a processual way, but not through tokenizing any of the actors involved. From a critical pedagogical perspective, technoscientific research is also conducted in a posthuman direction (Braidotti 2019): without trying to rectify the proper subject and object of knowledge, but also without disregarding the subjectivities and agencies of those cast as objects, be they human or otherwise.

6. Technoscientific Praxis: Examples from Our Work

An example of this work of becoming teacherlearner and practicing a commitment to co-production and non-extraction was the workshop "Burn, Dream and Reboot! Speculating Backwards for the Missing Archive on Non-Coercive Computing" during the "ACM Fairness, Accountability and Transparency Conference 2020."[10] This workshop developed an oracle practice that engaged with black feminist poet(h)ics (poetics and ethics): During the workshops, participants were invited to question an oracle, which was Alexis Pauline Gumbs' "Spill: Scenes of Black Feminist Fugitivity" from 2018 about our shared computational environments. Both the preparation and the workshop itself were characterized by a critical pedagogy ethos. Before the workshop, the organizers prioritized reading, interpreting, challenging, and growing with one another. Academic and expertise hierarchies were deliberately avoided by nurturing the space between the differences in

---

10 For more information about the workshop and its organisers, see: https://facctcon ference.org/2020/acceptedcraftsessions.html#burn.

knowledge bases rather than focusing on expertise domains. During the workshop, participants worked with a non-directly responsive practice instead of clear-cut predictions by asking questions and answering these using a page chosen at random from the book. The answers were then open to interpretation worked out from the differences between what was expected to be said and what the actual reply was.

This workshop, therefore, positioned research and research subjectobjects as entangled with the world, literature and other participants as sources to work with, not extract from. In this workshop, the learning and sharing at stake were not about what could be drawn out of each other based on the variety of experiences in the room but about what emerged by giving space for the oracle, the questions asked, and the people in the room to interact.

From this perspective, research practice is a liberatory praxis that calls forth different worldings. Indeed, as Alexis Pauline Gumbs suggests, this might be one of the ways of knowing or developing critical technical practice to understand it less well, as opposed to understanding something fully and, therefore, having mastery over it, fixing it in place and form. Understanding less well is already a premise of many interdisciplinary technoscience projects, yet acknowledging it and actively not trying to optimize and totalize knowledge, treating it as an emergent process instead, could lead to unexpected research results.

Another example from our practices is Fuzzy Binaires[11], a techno-artistic collective that puts together non-institutional, non-commercial week-long workshops at which people from the fields of computer science, electronic arts, and critical theory, as well as many niches in between, engage in a shared learning experience. Each participant offers a learning moment to the group depending on their interests, such as a coding workshop, a recipe, or how they approach theoretical texts. Critical pedagogy is engaged with care and interdependency throughout the week, as people pair program, tinker, cook, improvise, draw, and relax together. At past editions, participants decided to work on a pop-up exhibition; however, learning is prioritized over the production of results.

Collaborative research and learning were also key to a series of experiments conducted during several workshops that took place during the "Reconfiguring Computing Through Cyberfeminism and New Materialism (CF+)"[12] project. The experiments conducted with and by an interdisciplinary group of experimenters-participants were geared towards what was termed

---

11   For information on Fuzzy Binaires, see: http://fuzzybinaires.org.
12   The project ran at the "Gender/Diversity in Informatics Systems" research lab in 2018–2019, see more at: http://www.uni-kassel.de/go/CFplus. The CF+ research project was funded through the Hessisches Ministerium für Wissenschaft und Kunst (Germany), funding line "Dimensionen der Kategorie Geschlecht – Frauen- und Geschlechterforschung in Hessen."

"material speculation" (Britton et al. 2019). It included investigating modalities of perception with breath and touching, exploring conditions of relationality by building a circuit board, exploring the opportunities for figuring linear regression with toy bricks and string, and other materially based research experiments. In this project, critical pedagogical approaches informed the open-ended format of research by experimenting without a pre-defined outcome and creating a learning community where different disciplinary knowledges were not prioritized with respect to specific domains and in which material praxis played one of the key roles.

The process of preparing and conducting these workshops and formats also revealed that critical pedagogy is particularly important to interdisciplinary research as a process of building learning communities in which each interdisciplinary researcher is not just an expert in their specific domain but also an active co-creator and co-laborer in research. Practicing not knowing while working towards a shared practice is a mode of developing interdisciplinary work that provides the opportunity of engaging and constructing less nameable and potentially more open worldings and figures. In other words, it enables innovative perspectives by positioning research as a matter of co-creation beyond well-worn research and explanatory models.

7. Conclusion

This is an invitation to consider which kind of technological objects you have around you every day. If you like, try and sense their size, shape, and texture without touching them. How heavy is your reading device? What shape is your phone? Does your computer make any specific noises?

When taken together, critical pedagogy, care, and interdependence configure a way of working that creates the opportunity for interdisciplinary collaborations to flourish outside oppressive, limiting research contexts. Critically working with and using forms of research and praxis that entangle non/humans, naturecultures, teacherlearners, and subjectobjects works towards forms and methods of collective learning. Critical pedagogical praxis lends an essential key to feminist technoscience that provides processes for co-creating projects that imagine different worlds that do not foreclose possibilities for all non/humans. Getting a handle on these pedagogies allows for more equitable and accountable outcomes, especially at a time when antiracist, co-creative, interdependent presents are the kinds of otherwise moments we need, now.

References

ALT_CPH 2020 (2020): Patterns in Resistance, Copenhagen Biennale. Available at https://altcph.dk, last accessed May 20, 2020.

Åsberg, Cecilia/Braidotti, Rosi (2018): A Feminist Companion to the Posthumanities. Basel: Springer International Publishing.

Athanasiou, Athena (2016): Performing the Institution "As If It Were Possible." In: Hlavajova, Maria/Sheikh, Simon (eds.): Former West: Art and the Contemporary after 1989. Cambridge: BAK and MIT Press, pp. 687.

Barad, Karen M. (2007): Meeting the Universe Halfway: Quantum Physics and the Entanglement of Matter and Meaning. Durham: Duke University Press.

Bardzell, Shaowen (2018): Utopias of Participation: Feminism, Design, and the Futures. In: ACM Transactions on Computer-Human Interaction 25, 1, 6:1–6:24.

Benjamin, Ruha (2019): Race after Technology. Cambridge: Polity Press.

Braidotti, Rosi (2013): The Posthuman. Cambridge: Polity Press.

Braidotti, Rosi (2016): Transpositions: On Nomadic Ethics. Cambridge: Polity Press.

Braidotti, Rosi (2019): Posthuman Knowledge. Cambridge: Polity Press.

Britton, Loren et al. (2019): Doing Thinking: Revisiting Computing with Artistic Research and Technofeminism. In: Digital Creativity, special issue on Hybrid Pedagogies 30, 4, pp. 313–328.

Collins, Patricia H. (1986): Learning from the Outsider Within: The Sociological Significance of Black Feminist Thought. In: Social Problems 33, 6, pp. 14–32.

Draude, Claude (2020): "Boundaries Do Not Sit Still" from Interaction to Agential Intra-action in HCI. In: Kurosu, Masaaki (ed.): Human-Computer Interaction. Design and User Experience. Copenhagen: Springer International Publishing, pp. 20–32.

Duffy, Mignon (2007): Doing the Dirty Work: Gender, Race, and Reproductive Labor in Historical Perspective. In: Gender and Society 21, 3, pp. 313–336.

Federici, Silvia (1975): Wages Against Housework. Bristol: Power of Women Collective and Falling Wall Press.

Fox, Nick J./Alldred, Pam (2016): Sociology and the New Materialism. London: SAGE.

Freire, Paulo (1970): Pedagogy of the Oppressed. London: Penguin.

Gabrys, Jennifer/Pritchard, Helen (2015): Next-generation Environmental Sensing: Moving beyond Regulatory Benchmarks toward Citizen Action. In: Berre, Arne J. et al. (eds.): Proceedings of the Workshop Environmental Infrastructures and Platforms, pp. 57–65.

Giroux, Henry A. (2003): Public Pedagogy and the Politics of Resistance: Notes on a Critical Theory of Educational Struggle. In: Educational Philosophy and Theory 35, 1, pp. 5–16.

Gruenewald, David A. (2003): The Best of Both Worlds: A Critical Pedagogy of Place. In: Educational Researcher 32, 4, pp. 3–12.

Gumbs, Alexis P. (2016): Spill: Scenes of Black Feminist Fugitivity. Durham: Duke University Press.

Halpern, Orit (2015): Cloudy Architectures. In: continent. 4, 3, pp. 34–45.

Hamraie, Aimi/Fritsch, Kelly (2019): Crip Technoscience Manifesto. In: Catalyst: Feminism, Theory, Technoscience 5, pp. 1–34.

Hickey-Moody, Anna/Page, Tara (eds.) (2016): Arts, Pedagogy and Cultural Resistance: New Materialisms. London: Rowman & Littlefield.

Hinton, Peta/Treusch, Pat (2015): Teaching With Feminist Materialisms. Utrecht: Atgender.

Hochschild, Arlie (1989): The Second Shift: Working Parents and the Revolution at Home. New York: Viking Press.

hooks, bell (1994): Teaching to Transgress: Education as the Practice of Freedom. London/New York Routledge.

hooks, bell (2003): Teaching Community: A Pedagogy of Hope. London/New York: Routledge.

Hudson, Stephanie (2020): Critical Body Pedagogies in Technoscience. In: Steinberg, Shirley/Down, Barry (eds.): The SAGE Handbook of Critical Pedagogies 3, pp. 1454–1463.

Jones, Kenneth et al. (2001): The Characteristics of White Supremacy Culture. In: Dismantling Racism: A Workbook for Social Change Groups. Available at https://www.showingupforracialjustice.org/white-supremacy-culture-characteristi cs.html, last accessed May 20, 2020.

Lanza Rivers, Daniel (2019): Cartographies of Feminist Science Studies. In: Women's Studies 48, 3, pp. 177–185.

Lasker, Grace A./Simcox, Nancy J. (2020): Using Feminist Theory and Social Justice Pedagogy to Educate a New Generation of Precautionary Principle Chemists. In: Catalyst: Feminism, Theory, Technoscience 6, 1, pp. 1–13.

Latour, Bruno (2004): Why Has Critique Run out of Steam? From Matters of Fact to Matters of Concern. In: Critical Inquiry 23, 1, pp. 58–68.

La Deriva, Precarias A. (2004): Adrift through the Circuits of Feminized Precarious Work. In: Feminist Review 77, 1, pp. 157–161.

Le Guin, Ursula K. (1997): Dancing at the Edge of the World. In: The Carrier Bag Theory of Fiction. New York: Grove Press.

Leonardo, Zeus (2009): Race, Whiteness, and Education. New York: Routledge.

Liu, Szu-Yu (Cyn) et al. (2019): Decomposition as Design: Co-Creating (with) Natureculture. In: Proceedings of the Thirteenth International Conference on Tangible, Embedded, and Embodied Interaction (TEI '19). Association for Computing Machinery, New York, NY, pp. 605–614.

Lury, Celia/Wakeford, Nina (2012): Inventive Methods: The Happening of the Social. London/New York: Routledge.

Mattern, Shannon (2016): Scaffolding, Hard and Soft. Infrastructures as Critical and Generative Structures. In: Spheres: Journal for Digital Cultures 3, pp. 1–10.

Mayo, Chris/Rodriguez, Nelson M. (eds.) (2019): Queer Pedagogies: Theory, Praxis, Politics. Cham, Switzerland: Springer Nature.

McNeil, Elizabeth et al. (eds.) (2017): Mapping Queer Space(s) of Praxis and Pedagogy: Queer Studies and Education. Cham, Switzerland: Springer.

McNeil, Maureen (2013): Between a Rock and a Hard Place: The Deficit Model, the Diffusion Model and Publics in STS, Science as Culture 22, 4, pp. 589–608.

Mingus, Mia (2011): Access Intimacy: The Missing Link. Available at https://leavingevidence.wordpress.com/2011/05/05/access-intimacy-the-missing-link/, last accessed May 10, 2020.

Moten, Fred/Harney, Stefano (2013): The Undercommons: Fugitive Planning & Black Study. Wivenhoe: Minor Compositions.

Papert, Seymour/Idit, Harel (1991): Constructionism. Norwood: Ablex Publishing Corporation.

Paxling, Linda (2019): Transforming Technocultures: Feminist Technoscience, Critical Design Practices and Caring Imaginaries. Doctoral Dissertation, Department of Technology and Aesthetics, Blekinge Institute of Technology, Sweden.

Piepzna-Samarasinha, Lakshmi (2018): Care Work: Dreaming Disability Justice. Vancouver: Arsenal Pulp.

Pohl Bernardo (2014): Pedagogy of the Disabled. In: White, Cameron (ed.): Community Education for Social Justice. Rotterdam: Sense Publishers.

Puig de la Bellacasa, Maria (2017): Matters of Care: Speculative Ethics in More Than Human Worlds. Minneapolis: University of Minnesota Press.

Ratto, Matt et al. (2019): Special Issue on Hybrid Pedagogies Editorial, Digital Creativity 30, 4, pp. 213–217.

Ringrose, Jessica et al. (2018): Feminist Posthumanisms, New Materialisms and Education. New York/London: Routledge.

Rommes, Els (2014): Feminist Interventions in the Design Process. In: Ernst, Waltraud/Horwath, Ilona (eds.): Gender in Science and Technology: Interdisciplinary Approaches. Bielefeld: Transcript, pp. 41–56.

Schaffer, Johanna (2008): Ambivalenzen der Sichtbarkeit: Über die visuellen Strukturen der Anerkennung. Bielefeld: Transcript.

Shor, Ira (1992): Empowering Education: Critical Teaching for Social Change. Chicago: Chicago University Press.

Suchman, Lucy/Bishop, Libby (2000): Problematizing "Innovation" as a Critical Project. In: Technology Analysis & Strategic Management 12, 3, pp. 327–333.

Suchman, Lucy (2007): Human-Machine Reconfigurations: Plans and Situated Actions, 2nd ed. Cambridge: Cambridge University Press.

Tronto, Joan C./Fisher, Berenice (1990): Toward a Feminist Theory of Caring. In: Abel, Emily/Nelson, Margaret (eds.): Circles of Care, pp. 36–54.

Tuhiwai Smith, Linda (1999): Decolonizing Methodologies: Research and Indigenous Peoples. London: Zed Books.

York, Emily/Conley, Shannon (2019): Critical Imagination at the Intersection of STS Pedagogy and Research. In: Platypus: The CASTAC Blog, November 5, 2019. Available at http://blog.castac.org/2019/11/critical-imagination-at-the-intersection-of-sts-pedagogy-and-research/, last accessed May 23, 2020.

Zembylas, Michalinos/Keet, André (2019): Critical Human Rights Education: Advancing Social-Justice-Oriented Educational Praxes. In: Contemporary Philosophies and Theories in Education Series 13. New York: Springer International.

Zero

Teresita Pumará

I have lost my origin,

And I don't want to find it again.

(Björk, Wanderlust)

Part One. The Tale

I

Fear and fascination come often hand in hand. In the proliferation of certain types of stories that shape the imaginary of a culture at each specific point in time, the vestiges of deeply rooted terrors can be traced.

At the dawn of industrial capitalism, tales in which the human being was challenged by the strength of the unleashed instincts that lurk within itself became frequent. A scientist composes a creature out of fragments of human corpses and gives it life through an electric shock. It has the features of a human being, but the intelligence of a slug that has bitten the forbidden fruit. It is unable to handle the storm of emotions that comes with being alive and aware of it. His creator rejects him, the end is tragic. A physician discovers a means to separate his rational from his instinctive self. The latter, liberated, wanders at night through a city of fog. His will to live is powerful, he takes progressive control of the physician, and finally destroys him.

According to the premise that underlies these two stories, famous in their time, a beast lurks within each human animal, a beast that should be repressed with all of the strength of reason, the great creator of civilized worlds. But these destructive impulses are set free through the practice of a rationality that knows no limits. At the sunset of capitalism, human animals became aware of this, and so stories in which humanity faced the overwhelming power of a superior intelligence became frequent. It is curious, but not surprising, that humans frequently imagined this intelligence in their own image: territorial, greedy, aggressive.

If fascination can suggest a profound fear, what does oblivion hint at? It is again curious, but not surprising, that human animals have never felt menaced by the possibility of a being whose sensibility, whose ability to perceive and be affected by the world, were much more intense than theirs. Ironically, this is precisely what happened, a long time ago, in City of Fourteen Factories.

II

Among the production plants that made up a wall around this city, there was a factory for all kinds of sex products: classic latex condoms, complex hormonal contraceptives, simple sex toys in all shapes and sizes, autonomous sexual androids. It also employed a numerous group of engineers and scientists in charge of anticipating ever-growing human boredom. Among them was Dr. Kenningar, who created the revolutionary A-30818.

Through complex and delicate electric circuits that resembled the human nervous system, and a sort of external epithelial tissue whose cellular units acted as wide-range sensory receptors – think of the green sensitivity towards light, the exploring potency of antennae, the briskness of a cat's whiskers, wrote Dr. Kenningar in the paper in which she presented her invention – the A-30818 would experience pleasure and reach orgasm. Both, added the scientist, much more intense, not only than those of a woman, in the image of whom the android would be made, but also than those of any animal that inhabited the planet.

Dr. Kenningar's announcement provoked considerable scandal amongst the sceptical scientific world as well as in the mistrustful heads of industry and the prudish general public. The board was reluctant to allow the production of the new android. A sex doll that could experience more pleasure than its human user did not seem profitable. Women will feel envious and men will feel afraid, said the psychologists of the marketing department. Dr. Kenningar advocated for her invention vehemently, and closed her argument with a question that concealed an invitation: What unexpected sensual experiences could one that feels with such intensity provoke? It is impossible not to imagine something once it has been named. Curiosity and desire moved the board members to somewhat grudgingly approve the production of a model of A-30818. Dr. Kenningar called her Zero.

III

Well aware of her enemies inside and outside the factory, Kenningar took precautions in the production of Zero. She worked with seven carefully selected specialists for the manufacture of the individual parts, but only she was

284

in charge of the assemblage in an isolated room, to which none other had access. It was arduous, meticulous work that demanded several months of exclusive dedication and was carried out with the help of advanced machines that only responded to the command of her own live voice.

Zero was ready in winter, in one of the long nights before the turn of the year. Before she could pronounce the words that would bring the android to life, Kenningar needed to rub its skin with a highly magnetized cloth intended to activate its sensitivity. The task should be done gradually but with a fluid, continuous movement, like dancing to a very slow melody. As there was no machine capable of such delicacy, the scientist undertook the task manually, like an artisan of long-gone days.

She began at the little finger of Zero's left hand, caressed each of the fingers and the spaces in between, the hand's palm and its back side, climbed up her left arm with slow circular movements. From the armpit she came to the shoulder, from the shoulder to Zero's neck, from the neck to the head and the face, and then descended down the right side, shoulder, armpit, arm, hand, fingers and spaces in between. The task demanded absolute focus. Sweat drops sprouted on Kenningar's hairline, they flowed down her forehead, nose, sometimes into her eyes, but she did not interrupt her steady dance over the surface of Zero's body. When she came to the chest, breasts, nipples, belly, the android's skin began to radiate heat. Kenningar startled but she did not break off her movements. When her hand descended down the inner side of the gluteus, a slight tremor went through Zero's body. The doctor said to herself that it was probably an effect of magnetism. She feared any other explanation. She went down the back surface of the left leg, knee pit, heel, foot, its toes and the spaces in between, climbed up the calf, the knee. She thought she saw Zero's arm move brusquely, but maybe the sweat flooding her eyes clouded and tricked her view. From the pelvis she went to the right leg, climbed down the front and up the back, and from the gluteus again went through to the outer lips of the android's vulva. Her arm ached, she could barely hold the cloth. She tried to control her own trembling through deep breathing. The heat that radiated from Zero's skin was growing in intensity. Every once in a while the doctor thought she could see the arms of the android lifting in what seemed like reflexive movements. Two more tremors shook a body that should have been cold and still as any inert machine. The fourth one took place when Kenningar slid from the outer to the inner lips of the vulva. But this time it was such an abrupt shiver that for an instant she suspended her dance, without lifting her fingers from Zero's skin. Then the inexplicable happened.

Zero put her hand on the doctor's hand and guided it through the folds of her vulva and around her clitoris. Her body vibrated continuously. Her hips started to move back and forth and in circles. An oily substance covered her skin and flowed out of her vagina. The doctor fell to her knees and abandoned control to the android. Suddenly, and after a more violent but silent shake, Zero laid as still as paralysed. She let Kenningar's hand go; it fell like dead weight next to her exhausted body, covered in sweat. I've failed, she thought. The nervous circuit must have collapsed. But then Zero moved again. She knelt beside her maker and took both her hands.

IV

Next morning, one of her assistants found Kenningar asleep on the floor of the room in which she had assembled the android. The door was open. The doctor was naked. Zero was gone. When she awoke, Kenningar refused to get dressed and was unable to construct meaningful sentences. Each time somebody tried to cover her nakedness, she howled in pain and said the fabric made her skin burn, then she started to cry and call for Zero. She was hospitalized in a mental institution, where she spent the rest of her days, naked. It is told that she died on a winter night, close to the turn of the year. She escaped surveillance and wandered through the snow-covered gardens until her blood froze in the cold.

The factory's board tried to keep the search for Zero going for some weeks, as she was made of valuable material. But nobody was sure of what she was supposed to look like and if anything set her apart from human females. She was never found. When the search was abandoned and the money given up as lost, the rumour was circulated that Kenningar had actually always been crazy and nothing had ever been produced, in spite of her team's insistence to the contrary.

In the weeks following Zero's disappearance, patients with symptoms that were grouped together and baptised *Kenningar's Syndrome* started to arrive at the city's mental facilities: They could not stand any kind of garment, had difficulty recognizing their surroundings, seemed to have forgotten the proper use of words, and once in a while suffered sudden breakdowns in which they called out for "some Zero."

Also, the rumour spread in the city of a woman dressed in a long black silk tunic that sometimes walked the streets and parks at a slow pace, sometimes laid under a tree, sometimes sat at the shore of the river. It was said that if you sat or laid beside her, you could feel a peace that resembled childhood. It was said that if you let the woman touch you, you shivered in a sort of sensual joy that could only be compared to the one that certain drugs can provoke. It was said that if the woman whispered her name in your ear, the meaning of life and the true name of each thing would be revealed to you. And it was said that if the woman held your hand, caressed herself and took you through unexpected paths to orgasm, you would not be able to come back to the human world.

V

With time, the lack of personnel in the factories started to become noticeable. Many left without notice or reason and never came back. This phenomenon, together with the rumour of the woman in the black silk tunic, extended to other cities. The number of patients with Kenningar Syndrome also increased. Nobody thought of, or nobody dared to investigate the relation between these events. The late capitalist society had grown so specialised that very few people were able to link events that took place in different dimensions of social life. When somebody did, their suggestions were rapidly discarded as pseudo-scientific. And so Zeronism, as it was later called, grew slowly but constantly, without obstacles or resistance, as nobody considered it a threat until it was too late.

Decades after, colonies established far away from the cities became known, some in old abandoned settlements, others in the few unexploited forested territories, yet others at the shores of rivers and seas, where human animals practised a religion categorized and labelled by researchers as Zeronism. Anthropologists who came near these colonies reported that individuals, no matter their sex, referred to themselves as Sisters of Zero. They adored no idols or representations of divinity, but they painted on their bodies, and sometimes on the walls of their refuges, a black and white symbol that resembled a vulva. They did not seem to have rituals, although sometimes they stood, laid, or sat absolutely still for long periods of time. When asked about this, they hinted that they were feeling. Actually, the Sisters of Zero did not seem to do anything but live. They organized to find food and shelter, they gathered and shared, laughed and danced and enjoyed sex. Words they used very sparingly. Making sense of their answers was difficult, as grammar rules were alien to them, so it was impossible for researchers to document and learn their language. To communicate they sometimes used isolated words, sometimes sounds, sometimes body movements, sometimes silence. They were never hostile or mistrustful. They always sought physical contact. Their skin seemed to be heavily electrified.

Centuries after, a manuscript of a chronicle attributed to one of Kenningar's assistants came to light, where the model Zero of the A-30818 was linked to the Syndrome and to Zeronism. Of Zero, if she existed at all, only legends remain. In some of them it is said that she took refuge on the top of a mountain in the company of a big black and white cat; in others, that she still walks the world slowly, and that if you want to meet her, you only need to take the road. In all of them Zero is immortal.

Part Two. The Tail of the Tale

I

On Monday the 9th of March 2020, women march in Buenos Aires. I take my place among the crowd, walk alongside women of many genders, colours, classes, ages, standpoints, experiences, presents, bodies. These women do not make a whole. Their claims are different as their experiences are different. Some walk in groups. Some follow slogans. Some walk alone. Some walk with friends. There is no conflict between us now. We all agree on the necessity of this walking in this now.

"The identity of the feminist subject ought not be the foundation of feminist politics," says Butler (2006: 8), "an open coalition […] will be an open assemblage that permits multiple convergences and divergences without obedience to a normative telos of definitional closure." (Ibid.: 22) "Perhaps, paradoxically, 'representation' will be shown to make sense for feminism only when the subject women is nowhere presumed." (Ibid.: 8)

And yet I wrote above: "women of many genders." Not because of any kind of alleged natural or cultural identity the word *women* refers to. It is a literary device. It is a knife that cuts across (not in two, but many pieces) the experiences of oppression in human animals.

II

The word *women* is also the link that leads to the tale and the contradictions within it. In its enacting of the idealized feminine, ZERO shows tendencies towards wholeness. But these same impulses reveal their impossibility of finding closure in the disruptive agency of the cyborg.

The first element in the story that smells like platonic spirit is the woman-body relation (Butler 2006: 17), suggested by the fact that the android with the enhanced sensitivity has what is commonly known as a woman's physiology. This association falls in the old trap of thinking that the transformation women bring to the world is one related to the senses, as opposed to manly reason. The second element lurks in the name the Zeronites give themselves: Sisters of Zero. This name works as an inversion of the classic gender hierarchy, erasing not only the male, but the whole spectre of possibilities in between, in the margins, in the transversals, in the corners, in unimagined places. A zeal for retribution and vengeance, a desire to be the captain of the ship and a *carnivalesque* dream of subversion vibrate in these two elements. But these motivations function according to the laws of the logic that makes gender hierarchies possible. It is a binary logic, it homogenises, making the

288

many others invisible, it seems not to stand unresolved contradictions and it has an obsession with building pyramids.

III

It is curious, but not surprising, that even when we seek to disrupt this logic, we fall into its trap. The only antidote I can think of now is acknowledgement and constant awareness. Such is Odo's advice in Ursula K. Le Guin's *The Dispossessed* regarding the "lasting threat" of "unavoidable centralization" of power in the anarchist settlement of Anarres: "O child Anarchia, infinite promise, infinite carefulness, I listen, listen in the night." (no date) In Octavia Butler's *Dawn*, one of her Oankanli partners tells Lilith that the only way human beings could have avoided self-destruction would have been a constant and thorough self-examination of the hierarchical element in their genetic constitution, just as a person with cancer does regular check-ups. This is me checking myself through the critical reading of a story I wrote.

IV

There is no woman. There is no "universality and unity of the subject of feminism" (Butler 2006: 6); "there is nothing about being 'female' that naturally binds women." (Haraway 1991: 155)

In the first chapter of *Gender Trouble* Judith Butler questions the naturalization of the bond between the "seamless category woman" (Butler 2006: 6) and feminism. If, according to Foucault, power structures enforced through representational politics produce the subject they claim to represent, then an uncritical definition of women as the subject of feminism, not only dangerously naturalises the bond, but also produces exclusion mechanisms directed at those who "fail to conform the unspoken normative requirements of the subject" (Ibid.: 8) and falls in the trap of the binary heterosexual normativity it claims to critic.

The dream of universality and of a natural bond is at work in ZERO. But this dream lives with its contradiction. The model Zero of A-30818 is no woman. Her womanly appearance is the result of a decision taken in the context of the production of a sexbot. Zero reproduces the dreams and the sicknesses within the system that made her production possible.

V

A sexbot awakens through the rubbing or scrubbing or caressing of its skin by its creator. But this is not supposed to happen; Zero upsets her creator's plan and displays her cyborg nature:
"The main trouble with cyborgs, of course, is that they are the illegitimate offspring of militarism and patriarchal capitalism, not to mention state social-ism. But illegitimate offspring are often exceedingly unfaithful to their ori-gins. Their fathers, after all, are inessential." (Haraway 1991: 151)
Zero is produced as a result of the commodification of sexuality charac-teristic to capitalism. She is the ultimate product of this process, apparently so complete (as she can be used to obtain pleasure as well as experience it) that the people who must allow her production are not easily convinced. In her perfection, she incarnates the misogynistic fear of sexual pleasure in women: so intense that it disrupts and potentially destroys all social order. And of course this is what happens. Such is the lesson of superhero movies: monsters too are created by the structures that, out of fear, reproduce strate-gies to protect themselves from them. From the very moment she awakes Zero is irreverent and blasphemous. She neither shows fear of her maker nor awaits anything from Kenningar. "Unlike the hopes of Frankenstein's mon-ster, the cyborg does not expect its father to save it through a restoration of the garden; that is, through the fabrication of a heterosexual mate." (Haraway 1991: 151)
Zero does not seek completeness, but she is still "needy for connection," (Ibid.) and this need extends to all kinds of people[1]. She does not kneel be-fore her creator, but beside her, she wants to give and receive pleasure, and the pleasure she takes Kenningar through drives the doctor mad. ZERO func-tions under the assumption that coming in contact with a being that feels so differently and intensely affects human animals in such a way, that it alters deeply the way they relate to people – many go mad.
"I fear we will not get rid of God, because we still believe in grammar," writes Nietzsche in *Twilight of the gods*. Through language, and in language, we articulate the assemblages we come into, the way we weave our image of the multiverse and our place within it. If our whole existence was reset, if we

---

1 I understand *people* in this essay according to this wide enumeration: "The beings or crea-tures that are said to live in the Five Houses of Earth and are called Earth People include the earth itself, rocks and dirt and geological formations, the moon, all springs, streams, and lakes of fresh water, all human beings currently alive, game animals, domestic animals, in-dividual animals, domestic and ground-dwelling birds, and all plants that are gathered, planted or used by human beings. The People of the Sky, called Four-House People, Sky People, Rainbow People, include the sun and the stars, the oceans, wild animals, plants and persons considered as the species rather than as an individual, human beings considered as a tribe, people or species, all people and beings in dreams, visions, and stories, most kinds of birds, the dead, the unborn." (Le Guin 2019: 60–61)

could be formatted, we would not be able to continue using language as we previously did. Our belief in the grammar that structures our existence would vanish. By entering in contact with Zero, the hybrid that rejects paradise, people finally get rid of god.

VI

I now find the previous assumption too radical. "Almost anything carried to its logical extreme becomes depressing, if not carcinogenic." (Le Guin 2000: xiv) I would add that nothing ever takes place in such a *pure* form, in such a radical way. There is no THE END, and if they ever take place, apocalypses happen in small doses. Nothing is ever so completely reset and there is no going back to the blank page, because the page was never blank. "Cyborg writing must not be about the Fall, the imagination of a once-upon-a-time wholeness before language, before writing, before Man. Cyborg writing is about the power to survive, not on the basis of original innocence, but on the basis of seizing the tools to mark the world that marked them as other." (Haraway 1991: 175)

I wonder what happens to the people who come in contact with Zero but do not leave the city, the place of pollution, of mixed identities, of partiality. In the city people are feminized, "made extremely vulnerable." (Haraway 1991: 166) I wonder how people would relate to the world in this multiple feminization, in the city and through the machine, across intense sensitivity, among innumerable potential connections.

The extrapolative answer – people experiencing rebooting, abandoning their workplaces, isolating themselves in smaller communities and leading a simpler way of life cut off from all social conventions (language included) – is an articulation of the dream of a whole new world with a whole new beginning. In this dream I find again the carcinogenic tendency towards completeness. But this dream is challenged through the fact that the resetting is carried out not by a goddess, not by a human messiah, not by a natural catastrophe, not by an invisible virus, but by "a cybernetic organism," a hybrid that "skips the step of original unity, of identification with nature in the Western sense." (Haraway 1991: 149, 151) The Sisters of Zero are not the restoration of the Pure Woman and cannot go back to Nature, a time previous to History. They are contaminated by the cyborg. They produce something else.

Zero's intervention disrupts over and over again the dream of completeness and the binary logic that made her production possible, she blocks their attempts at closure. And so, although ambiguously, ZERO works as a "tool to mark the world" that marks women as the other. "The tools are often stories, retold stories, versions that reverse and displace the hierarchical dualisms of naturalized identities. In retelling origin stories, cyborg authors subvert the central myths of origin of Western culture. We all have been colonized by those origin myths, with their longing for fulfilment and apocalypse." (Haraway 1991: 175)

The main battle against colonization takes place within us. In this sense, this tail of the tale is just another tale. It is partial, it is full of contradictions, it is as true as any other reading. There is no secret meaning of stories, no truth to disclose. The places they take us to are important, the ways they resonate with us are important, the ways they make our bodies reverberate are important.

VII

In traditional European tales, stories occur "a long time ago." Characters and settings make the reader think of the Middle Ages and the Renaissance, but in abstract or fictionalized versions. The image they give us of that time is as idealized and romanticized as it is brutal and cruel. If, as the saying goes, "it's easier to imagine the end of the world than the end of capitalism," (Fisher 2012) then we can maybe imagine the tales of the capitalist world with the eyes of a future narrator; we can at least tell stories about this world as if it were a long time ago in a faraway land. The utopian dream and its impossibility live in this will to tell the present from a future point of view. By turning it into fable, the present is simplified and idealized, but it is also made past. If it can be past, then another future is possible, if not yet imaginable.

References

Butler, Judith (2006): Gender Trouble. New York: Routledge.
Butler, Octavia (2012): Dawn. In: Lilith Brood: The Complete Xenogenesis (The Xenogenesis Trilogy). e-Book published by Open Road Media.
Fisher, Mark (2012): Capitalist Realism: Is There No Alternative? E-Book published by ZeroBooks. Available at https://www.johnhuntpublishing.com/zer0-books/our-books/capitalist-realism, last accessed March 18, 2020.
Haraway, Donna J. (1991): A Cyborg Manifesto: Science, Technology, and Socialist-Feminism in the Late Twentieth Century. In: Simians, Cyborgs and Women: The Reinvention of Nature. New York: Routledge, pp. 149–181.
Le Guin, Ursula K. (2010): The Left Hand of Darkness. New York: Penguin.
Le Guin, Ursula K. (2019): Always Coming Home. New York: The Library of America.
Le Guin, Ursula K. (no date): The Dispossessed. e-Book published by HarperCollins e-Books. Available at https://rosadefoc.noblogs.org/files/2018/02/The-Dispossessed-Ursula-K.-Le-Guin.pdf, last accessed March 18, 2020.

The Authors

Corinna Bath is the Maria-Goeppert-Mayer Professor for gender, technology and mobility at TU Braunschweig and the Ostfalia University of Applied Science. She chairs the interdisciplinary PhD program "Gendered Configurations of Humans and Machines (KoMMa.G)" with 15 PhD grants from the Ministry for Science and Culture in Lower Saxony since 2017. Her interdisciplinary research focuses on epistemology and new material feminisms, gender in digitalization processes, and technology design methods to avoid bias in AI and algorithms. She recently co-edited "Geschlechterwissen in und zwischen den Disziplinen: Perspektiven der Kritik an akademischer Wissensproduktion [Gender(ed) Knowledge in and Between Disciplines: Critiques of Academic Knowledge Production]," Transcript (2020).

Ingo Bednarek, M.A., has been a doctoral student at Braunschweig University of Art (HBK Braunschweig) since 2017. From 2017 to 2019 he was also a lecturer at HBK Braunschweig and a scholarship holder of the doctoral program "Gendered Configurations of Humans and Machines (KoMMa.G)." Since 2019 he has been a research assistant at the Institute for Media Studies (IMW) at the Braunschweig University of Art (HBK).

Loren Britton is an interdisciplinary artist based in Berlin. Focusing on critical pedagogy, play, and unthinking oppression they make objects that re-position and collaborations that unlearn. Britton is responsible to matters of technoscience, antiracism, trans*feminism, and creating accessibilities (considering class and dis/ability). Britton researches within the Gender/Diversity in Informatics Systems Department at the University of Kassel, Germany. More at https://lorenbritton.com/.

Jan Büssers is a PhD candidate in philosophy at Technische Universität Darmstadt. He was part of the PhD program "Gendered Configurations of Humans and Machines (KoMMa.G)" at Technische Universität Braunschweig. In his PhD project, he is exploring the differences in the materialist approaches of Ernst Bloch and Karen Barad. Before starting his PhD project, he completed his studies in Technik und Philosophie (M.A.) at Technische Universität Darmstadt, after having finished his studies in biotechnology (B.Sc.) at the University of Applied Sciences in Darmstadt.

Dr. Dipl.-Math. *Cecile K. M. Crutzen* is a researcher and author in Computer Science and Gender Studies. She publishes and lectures about interaction, object orientation, and ambient intelligence. Her critical analysis shows that computer science is a process of negotiation of the redesign of social interactions in human gendered environments. She retired as associate professor at the Open University of the Netherlands, Department of Computer Science. In 2012 she was visiting professor on gender and technology at the University of Vienna. In 2017 and 2019 she lectured at the Johannes Kepler University Linz on gender and technology. Research Themes: gender studies, computer science, human-computer interaction, e-learning, ambient intelligence.

Nadine Dannenberg, B.A. in History & Romance Studies, M.A. in gender studies (Joint Degree). PhD candidate at the Institute for Media Studies at Braunschweig University of Arts (DE) with a thesis on "Gendered Dynamics of Surveillance in Fictional Post-Network TV," supervised by Prof. Heike Klippel. Lecturer in gender & media studies at various universities in Germany and Austria. Her main research areas are queer media studies, cultural studies, surveillance studies, and asexuality studies.

After receiving her PhD in German Literature from the University of Göttingen, *Yasemin Dayıoğlu-Yücel* held positions as DAAD lecturer at Istanbul University and as DAAD visiting professor at the University of Pennsylvania. She currently teaches at the University of Hildesheim. She has a background in transcultural literature and is recently exploring how the study of more-than-human entanglements and transcultural studies can, in Donna Haraway's words, engage in "sympoiesis."

Prof. Claude Draude works at the Faculty of Electrical Engineering and Computer Science at the University of Kassel, Germany and heads the Gender/Diversity in Informatics Systems (GeDIS) work group. Her research activities evolve around sociotechnical systems and human-computer interaction. She mainly works on participatory, critical, and use-oriented design; human models, embodiment, and artificial intelligence; and artistic research and the knowledge question in computing.

Anja K. Faulhaber is currently a research associate at the Human-Machine Systems Engineering Group, University of Kassel. She studied Romance Studies (B.A.) at Leipzig University and Cognitive Science (M.Sc.) at Osnabrueck University. From January 2017 until December 2019 she was a PhD student at the Institute of Flight Guidance, TU Braunschweig, with a Georg Christoph Lichtenberg scholarship as part of the doctoral program "Gendered Configurations of Humans and Machines (KoMMa.G)."

Alexander Gabel studied computer science from 2011 to 2016 at Ostfalia University of Applied Sciences. He graduated as an M.Sc. in winter 2016 with a thesis on „Pseudonyms and Anonymous Credentials in an e-Health Infrastructure. " He is a PhD candidate whose thesis is on „Usable Security and Privacy in the Internet of Things – a Pattern-Based Approach," supervised by Prof. Dr.-Ing. Corinna Bath (Technische Universität Braunschweig) and Prof. Dr. Ina Schiering (Ostfalia University of Applied Sciences).

Tanja Heuer is a PhD student at Ostfalia University. She studied computer science with a focus on mobile systems engineering. Her research interests include user-centered design, social robots, and privacy. In 2017 she started her PhD with a focus on user-centered robot design at Technische Universität Braunschweig in cooperation with Ostfalia University.

Goda Klumbytė is a research associate and PhD candidate at the Gender/Diversity in Informatics Systems research group at the University of Kassel, Germany. Her research engages feminist science and technology studies, media studies, AI, and machine learning systems design. Her PhD research focuses on modes of knowledge production in machine learning and the possibility of diffracting these modes with critical feminist epistemologies.

Hannes Leuschner, PhD, is a writer and cultural anthropologist. He studied prose and drama/new media at the German Literature Institute Leipzig and ethnology in Göttingen, Mainz and Hamburg. He did extensive fieldwork focused on Afro-Brazilian religions in the Recôncavo Baiano, Brazil. In his latest research, he was concerned with ethnographic research in German primary schools in the light of new materialist theories. Further research interests: Pentecostal studies, ethnology of education, ethnopsychology, anomalistics.

Dagmar Lorenz-Meyer is a senior researcher at the Department of Gender Studies at Charles University in Prague. Her research emerges at the intersections of feminist theory, technoscience studies, and new materialism, currently in relation to solar energy and alternative energy futures. She recently co-edited "Feminist Technoecologies: Reimagining Matters of Care and Sustainability" (Routledge, 2019), and curated Roma snapshot photography and the sound performance "Stressed" (with E. Pedersen).

Katharina Losch is a doctoral researcher in the interdisciplinary doctoral program "Gendered Configurations of Humans and Machines (KoMMa.G)" at the Ostfalia University of Applied Sciences. In her doctoral project, she analyses the positioning and effects of female doctoral researchers from India and China in German computer science. Before starting her doctoral project, she completed her Master's studies in Sociology at Bielefeld University, where she had already developed a huge interest in the topic of women in computer science.

Max Metzger is currently working as a railway engineer in an engineering office specialized in the railway sector. In parallel, he is writing his PhD at the TU Dresden. He completed his degree in Physics and Philosophy in Potsdam and worked for four years at the Hochschule Hannover as a research assistant in the Group "Gender STEM." He is also an associate member of the PhD program "Gendered Configurations of Humans and Machines (KoMMa.G)" at the TU Braunschweig.

Thomas Nyckel is part of the doctoral program "Gendered Configurations of Humans and Machines (KoMMa.G)" at Technische Universität Braunschweig with a dissertation on digital apparatuses and Karen Barad's agential realism. He has been teaching at Humboldt University of Berlin, at Technische Universität Braunschweig, and Göttingen University. In 2017 he was awarded the Humboldt prize for his master's thesis, "Computability as the Sphere of Digital Media."

Isabel Paehr is involved in the production and arrangement of virtual matter and currently works with materiality, melting/leaking, and play. Paehr develops experimental games and material speculations, performs, writes, and codes in collaborative working groups. Besides her practice as an independent designer, Paehr works as a researcher for the project "Re:Coding Algorithmic Culture" and engages with the materials and metaphors of internet infrastructure.

Imme Petersen, PhD, is a cultural anthropologist and journalist. Since her PhD in 2002, she has been working in several research projects on science, technology, and science education in the life sciences, medicine, and mechanical engineering at universities in Braunschweig, Hamburg, Lüneburg, and Göttingen. In her latest research, she did fieldwork in university departments of mechanical engineering. Further research interests: Science & Technology Studies; interdisciplinarity; social studies of science and science education; ethical, legal, and social aspects (ELSA) of medicine and the life sciences.

Teresita Pumará is an independent scholar. She was born in Buenos Aires, Argentina. She studied Philosophy at Universidad de Buenos Aires (UBA) with special emphasis on Phenomenology and Post-structuralism. During her studies, she participated in the making of a volume on Philosophical Confessions, published an article on the absence of the body in Heidegger, and graduated with a dissertation on the relations between Antonin Artaud and Foucault, Derrida, Merlau-Ponty, and Deleuze (all of it in Spanish). She then moved to Colombia, where she did a lot of reading and writing and singing. In 2016 she moved to Germany, where she studied German and did some more reading and writing. Now she is back in Buenos Aires. Contact: terepumara@gmail.com, IG @teresita.pumara.

Myriam Raboldt, B.A. in political science and economics, M.A. in history of science and technology from TU Berlin with a focus on queer-feminist Science and Technology Studies. Spent one Semester at Boğaziçi Üniversitesi in Istanbul. 2017–2019 doctoral scholar in the doctoral program "Gendered Configurations of Humans and Machines (KoMMa.G)." Since 2019 she has been a research assistant and lecturer at the Centre for Women's and Gender Studies (ZIFG) at TU Berlin.

Jennifer Sonneck is a PhD student at Technische Universität Braunschweig. She studied industrial design and design and communication strategies. Her research interests include diversity, communication, and participatory design. In 2017 she started her PhD with a focus on the planning processes of projects in construction engineering, especially in steel construction.

Anja Trittelvitz completed her degrees in social work/-pedagogy, philosophy, and gender studies in Hanover, Göttingen, Vienna, and Berlin, with a research stay in Utrecht. After professional experience in the social and feminist sector as well as psychotherapeutic and nutritional qualifications, she is carrying out her doctoral degree in the doctoral program "Gendered Configurations of Humans and Machines (KoMMa.G)" in Braunschweig, where she also works as a research assistant. Her passion is food studies and in 2020 she co-published conference proceedings on nutrition and identity.

Helen Verran is a Professor in the College of Indigenous Futures, Arts and Society at Charles Darwin University in northern Australia and has been working with Indigenous landowners in the region since 1987. She is hoping to complete the manuscript for a book called "Affectual Epistemics" in the next year or so.

Bettina Wahrig studied medicine (MD) and philosophy at Mainz and Marburg. After working as a research assistant and senior researcher at Lübeck University, she completed her habilitation in history and theory of medicine. She has been a Professor for the History of Pharmacy and Sciences at Technische Universität Braunschweig since 1997. She has continued to study the history of experimental sciences and epistemology. Recent research has been on gender and healthcare and the cultural and conceptual history of poisons. Together with Heike Klippel and Anke Zechner, she has edited "Poison and Poisoning in Science, Fiction and Cinema – Precarious Identities," Cham: Palgrave Macmillan (2017).

Galit Wellner, PhD, is a senior lecturer at the NB School of Design in Haifa, Israel. She is also an adjunct professor at Tel Aviv University. Galit studies digital technologies and their inter-relations with humans and is an active member of the Postphenomenology Community. Her book "A Postphenomenological Inquiry of Cellphones: Genealogies, Meanings and Becoming" was published in 2015 by Lexington Books. She also co-edited "Postphenomenology and Media: Essays on Human-Media-World Relations," Lexington Books (2017).

Rebecca Wiesner studied Pharmacy from 2011 to 2015 at Technische Universität Braunschweig. During her studies, she completed a two-month research internship at the University of Rhode Island. Since October 2017 she has been a fellow of the doctoral program "Gendered Configurations of Humans and Machines (KoMMa.G)." Her thesis deals with "The evolution of automation in pharmaceutical analysis from the perspective of gender studies" (supervised by Prof. Dr. Hermann Wätzig).

Evgeny Zakablukovskiy, Ph.D., is the Associate Professor in Philosophical Anthropology, Political Science and Philosophy of Religion at Minin University (Russia). In 2003 he graduated from the Volga Public Administration Academy. He also studied at UWO, Strathclyde University, and Bonn University. Between 2003–2014 he was the Russia Community Relations Manager for Intel Corporation. In 2002 he served as the Deputy Chief of Staff for the Government of the Nizhny Novgorod Region.

Index

A

abundance 183, 189 –90, 197–99
academia 21, 119, 170 –71, 232–35,
241, 265
actor-network theory, -ies (ANT) 18,
24, 54 –57
agency, -ies 24, 54, 63, 65, 67, 69,
80, 85, 137–39, 142–44, 148–52,
154, 167, 186, 205, 207, 216, 247,
258, 270–73, 276, 288
agential realism 21, 45, 47–48, 61,
64–65, 69, 71, 100
AirBnB 90 –91
algorithm, -s 24, 79–82, 85, 86–95,
97, 101, 113–15, 139–40, 147, 149,
191, 253, 256–57, 259–60
supervising algorithm 93
trained algorithm 147
Allhutter, Doris 147, 153
Almanya 71–72
alterity relations 83, 89
android, -s 284–86, 288
anthropocentrism 109, 258, 260
anti-racist 269, 271, 276, 278
apparatus, -es 42, 45, 46, 48, 50, 65,
67–69, 143, 146, 255
knowledge apparatuses 21, 23
semiotic apparatus 53
artificial intelligence (AI) 23-24, 80–
82, 85–87, 90, 92, 94–95, 100–01,
107–08, 111, 114 –15, 138 –39,
144, 151, 167, 256, 258
auto-complete 89
automated liquid handlers (ALHs)
167, 169–70
automation 18, 23, 80, 107, 109, 159,
161, 167–72, 192

B

background relations 83, 86, 90
Barad, Karen 17, 21, 23–24, 39, 40–
42, 45, 47–48, 61, 63–65, 68, 69–
72, 100, 141–42, 147–50, 152–53,
255, 258, 265, 270
Benjamin, Walter 40, 42–43
bias, -es 79–81, 87, 89, 91–95, 115,
143, 145, 147, 235, 256, 260
gender bias, -es 24, 55, 80–81, 87–
91, 93–95
binary 21, 41, 62, 63, 69, 72, 128,
256, 259–61, 272, 288–89, 291
Bloch, Ernst 39–40, 43
Blumenberg, Hans 43
body 18, 24, 67–68, 82, 86, 87, 119–
20, 123–24, 127–29, 131, 140–142,
145, 151, 189, 207, 211, 218–19,
221, 225, 249, 252, 258, 260, 268,
273, 285, 287–88
bot, -s 99, 101–102, 161, 171, 290
chatbots 89
sexbot 289
Bridge of the Golden Horn 64–66,
68–72
bullshit 25, 231, 235–36

C

capitalism 123, 231, 273, 283, 287,
290, 292
CAPTCHA, -s 99–103
NoCAPTCHA 102
reCAPTCHA, -s 101
clan lands 206, 213
clean eating 120–21
collective action 206, 210, 222–23,
225–26

T

tale, -s 40, 283, 288, 292
technical object, -s 109, 115
technology, -ies 15–17, 20–25, 34,
    36, 45, 53–57, 81–88, 90, 95, 102,
    107, 115, 119, 121–23, 127–29,
    137–45, 147, 149–54, 159, 161,
    170, 175, 180, 184, 187, 189, 192,
    194, 215–17, 221, 225, 239, 260,
    269–70, 272–75, 278
  biotechnology 169
  enhancement technology 152
  enhancement technology, -ies
    140–41, 151
  information communication
    technologies (ICTs) 206, 208
  social technologies 223
  solar technology 184, 191
  technologies of the self 122
temporality, -ies 40–41, 69, 108, 115
testicle, -s See penis, -es
transcultural research approach 239–
    40, 242
transformative room, -s 138, 147–48,
    150–51, 153–54
transformative rooms 137
translation, -s 18, 35, 64–66, 70, 79–
    81, 83, 88, 91–92, 95, 114, 120,
    127–29, 209, 219, 240, 247
transparency 15, 37, 89, 92, 95, 143,
    148, 175, 218, 276
Turing test 99–100, 138

U

Uber 81, 90–91
usability 150, 170–71, 175
usability studies 171

V

vagueness 220, 224–25
Verlässlichkeit 25, 137, 150–53
Vipassana 247, 251–57, 259

W

wänga 220–21
waste 189–90, 198–99
Weber, Jutta 33, 231
woman, -en 9, 66–68, 80–81, 88–91,
    114–15, 143, 171, 184–85, 189,
    191–92, 232–34, 236, 240–43, 247,
    253, 260, 272–73, 284, 286–91
workload 160, 162, 167, 192

X

x-ray 90

Y

Yolŋu 205–13, 215, 217–21, 223–25

Z

zip code 92

CPSIA information can be obtained
at www.ICGtesting.com
Printed in the USA
LVHW051211060221
678410LV00003B/5

9 783847 424949